Women in American History

Series Editors

Mari Jo Buhle

Jacquelyn Dowd Hall

Nancy A. Hewitt

Anne Firor Scott

A list of volumes in the series appears at the end of this book.

Natural Allies

Natural Allies

WOMEN'S ASSOCIATIONS IN AMERICAN HISTORY

ANNE FIROR SCOTT

UNIVERSITY OF ILLINOIS PRESS
Urbana and Chicago

Illini Books edition, 1993

© 1992 by the Board of Trustees of the University of Illinois
Manufactured in the United States of America
P   5   4   3   2   1

This book is printed on acid-free paper.

Library of Congress Cataloging-in-Publication Data

Scott, Anne Firor, 1921–
    Natural allies : women's associations in American history / Anne
Firor Scott.
        p. cm.—(Women in American history)
    Includes bibliographical references and index.
    ISBN 0-252-06320-1
    1. Women—United States—Societies and clubs—History. 2. Women—
United States—Social conditions. 3. Women volunteers in social
service—United States—History. I. Title. II. Series.
HQ1904.S28 1992
305.4'06'073—dc20   91-10979
                                                                  CIP

For
Rebecca, David, Donald, Anne, and Peter
with love

γυνὴ γυναικὶ σύμμαχος πέφυκέ πως.

Woman is woman's natural ally.
Euripides,
Fragment 108 [ed. Nauck]

Contents

Illustrations follow page 110.

Acknowledgments

The list of people who have helped me along the way, sometimes without knowing that they did so, is too long for enumeration. I must content myself with a heartfelt "Thanks so very much" directed toward all the highways and byways inhabited by social historians, especially those who study women.

Colleagues who read the entire manuscript and wrote many pages of astute commentary slowed me down, but much to the benefit of the book. Mari Jo Buhle, Jack Cell, Bill Chafe, Ellen DuBois, Maurine Greenwald, Jacquelyn Hall, Nancy Hewitt, Suzanne Lebsock, Gerda Lerner, Rebecca Scott, each from a different perspective, helped me formulate what I was trying to do and to do it better. I wish I could publish their comments as an example of collegiality at its best. Rejean Attie, George Gopen, Dolores Janiewski, Linda Kerber, and Peter Railton helped with certain chapters. Evelyn Brooks Higginbotham, Darlene Clark Hine, and Deborah Gray White have done their best to teach me something of the history of black women. Students in women's history classes and lecture audiences around the country have asked the kinds of questions that send one back to the drawing board. At the eleventh hour Connie Pearcy picked up errors and infelicities that the jaded authorial eye could no longer see. The best thing I can wish for all these good folks is similar conscientious critics for their own work.

It is hard to find adequate ways to thank the supportive staff members of the National Humanities Center in North Carolina and the Center for Advanced Study in the Behavioral Sciences in California for all they did, finding books, editing disks, sharpening computer skills, and expecting something to come of it all. Both centers, with funds from the National Endowment for the Humanities, the Commonwealth Fund, and the Andrew W. Mellon Foundation, provided ideal working conditions, the first in 1980–81 and the second in 1986–87. The Ford Foundation, the Duke University Research Council, and Charles Clotfelter, director of Duke's

Center for the Study of Philanthropy and Voluntarism, also provided essential support.

The endlessly helpful people at the Schlesinger Library at Radcliffe College have borne with this research and the researcher for many years. My semester there as visiting scholar in 1984 made the book possible. Other manuscript depositories whose unfailingly welcoming staff members contributed vital data include the Bentley Library at the University of Michigan, the Department of Special Collections at the University of Colorado in Boulder, the Manuscript Department of Perkins Library at Duke University, the Henry Huntington Library, the Southern Historical Collection at the University of North Carolina in Chapel Hill, the North Carolina Department of Archives and History in Raleigh, the Oberlin College Archives, Tulane University, the Berea College Library, the Virginia State Library, and the Western Reserve Historical Society. Many others have provided help by mail.

Some of the material in the book appeared in a different form in three articles and one working paper and is used here by permission:

"On Seeing and Not Seeing: A Case of Historical Invisibility," *Journal of American History* 71, no. 1 (June 1984): 7–21.

"Most Invisible of All: Black Women's Voluntary Associations," *Journal of Southern History* 56, no. 1 (Feb. 1990): 3–22.

"Women's Voluntary Associations: From Charity to Reform," in Kathleen D. McCarthy, ed., *Lady Bountiful Revisited: Women, Philanthropy and Power* (New Brunswick, N.J., 1990), 35–54.

"To Cast Our Mite on the Altar of Benevolence," *Working Paper of the Duke University Center for the Study of Philanthropy and Voluntarism* (Jan. 1988).

Carole Appel and Richard Wentworth, exemplary publishers, practiced the cardinal virtues of faith, hope, and charity. I hope they won't have to wait for heaven for their reward. Every author hopes for a skillful copy editor. It has been my good luck to have Carol Bolton Betts, who has done a splendid job.

For more than twenty years, Marie Alston Lee has provided a support system nonpareil. My debt to her is enormous.

I wish there were some less stereotypical way to say that Andrew Scott has been an indispensable critic from the beginning. No one will be happier than he to see a book on the shelf rather than a manuscript on his desk, with a note "Could you bear to read this just once more?"

Introduction

Once he tried to feed all the animals in the world in one day, but when the food was ready an Animal came out of the deep sea and ate it up in three mouthfuls. Suleiman-bin-Daoud was very surprised and said, "O Animal, who are you?" and the Animal said, "O King, live for ever! I am the smallest of thirty thousand brothers, and our home is at the bottom of the sea. We heard that you were going to feed all the animals in the world, and my brothers sent me to ask when dinner would be ready." Suleiman-bin-Daoud was more surprised than ever. "O Animal, you have eaten all the dinner that I made ready for all the animals in the world." And the Animal said, "O King, live for ever, but do you really call that a dinner? Where I come from we eat as much as that between meals. . . . "[1]

If I had known in 1979 what I know now, this book might not have been written, for, like Kipling's naïve potentate, I had no idea of the magnitude of the task. In what was intended as an honest statement I told the National Humanities Center that I had been working on this subject for twenty years, and all I needed was time to write. My curiosity about "organized womanhood," as the nineteenth century labeled it, had begun long before when I had discovered women in their missionary societies, temperance organizations, and literary societies remaking the social and political landscape of the early-twentieth-century South, and was puzzled that this activity had never found its way into any of the standard histories. The effort to understand what was happening among southern women had led me to examine women's associations elsewhere, and I thought I knew enough to write a definitive book.

So I began—but every time I followed some lead or went looking for some missing piece of information, another of the thirty thousand brothers (in this case sisters) popped up. By the end of my year at the Humanities Center I understood just how big the subject might be and, turning to a familiar academic device, offered a course called Women's Voluntary Associations in the Shaping of American Society. This only led me deeper into the thicket as my students, with admirable diligence, turned up more societies that I had never heard of.

It soon became clear that women's associations were literally everywhere: known or unknown, famous or obscure; young or ancient; auxiliary or freestanding; reactionary, conservative, liberal, radical, or a mix of all four; old women, young women, black women, white women, women from every ethnic group, every religious group had their societies. Before long, as the scope, magnitude, and diversity of this phenomenon came into view, I realized that it lay at the very heart of American social and political development. It became clear that the first task was not to write a comprehensive survey of the thousands of associations but to make the case for their centrality to this development. That is what this book seeks to do.

The argument runs like this. Since the early days of the Republic women have organized to achieve goals that seemed to them important. In retrospect it is clear that such women, constrained by law and custom, and denied access to most of the major institutions by which the society governed itself and created its culture, used voluntary associations to evade some of these constraints and to redefine "woman's place" by giving the concept a public dimension. Many years later a participant summed up the matter succinctly: "Suddenly they . . . realized that they possessed influence; that as organizations they could ask and gain, where as women they received no attention. . . ."[2]

The complex network of women's organizations had many social consequences. At the most general level, as Darlene Roth phrased it, "A separatist tradition has developed, which has supported both 'liberal' and 'conservative' causes, both status-quo and change-oriented issues, and which manifests itself in a wholly separate entity within the domain of public affairs—an interconnecting network. . . ."[3]

Within this network women learned how to conduct business, carry on meetings, speak in public, manage money. Experiences in small-scale voluntary associations ("our little republic," one woman called hers) prepared women for politics, broadly defined. By finding a way to take up public concerns, they were contributing to the expansion of American democracy, first indirectly and then, in 1920, directly. As significant as this transformation was, it has not attracted the attention of the numerous historians who see the expansion of democratic participation as a major theme of American history.

Another result is less immediately obvious. For some women, working toward collective goals tapped wellsprings of creativity that had been quiescent in the narrow round of domesticity. These individuals were exposed to a wider range of social experience than would have been common in family life. When one woman began speaking her mind and discovered she had powers of persuasion, or another, knocking on doors in fear and trembling, found she could make a good case to the skeptic for the abolition of slavery; when one took charge of a successful fair to raise money, or another conducted a piece of original research; when a woman undertook to administer an orphan asylum or a home for aged widows, and found she could do so with skill and ease—confidence grew. Some kinds of self-discovery occur in lonely introspection, other kinds require experience, feedback, and the support of people who recognize one's gifts. I have long been both fascinated and puzzled by the fact that so many late-nineteenth-century men spoke of their own time as "the woman's century," and have wondered what process brought to public view so many talented women in such a comparatively short time. The records of women at work in their associations show talents rapidly developing and becoming visible. Such women inspired others to believe in themselves, and thus influence ramified. Personalities changed, and as the numbers of "new women" grew, the society also changed.

Not only personalities, but values and attitudes were developed and reinforced by collective experience. This was true no matter what the orientation of any particular group—in moral reform as well as in the Women's Trade Union League; in the DAR as well as in the YWCA.[4] Associations provided careers for many women, careers from which the income was psychic rather than material. In their own groups women learned to be professionals before the traditional professions were open to them, and developed a recognizable female style of professional behavior that relied heavily on cooperation. Reflecting their voluntary-association training, the first women doctors, lawyers, teachers, and ministers often functioned differently from their male counterparts.

A further consequence has been structural. As each chapter of this book will show, women's associations have been prolific builders of vital community institutions. In the early days women built orphan asylums and homes for aged widows and spinsters; by the 1930s the landscape was covered with libraries, schools, colleges, kindergartens, museums, health clinics, houses of refuge, school lunch programs, parks, playgrounds, all of which owed their existence to one or several women's societies.

As women tried to shape public policy they sometimes functioned as a kind of early warning system, recognizing emergent problems before they were identified by the male-dominated political process. Perhaps women had an advantage when it came to understanding the negative consequences of what were generally seen as the great positive accomplishments of the urban-industrial revolution. When their husbands or fathers lived and prospered, middle-class women were insulated, to a degree, from the daily struggle for economic gain and the sharp competition of the marketplace. Socialized to believe in their own compassionate instincts, living as close as they often did to the daily requirements of child raising and household management, they seem to have been more likely to empathize with people whose lives were a struggle against heavy odds. Men, whose life experience was different, and who were busy seizing the opportunities of an expanding economy, often failed to recognize (or closed their eyes to) negative side-effects of what they were doing. It was left to the women to identify certain kinds of problems and force them on the attention of the formal power structure.

Of course, women were not the only "outsiders." Many men, too, questioned the dominant ideology: spokesmen for wageworkers and African Americans, itinerant printers, ministers dedicated to the social gospel, and college professors inspired by European social thought were among those whose critiques of existing social and political arrangements influenced pragmatic reformers in women's associations. Largely through separate efforts, though with shared ends, these various outsiders attempted to challenge or humanize the emerging industrial order.

As they sorted themselves into groups, women helped define and shape the emerging class structure. Most of those who appear here came not from the ranks of the very well-to-do nor from those of wage earners; they were wives and daughters of middling businessmen, professionals, landowning farmers. Some consciously tried to build bridges to bring people from different parts of the class structure together. One can watch members of some associations carefully delineating the class boundaries within which they feel at home, and others seeking to dissolve those boundaries. With respect to the much disputed notion that in their associations middle-class women were attempting to assert control over the behavior of the "lower classes," I think the evidence does not support any simple hypothesis. The women we see in these pages, though often, perhaps nearly always, conscious of the difference between "our own people" and other people, did not always draw distinctions in terms of economic or social class. Their world might be divided into the saved and the lost, the abstemious and the intemperate, the chaste and the licentious, native born and immigrants, workers and loafers, those who cared about children and those who exploited them, the worthy and the unworthy—and they did not assume that these categories were necessarily connected to class. There is a difference, too, between trying to promote social order by keeping people "in their place," as the phrase went, and trying to help them develop characteristics that—if accomplished— might admit them to the middle class.[5]

All these streams of development and the transformation of personalities which accompanied them came together in the second decade of the twentieth century to make woman suffrage inevitable. For skillful organization, astute lobbying, mobilization of the grass roots, effective human relations, and powerful emotional appeal, the final suffrage campaigns have seldom been equaled. The élan of success carried over into the first years of the difficult decade of the 1920s as women took their habits of cooperation into legislative action and into the welfare agencies of many states.

I have tried to get as close as the data permits to the inner workings of local groups in order to see the reality behind summary annual reports and the view-from-the-top. As a member of a local League of Women Voters who had once worked in the national office, I quickly learned about the gulf that separated what the national board thought the local units were doing and what they were really doing. Not that the local work was unimportant, but it was determined locally to a greater extent than any but the most perceptive national leaders quite realized. This point is hard to document since local records are rarely as complete or as available as those of organizations' national headquarters. The examples of local groups at work included here are built from shards of the past, comparable to those pieces of ancient pots from which the archaeologist extrapolates whole schools of artistic development. Many more such fragments are buried in mountains of as yet unexamined manuscript material awaiting patient and imaginative historians.

The book is divided into two parts and eight chapters. The three chapters in Part I cover the years before the Civil War, and are roughly though not entirely chronological. They describe what I perceive as three successive phases in the early evolution of women's voluntary associations, beginning with the benevolent societies, followed by groups dedicated to reform, and then by the massive effort to provide what was called "soldiers' aid" in the Civil War. Part II, after a brief introduction, deals successively with three major types of organization: those based on religion, those designed for self-improvement, and those focused on community improvement. All three contributed in important ways to the movement for social justice, which is the central focus of Chapter 7. The final chapter harks back to this introduction and summarizes the major themes of the book.

PART I

The New Republic

This book is about women. For that reason many of the familiar land-
marks of American social and political history will appear in a new light.
However, the general picture of "what happened" does not disappear, and
it is necessary to bear its general outline in mind as we watch women
organize their voluntary associations.

Part I begins just after the launching of the Constitution and ends with
the freeing of the slaves and the beginning of Reconstruction. The seventy-
odd years encompassed in this section of the book—barely a biblical
threescore and ten—were years of growth and change. At the outset the new
United States was what we now call a pre-industrial society. The people
alive in 1795 surely did not think of themselves as "pre" anything; this was
their world; life was shaped by economic patterns not very different from
those of their parents and grandparents. A sophisticated late-nineteenth-
century historian would describe the nation in 1800 in these terms: " . . . the
land was still untamed; forest covered every portion, except here and there
a strip of cultivated soil; the minerals lay undisturbed in their rocky beds,
and more than two thirds of the people clung to the seaboard within fifty
miles of tidewater, where alone the wants of civilized life could be supplied."[1]

Despite the absence of means to meet what Henry Adams perceived as
"the wants of civilized life," this almost entirely rural society must have
seemed to its own people well developed, and a great improvement over
what they or their ancestors had left behind in Europe.

True, almost everybody lived in rural villages or in the countryside. A
few seaboard "cities," connected with each other by sailing vessels, exhibited
a lively urban culture. Elsewhere communication and transportation were
limited; many of the five million people counted in the census of 1800
lived their whole lives in a circle of thirty or forty miles. Others, of course,
were part of the never-ceasing movement to the west where they could
manage even less of what a Bostonian might view as civilization.

By 1865 all this had changed dramatically. For one thing there were ten times as many Americans, and in states like Massachusetts or Rhode Island half the citizens lived in towns. Cheap printing and railroads accelerated the circulation of ideas. What was called the Second Great Awakening had persuaded many people that they could by an act of will give up sin and approach perfection.

The enormous and ever-increasing variety of American experience argues against any single interpretation of the antebellum society or its *zeitgeist.* It is possible to find evidence for almost any spirit one can imagine, from the despair of a man growing old in a new settlement, bemoaning the absence of friends or family to sustain him, to the boundless optimism of men and women who expected to see the millennium in their own lifetimes. The human types were diverse and numerous: the taciturn New England farmer, the refugee from the Irish potato famine; the prosperous Philadelphia Quaker and his frugal German neighbor; the land speculator and the reckless entrepreneur; the displaced craftsman and the new wageworker, male or female. The proud, provincial southern planter and his southern-lady wife; male and female slaves; the stern Mormon family with its multiple wives; the lady out of *Godey's;* the sunbonneted, if not sunburned, woman walking beside the covered wagon headed for Oregon, and the Native Americans they encountered en route—behind each stereo-type stood numerous real people, characters enough to supply American novelists, poets, and playwrights for a hundred years to come. Each one saw and judged the world through the prism of his or her own experience, shaped by class, race, gender, region, experience, and the peculiar contour of an individual psyche. Optimism said that God had planned for Ameri-cans to control a vast continent and teach the world about representative government; pessimism said the republic was already falling into luxury and decay and would soon go the way of the Roman empire. What one person viewed with alarm (factories, competition, slave labor, immigration, westward expansion) another saw as a great opportunity to rise in the world. Even as evils were perceived and described in dramatic terms—especially by the great evangelical ministers—there was a pervasive opti-mism that things gone wrong could be set right if only enough people could be converted. A more secular view saw education as the force that would sustain the republican experiment and provide a way for children to go beyond their parents. Two pervasive strains of thought, millennialism—the belief that the society could become perfect—and per-fectionism—the faith that individuals could—fueled much of the activity here described.

The horrifying loss of life in the Civil War, the failure of the South to make good on its determination to be independent, and the consequent freeing of the slaves wrought momentous changes in American life; opened, it was said, a great chasm between what had gone before and what came after. It is appropriate, therefore, to begin the second part of the book in 1866.

1

To Cast Our Mite on the Altar of Benevolence: Women Begin to Organize

> Benevolence: Disposition to do good, desire to promote the happiness of others, generosity, charitable feeling.
> —*Oxford English Dictionary*

In the last quarter of the eighteenth century, as the song had it, the world turned upside down. The whole complex of events and experiences encompassed in the Revolution and the formation of the Constitution created a sense of ferment, of new opportunities, but also of fear that the new experiment might fail if citizens were not up to the challenge. Women sensed new possibilities. John Adams was more prescient than he knew when he joked, in response to Abigail's exhortation that he and his colleagues should "remember the ladies" when they wrote a new constitution, "We have been told that our Struggle has loosened the bands of Government every where. That Children and Apprentices were disobedient—that schools and Colledges were grown turbulent ... But your Letter was the first Intimation that another Tribe more numerous and powerfull than all the rest were grown discontented. ... "[1]

By the 1790s, as President Washington, departing from office, was advising his fellow citizens to cherish virtue, education, and the new federal government, and Judith Sergeant Murray was announcing that young women were about to "form a new era in our history," the first female benevolent societies began to appear.[2] They were the first step toward what Linda Kerber has called "a synthesis ... that would facilitate women's entry into politics without denying women's commitment to domesticity."[3] Their self-imposed task was to fill at least part of the gap as the numbers of people in need increased and local government aid did not.[4]

While economic development had brought a rapid increase in the number of poor people, it also increased the number of business and professional men and skilled artisans who could support their families without relying on the full-time economic production of wives and daughters; such women were in the vanguard of benevolent organization. In 1800 even very prosperous families still relied on women for plenty of productive work, but as some goods once made at home began to be available in the market there was a margin of time that could be devoted to the kinds of collective enterprises hitherto the domain of men.[5]

There were precedents. Men had created voluntary associations for many years and women had occasionally made their own experiments, though none had lasted long.[6] In Boston in 1778, for example, young Hannah Mather had organized a "woman's lodge," for the purpose of "improving the mind, that by *Strength* and *Wisdom*, we might beautifully adorn the female character, . . . " but it disappeared when members married and began to have children.[7] During the Revolution some women (probably more than were recorded) banded together to raise money, provide amenities to the soldiers, and support the movement for independence. These groups dissolved when the war was over, but memory of their accomplishments lingered.[8]

Women were also accustomed to the idea of benevolence; it meant a quality that good Christians were expected to exhibit, especially those whom God had favored with health, wealth, and standing in the community. Taking care of the less fortunate was not only a Christian duty, it might also insure one a place in heaven, and certainly enhanced the reputation of one's family. Individual women had engaged in charity as far back as the record ran; now they proposed to join together for greater effectiveness.

The women set out to provide help for people in trouble: poor people, particularly those recognized as "worthy," and especially women and children. The desire to do good was a powerful motivation, but it was not the only one. From the beginning, benevolent women—still under the influence of the challenges of the revolutionary age—were intent on their own spiritual and intellectual improvement. An increasing number of women were acquiring some education and developing a desire for more. While young women would soon begin flocking to female seminaries, their mothers and married sisters tried to make benevolent societies educational institutions for themselves.[9] Here and there a female "reading circle" or a literary society appeared— groups, usually of young, single women, intended entirely for self-education— but for the most part adult women seemed to feel more at ease seeking to improve themselves in a context of carrying out significant community responsibilities. Murray's "new era in female history" was underway.

While development took place at different times in different places, over the first two decades of the nineteenth century most settled parts of the United States experienced rapid growth and increased interaction with the rest of the country. Voluntary associations of all kinds proliferated, to supplement the old institutional structures of family, church, and local government.[10]

The first "female societies" appeared in coastal cities from Savannah to Boston, but within two decades women in towns and villages all over the country, usually led by wives and daughters of the most visible and respected families, had begun to follow suit. In the rapidly growing cities poverty was increasingly visible, but in many prosperous towns and villages it was not yet a pressing problem; something more than simple need attracted women to collective activity. Though the swift rise of the benevolent society is often described as a response to the Second Great Awakening, the impulse to organize was not limited to places where the revival spirit had struck. Many women felt, however vaguely, that in the new age now coming into being a new kind of participation in community life was expected of them.

Societies took various forms and various names. In Philadelphia there was a Female Association for the Relief of Women and Children in Reduced Circumstances; in New York one group, inclined to specificity, called itself the Female Association for the Relief of the Sick Poor, and for the Education of Such Female Children as Do Not Belong To, or Are Not Provided For, by Any Religious Society; the Female Benevolent Society of St. Thomas and the Daughters of Africa were only two of many groups of free black women; in Savannah, Boston, and Petersburg, Virginia, white women combined to establish and administer asylums for female orphans; and in Baltimore to create a charity school for girls. Mite societies, cent societies, missionary societies, mutual aid, charitable and sewing societies were all variations on the same central idea. Whatever they called themselves, their essential activities were similar. Missionary societies began by raising money to send young men to preach in foreign parts or in the West, but very shortly many of them were engaging in local charity as well. Sunday school societies set out to provide a modicum of education for laboring children, but soon found that clothing and shoes were a necessary prerequisite to learning. Charitable societies distributed Bibles and preached temperance. Some groups were affiliated with a particular church, others were ecumenical, based on neighborhoods, kinship, or class.[11] Protestant groups were most numerous, but Catholic and Jewish women set up their own associations.

No matter where they were, who the members were, or what they called themselves, organizational forms were remarkably similar. Written constitutions were universal: every society established rules about meetings, the uses of money, and qualifications for potential recipients of charity.[12]

Free black women in New England and Pennsylvania were among the first to organize. Their motivation was in many ways quite different from that of their white contemporaries. Limited on all sides by prejudice and poverty, they began to establish societies for mutual aid and self-education. Despite the meagerness of their resources, they undertook to help one another and those even less fortunate. In 1809, for example, when the men in the African Benevolent Society of Newport, Rhode Island, though welcoming women's labor, would not permit them to vote or hold office, the women set up a separate association. In 1818 the Colored Female Religious and Moral Society of Salem (Massachusetts) drew up a forthright constitution which could be distinguished from those of its white neighbors in Boston or Cambridge by its plain speaking and its focus on mutual aid and self-help. Article 4, for example: "We promise not to ridicule or divulge the supposed or apparent infirmities of any fellow member, but to keep secret all things relating to the Society, the discovery of which might tend to do hurt to the Society or any individual." Or article 5: "We resolve to be charitably watchful over each other, to advise, caution and admonish where we may judge there is occasion, and that it may be useful; and we promise not to resent, but kindly and thankfully receive such friendly advice or reproof from any one of our members."

The society announced that it was formed for the benefit of sick and destitute *members,* and that if any member committed a "scandalous sin, or walk unruly, and after proper reproof continue manifestly impenitent, she shall be excluded from us, until she give evidence of her repentance."[13]

These strenuous requirements for self-monitoring and self-improvement reflected black women's conviction that the behavior of one affected the image of all. For them, mutual aid was to be psychological as well as material.

While they read and talked, women knitted, sewed, or made palm-leaf hats to supply the needs of the poor, either directly or by selling their handiwork for cash. They solicited money and goods from sympathetic men and used the money to organize schools, orphans' homes, homes for elderly women, soup kitchens, and employment services. For the most part members ran these institutions themselves, or hired needy women of their own social group to do so. "Managers" were assigned to visit people who needed help, and "prudential committees" allocated goods and money between meetings. A few societies experimented with work relief.[14]

White women's societies nearly always made a distinction between the "worthy" and the "unworthy" poor. The first group was made up of what might be called the working poor: people they considered respectable and self-respecting but who had met with unemployment or illness or the common misfortune of having too many children. Once-prosperous widows who had fallen on hard times or were too old to work were viewed with special sympathy. On the other hand, people who seemed unembarrassed by their poverty, who loved rum, or were thought to be ingenious beggars who were able to take advantage of their benefactors, were deemed unworthy.[15] Foreigners were often viewed with suspicion. In cities like

Boston and New York, women worried lest they mistakenly help professional beggars or people who would sell their gifts to buy liquor. In small towns where most people knew each other, identifying people was easier. Occasionally some maverick member would raise the issue: Do we really *know* what "worthiness" is and who possesses it? But usually the concept was taken for granted and required no justification. Black women, by contrast, made few such distinctions; from their perspective virtually all African Americans who needed help were worthy of it.

Benevolent women brought their domestic habits into the public arena. Not only did they sew and knit for the poor just as they did for their own families, they also behaved as good mothers were supposed to: rewarding virtue, attempting to cure bad habits, and concentrating special attention upon children and old women, precisely as they did in their homes. They visited people in need, and liked to believe that warm relationships were established. Deaths of long-term clients were noted in the same words as those of longtime members.

Depending very much upon the capability of local leaders, societies varied in effectiveness and degree of sophistication. For example, one of the earliest—the New York Widows' Society as it came to be called—was a well-run and wide-ranging operation from the start. Isabella Graham, the founder, a highly educated, self-confident Scottish woman, had considerable experience as a teacher, and had herself been a self-supporting widow. An intensely religious person who was never happier than when writing on theological issues, she was also an astute politician who gained support for her enterprise from powerful men in the government of New York.

The Widows' Society was a prolific creator of long-lasting welfare institutions: schools, orphanages, workrooms for indigent women, for example.[16] The intensity of members' commitment might be measured by the fact that so many risked their lives by remaining in the city to provide aid to their clients during successive epidemics of yellow fever.[17]

A generation later Sarah Josepha Hale offered similarly creative leadership to the Boston Seaman's Aid Society. Graham and Hale were well-known women; many others, never heard of beyond the boundaries of their own communities, demonstrated administrative skills and imagination in the pursuit of their goals. When no natural leaders emerged, societies formed in an initial burst of enthusiasm often dwindled and died.

Thousands, however, survived, in old communities and new ones, in cities and country towns—anywhere there were women. In the frontier settlements charitable societies appeared almost as swiftly as town government.

Simple as these early collective efforts may seem on the surface, when they are viewed as a widespread social phenomenon, puzzles appear: Why were many so similar, despite wide differences in geographic location and original purpose? Why did they appear in places where poverty was only barely visible as well as in rapidly growing cities where it was an obvious problem? Were they, as some historians believe, one of the ways an increasingly self-conscious elite, black as well as white, began to define itself as separate and different from "the poor"?[18] Did women use benevolence as some men did philanthropy to consolidate their positions as community leaders?[19] Why did some women belong to two, three, or four such societies—spreading themselves and their resources thin, rather than concentrating both? Why did benevolent women feel free to invade the privacy of those they sought to help in ways that they would have found most offensive had they been the subjects of such invasion?[20] Most of all, one would like to see the benevolent societies through the eyes of those they presumed to help—but alas, no recipient seems to have left her reflections.

It is not possible to find complete answers to these questions, but the surviving records of individual societies reveal something about the consciousness of the women themselves, a sensibility so different from our own that only a strenuous effort of historical imagination enables us to begin to see the world as they saw it. As benevolent-society members met and talked and wrote minutes and went about helping and exhorting their poorer neighbors, they revealed the values that pushed them on. In language that owed something to sermons and the King James Bible, and something as well to sentimental novels, they offered their perception of the world outside their own social class. We can see limitations and possibilities revealed and anxieties expressed.

Now and then, through the veil of sentimental language, it is possible to detect a skeptic who questioned the way things were being done, or who preferred blunt speech to euphemism, but for the most part benevolent women, particularly those who were white, spoke and thought like the characters in *Little Women*. Marmee and Meg existed by the thousand; only an occasional Jo, an occasional Amy, added variety to the landscape.

Black women, perhaps because the language of oppression had made euphemism anathema to them, spoke more plainly. Their situation was different from that of white benevolent women in fundamental ways. "Worthy" and "unworthy" were not so much part of their vocabulary: the fact that they shared with their poorer sisters all the indignities of racial prejudice and the stigma attached to black women gave a different tone to their statements and to their work.

Variations in the spirit and activity of benevolent societies across the country tell us something about the variety of American communities and of American women.

The Cambridge (Massachusetts) Female Humane Society was founded in 1814 in the setting of a small, semirural, homogeneous village.[21] It began with a concern "for the relief of the Indigent sick, particularly Females residing in Cambridge and the Port." Any woman who cared to join was welcome and the society denied vehemently that it intended to represent any one social group or religious view. Class lines were fluid; members were entitled to ask for assistance from the society. Recognizing sickness as a great threat to people whose income depended upon being able to work daily, the society decided to pay for doctors and apothecaries as necessary. In summer when wood was cheap the women bought a large supply in order to sell small quantities at cost when cold weather had driven the price up.

Frequent comments on the general good health and comfortable circumstances of most Cantabridgians suggest that no perception of pressing need had called this group into existence. The women had simply caught the prevailing contagion for organizing. Unlike many of their sister societies, this one put no special emphasis upon doing God's work or on the good that members were doing their own souls. They were not much concerned with the issue of worthiness. The president urged members not to worry too much about being imposed upon, but to give freely when need was perceived since it was better occasionally to help someone who was not much in need than to overlook someone who was. The Humane Society assumed that able-bodied people of either sex would work to support themselves; their aid was for those unable to work. In 1842, when the Washingtonian temperance revival was in full swing, the minutes recorded "a great improvement in the habits of many of the suffering poor."

Just to the south, Rhode Island women were intent on education as the sovereign remedy for poverty. In Providence a Female Society for Relief of Indigent Women and Children had begun in 1801 with education, a school for children, and a plan for work relief as the first order of business.[22] In 1811 in the small town of Bristol, eighty-eight women had joined together announcing that a third of whatever money they raised would be used for the education of children.[23] Further west, in Shrewsbury, Massachusetts, in 1832, about one in five of the town's adult women, wives of ministers, merchants, professional men, and substantial farmers, joined the Shrewsbury Charitable Society.[24] Their constitution forbade gossip, and serious subjects for discussion were assigned for each meeting.[25] The society met in homes (always designated as "*Mr.* So-and-So's house," though only women were present); tea was served, but the rule was that it should be kept simple. Occasionally a "dear sister of the society" was in need and was promptly helped. The typical client was a widow, or the wife of an alcoholic or disabled breadwinner. A third needed help only once; another third received help twice; the final third were regulars.

Not far away, in Hopkinton, New Hampshire, the Chesterfield Female

Benevolent Society, which began with such enthusiasm that it met weekly, represented a somewhat different version of the familiar story.[26] The society decided to set up a library for the use of the community, dividing the books between the north end of town and the south—presumably so that they were within walking distance of all the inhabitants. Hopkinton women increased their resources by trading some of their handicrafts for palm leaf which they made into hats to sell. In so doing they were—though there is no mention of this fact in the record—competing with young single women for whom such hatmaking was a principal means of self-support. For a while the society flourished; then enthusiasm began to lag, and finally—after four years—the minutes ended on a sad note: "Met at Mr. Cook's, agreeable to adjournment, three in number, finished three hats, no appointments made." Perhaps there were simply not enough poor people in Hopkinton to keep the flame of benevolence alive, or perhaps sustained leadership never emerged.

In Lynn, the center of boot and shoe manufacture in Massachusetts, two societies competed for philanthropic resources: the Female Benevolent Society, founded in 1814 when the town had four thousand inhabitants, and the Lynn Fragment Society, which first met six years later.[27] Their constitutions were identical and there was a striking similarity of names between members and recipients. Most mysterious of all is the fact that a considerable number of women belonged to both societies.

The constitution of the Lynn Fragment Society suggests something about ideology as well as about practicality. The women announced that they wanted to exert their feeble efforts to "alleviate the distresses of the indigent, to cast our mite on the altar of benevolence—and though our means may be small, yet we think by proper economy in our domestic concerns, and by gathering up the fragments, and applying them to objects of need, the blessing of the poor may rest upon us, and the rich bounty of Heaven reward our philanthropy."

Article 6 authorized the treasurer to receive money and donations and required her to exhibit an *accurate* account with *proper vouchers* at every annual meeting.

In Morristown, New Jersey, another town of fewer than four thousand inhabitants, seventeen Presbyterian women founded the Female Charitable Society in 1813. There is no record that the society ever helped a man. Recipients were classified as: 1) Irish, 2) colored, and 3) "our own people." The historian of this society notes that from 1813 until 1870 there was "very little change in the scope of its work, or in its structure, standards and procedure. Many of the early members remained active for as long as two or three decades."[28]

In Salem, Massachusetts, the Female Charitable Society began early to place female orphans and children of disabled parents in foster homes for training. Though they used the existing laws of apprenticeship to "bind" these young girls for a fixed period of labor, in the early days the women made an effort to supervise the treatment the children received. In the 1830s a serious economic decline was too much for this system, and the practice of binding out was abandoned.[29]

The Daughters of Africa in Philadelphia was made up, Dorothy Sterling tells us, of nearly two hundred working-class women who banded together in 1821 to help each other. Their minutes may be epitomized by such entries as: "November the 15th 1822, Mary Brown borrowed of committee the sume of 4 wich she is to pay in 3 month to th Society for the Burial of her child" or "Sarah Pratte ten dollar for the lost of hir housband." The Female Benevolent Society of St. Thomas, also in Philadelphia but enrolling members of better-off black families, differed principally in its ability to help people beyond its own members. "Visited Mrs. Jones with the Committee and gave her 50 cts worth of groceries. She had been confined 10 days. [signed] Grace Douglass."[30] Unlike white women, these black women had very few wealthy patrons and no hope of receiving help from the government.[31]

Benevolent societies abounded in New England, New York state, the Western Reserve, and the Middle Atlantic states. In the South, too, despite its thinly spread population and comparatively small number of urban areas, the first society had appeared in 1801 when women in Savannah organized and administered a home for orphan girls.[32] The entire Board of Managers was female. Records survive of benevolent societies in Baltimore, Richmond, Raleigh, Nashville, Augusta, Petersburg, Charleston, and New Orleans. An obscure note in a local history tells us that in 1819 women from three Protestant churches met in Clarke County, Georgia—here there was no town of any size—to form a Female Mite Society.[33]

Southern towns produced benevolent societies that were indistinguishable from those in the North or the Middle West. In Petersburg, Virginia, in 1811 women undertook to raise money, organize, and manage an orphan asylum for girls. Securing a corporate charter from the state allowed them, in Suzanne Lebsock's phrase, to open "a large loophole in the common-law doctrine of civil death for married women," for under the common law, married women could not own property.[34] From that point forward, Petersburg women, black and white, multiplied associations: benevolent, missionary, and educational. Each church had a cluster of women's societies, though only the black Baptist church recognized this fact in its formal records. As elsewhere Petersburg churches depended heavily on women's societies to raise money, and the characteristic dense network of kin relationships prevailed.

In Charleston, Barbara Bellows discovered records of a vigorous and hard-working Ladies Benevolent Society, founded in 1813, made up of elite women who were not reluctant to visit lepers or to rescue children from houses of prostitution; they "typically encouraged the poor to become self-sufficient rather than fostering dependence...."[35] In another coastal town, Wilmington, North Carolina, the Female Benevolent Society in 1817 secured a charter for a school "for poor children and destitute orphans" which was later described as the beginning of a common school system in that area.[36]

The Female Bible and Charitable Society of Nashville, organized in 1817, had a secretary who had read law with her father. Surmounting the challenge of the 1819 depression, by the 1830s Nashville women were in full swing, as they established an orphan school, a house of industry, and other such institutions.[37]

By the 1820s the Raleigh (North Carolina) Female Benevolent Society had established an important place for itself in that small state capital. In addition to the usual commitment to aged widows and other distressed females, the Raleigh society was determined to provide employment for women who wanted to work, and education for destitute children. Younger members were expected to teach in the society's school, which enrolled twenty-six children on weekdays and more on Sundays. Managers took turns visiting each week to examine the pupils on their scholastic and religious progress. The women believed that education would rescue the children from poverty and "render them useful and respectable in the sphere to which it has pleased God to place them." Apparently they did not consider it necessary or inevitable that the children remain in that sphere, since they asserted that children who had "received the first rudiments of education from charity" might go on to become "shining lights in the world both for talents and for piety."

In 1821 the annual report noted the "great utility of providing work for females" and recorded that the society had supervised the manufacture of 195 pounds of donated cotton into cloth. The women who had spun and woven had together earned $141.78, and "thus in some degree obviated the necessity for private charity." Unfortunately the record does not show whether the society paid better wages than commercial establishments. The Raleigh women were among those who expressed qualms about their own ability to discern who was "worthy" and who was not. "It has been observed of this society," they noted, "that the managers ought to discriminate so as to bestow the largest portion of their favor on the most deserving. To this they can only answer that the most deserving may not be the most necessitous and though evil may have previously been committed, who shall say what has been resisted?"

They clinched the argument by quoting the Bible: "There is more joy in

Heaven over one sinner that repenteth than over ninety and nine just persons."[38]

People moving west took the habit of benevolence with them. By 1829 Cincinnati had its network of women's organizations. Settlers had barely arrived in Cleveland when the women began to organize. In Chicago, where the first lots were platted in 1832, there was a Dorcas Society by 1835, followed by the Ladies Benevolent Society in 1843, and the Chicago Orphan Asylum in 1849. In 1858 came the Home for the Friendless. In the latter two institutions members of the board did the day-to-day work. Like many of their counterparts elsewhere the earliest institutions of this sort were characterized by limited funds, informal organization, and intense personal involvement.[39]

In Detroit the first recorded benevolent society was established by Catholic women in 1834 to oversee the poorhouse and establish an orphanage. In 1836 Protestant women set up an orphanage of their own.[40] Seven years later black women organized a Colored Ladies Benevolent Society which met in the Colored Methodist Church.[41]

Bearing witness to the nearly universal assumption that women were responsible for community welfare, when the Mormons set about establishing what they thought would be a permanent community in Nauvoo, Illinois, Joseph Smith took care to organize the women into a Relief Society. In addition to the usual benevolent functions, the society accepted responsibility for reinforcing the tenets of the evolving faith of the Church of Jesus Christ of Latter-day Saints and for providing help in the building of a temple. After Brigham Young led the Saints to Utah, the Relief Society was revived and became one of the most significant institutions in the carefully structured Mormon hierarchy.[42]

In San Francisco, four years after the gold rush began, it was clear that many "unprotected" women had followed husbands, brothers, and lovers to the gold fields, only to find that the men had died or disappeared.[43] The polyglot California population was heavily male, and a single woman was thought to be at considerable risk. Though by 1853 there were eighteen churches, several orphanages, and an almshouse, as well as some "secret and racial benevolent societies," a group of well-to-do women thought something else was needed. In August of that year they formed an association to "render protection and assistance to strangers, to sick and dependent women and children." The first challenge was to find employment for women whose male breadwinners had disappeared, and in a very short time the Ladies' Protection and Relief Society had put up a building as a refuge for such women. The second president (who remained in office for thirty years) was a Vermonter married to a lawyer-turned-tract-distributor who had gone to California to represent an undertaking firm. After her own demanding trip across the Isthmus of Panama during which she knew not what might have happened to her husband, Mrs. Gray had had no trouble imagining the situation of other women. Building on by now half a century of eastern experience, the San Francisco society immediately asked the legislature for five thousand dollars to carry on its work. The petitioners came back with three thousand dollars and promptly set out to raise the rest—members were firmly instructed to collect no less than two hundred dollars apiece, which they proceeded to do. When a local businessman gave the society a full city block in an undeveloped part of San Francisco, the women enthusiastically undertook to be managers of property as well as benefactors of the poor.

Perhaps because the lone women who first aroused concern found an extensive choice of husbands, the society's charitable focus quickly shifted to children. Members took orphans into their homes and tried to raise them to be clean-living, right-thinking, and hardworking. The society welcomed children of any ethnic group and did not hold them responsible for their parents' failings.[44] Nor did they insist that the boys, at least, stay in "the station to which God has appointed them." On the contrary, they begged local businessmen to provide opportunities for their young charges: "A boy who would be a laggard at the plough, might become a brilliant inventor . . . " if only he had a chance. "Remember your hopes and fears and aspirations . . . remember the strong preference that stirred within you for one occupation or craft more than another, so that you felt it easy and joyful to earn your bread in one way, and repulsive or well-nigh impossible in another."

The women made no such plea for the girls, who were taught housewifery and, presumably, prepared for marriage. Given the early California sex ratio, this was doubtless realistic, but it showed some myopia on the part of these energetic and effective women who had themselves found it "easy and joyful" to engage in a very active life away from housewifery.

The 1906 earthquake tested the organizational resilience of the society. With energy and imagination the women moved large numbers of children to places of safety despite the chaos around them, and nursed those who fell victim to the post-earthquake epidemics. Only two children in their care died.

Fashions in welfare changed, foster homes became the accepted mode of dealing with orphans, and by the 1920s the San Francisco society was again concentrating on the needs of women, especially old women. Symbolic of continuity, and despite changing fashions, three members of the Board of Managers in 1953 were descended from members or associates of the first society in 1853.

These examples are a tiny but representative fraction of nineteenth-century benevolent societies. The patterns they established in the early nineteenth century have lived on. On 2 March 1983, the weekly newsletter of the First Methodist Church in Athens, Georgia, carried the following announcement:

> Circle 9 enables us to grow in three ways as Christian women through: study that fosters our spiritual and intellectual growth, service projects that express our concern for others, and fellowship that binds us together as friends.
>
> Our monthly programs have been quite varied, on Isaiah, worship, the Nestle boycott, computers, and the interior spiritual life. . . .
>
> Our annual bake sale has provided the funds for making linens for the Ethel Harpst Home and gifts for its children, and for sending an underprivileged child to summer camp.[45]

Except for the Nestle boycott and the computers, this notice might have appeared in almost any town in any year since 1812.

How did women's benevolence, expressed through their voluntary associations, compare with that of men? The material for a detailed comparison would have to be drawn from widely disparate sources, but there is enough evidence to support some impressions. First, some men were more likely than women to operate as individuals. Robert Dalzell's description of Amos Lawrence, one of the Boston Associates, shows him to be a one-man benevolent society who spoke and acted much as the women's groups did. Similarly, one Alexander Henry, an Irish immigrant merchant in Philadelphia and one of the early enthusiasts for Sunday schools, made it a practice to buy wood in large quantities for needy citizens and to pay for the education of young men training for the ministry.[46] Other men tended to make large gifts to institutions, particularly those that might bear their names. When men undertook to organize charitable associations the differences at first glance seem minor. In New York, for example, in 1787 a group of professional and business leaders had established a Society for the Relief of Distressed Debtors to provide food and clothing for men in debtors' prison. Because wives and children of those imprisoned for debt were sometimes permitted to share the erstwhile breadwinner's cell, such aid might feed a whole family. Gradually members of the society expanded their concerns to include vice, immorality, and drunkenness in the jails, and in 1791, in concert with the Medical Society of New York, they set up the New York Dispensary to serve the medical needs of the indigent. It is not clear how long this society persisted.

In another case, a group of New York men, declaring themselves tired of amelioration, set out to identify and then prevent the causes of pauperism. They wound up with much the same diagnosis as their compatriot women, which is to say they decided poverty was caused by intemperance, gambling, and lack of character. Indeed their whole effort was astonishingly revealing of the difficulty comfortable people had in analyzing the structural causes of poverty, and of the dismay they felt when "solving" the problem turned out to be a mirage. After a few years of effort the Society for the Prevention of Pauperism tacitly recognized defeat and resolved itself into a less ambitious Society for the Reformation of Juvenile Delinquents, which established, in 1824, a refuge to which juveniles could be committed by the courts.[47]

The only serious effort on the part of a historian to compare male and female associations in the antebellum years is found in Suzanne Lebsock's *Free Women of Petersburg*. Asking whether the organizational lives of men and women were indeed separate, and whether women's collective behavior differed from that of men, Lebsock answers yes to both questions. Women, acting collectively, were, she suggests, more apt to be highly personal and to direct their efforts toward other women. However, she also discovered in examining local records that after years during which poor relief had been accepted as women's responsibility, by the 1850s mixed associations began to take over responsibilities once carried by all-women groups. When this happened women constituted themselves as auxiliary to male societies.[48] A similar shift in Cleveland in the same decade suggests that some change in prevailing perceptions of responsibility was taking place, but whether the initiative came from men or women—or both—is not recorded.[49]

The most significant difference between male and female benevolence was this: for men, philanthropy or benevolence, whether conducted individually or in associations, was generally only part of a larger career. Much time was devoted to making the money of which they would then give some to worthy causes. Benevolence figured in the building of a man's career, both as a means of forming associations with other men and as a means of promoting a favorable public image, but it was rarely his central concern or source of identity. Women's benevolent societies by contrast *were* their "careers," an accepted extension of their defined role as wives and mothers.

Like some simple life-forms that persist for millennia while more complex forms appear and disappear, the benevolent society has survived for nearly two centuries, through tumultuous change, and despite the proliferation of many more complex women's associations and the growth of the welfare state. The forms of organization invented by the founders of the benevolent societies shaped the future of voluntary associations of the most diverse kinds.

Although the founding of many early societies reflected the religious enthusiasm of the early nineteenth century, once they came into existence these groups took on a complex life that met both personal and collective needs beyond religious or spiritual ones. For individuals there was sociability with women of their own class or cast of mind and reassurance that as dispensers of benevolence they were important people in the community. Some women enjoyed the craftsmanship they practiced on behalf of the poor. Working together, black women found the kind of support white society denied them, and that they did not always receive from black men. And although their search for respectability was of a different order from that of white women, for them, too, the voluntary association provided a measure of status.

Visiting the needy offered a protected way to look across class boundaries and obtain a wider experience of life without risking one's own position. Some felt their souls benefited from exposure to the vicissitudes of life among the working classes; others, no doubt, simply enjoyed the sentiment of pity, the assurance, by contrast, of their own good fortune. In the early days the teaching or preaching which went along with charity allowed women to do things not otherwise permitted. A few—very few as far as the record goes—began to ponder the reasons for the extreme poverty they sometimes encountered and to make their own, often naïve, social analysis. At the same time their encounters with clients increased awareness of class differences on both sides.

Over the years benevolent societies rarely stirred significant community opposition.[50] They have tended to fulfill the basic cultural expectation that women should be compassionate and nurturing; they have provided women with a public way to practice these virtues without calling their fundamental womanliness into question in any way. Perhaps this is one secret of their persistence.[51]

The concrete accomplishments of nineteenth-century societies were considerable. At a time when poverty was spreading and municipal governments felt hard-pressed to meet minimum needs, food, clothing, and medical care were very important to people who did not have these things. For at least the first half of the nineteenth century municipalities were often quite unable to keep up with multiplying demands for aid, and women's associations strove to fill the gap. At the most elemental level a child with shoes is better off than a child without shoes, no matter what complex motivation provided the gift.

From the beginning, women's societies created community institutions. First came orphan asylums, then schools, employment services, homes for wayward girls, libraries, old ladies' homes, and the like. These institutions were run on limited resources and depended heavily on the day-to-day work of benevolent women. Paid staff members were generally members of the societies who needed to earn their keep. Providing a setting for a dignified old age for even a minority of aged widows and spinsters and caring for orphan children met pressing community needs.

In the beginning, benevolent women thought vice led to poverty; in time they reversed the order: poverty might lead to vice, and their favorite cure was education.

What do the records of benevolent societies tell us about the women who built them? Clearly by the end of the eighteenth century numbers of women had acquired some education despite the scarcity of formal schools. The handwriting of members and subscribers, the skillful minutes, the carefully constructed constitutions, the precise records and accounts, the willingness to handle money—all suggest that the kind of female education Benjamin Rush had declared to be necessary for the new nation was already taking place.[52]

There is also evidence that many married women had some money of their own; furthermore, they seem to have had few qualms about asking men, in their families and out, for money to carry on charitable endeavors. From the earliest days women not only handled money in significant amounts but even in small communities they invested resources in local business enterprise.

From the beginning, white women's associations had a political dimension. Isabella Graham went to the legislature for a charter for the New York Widows' Society in the 1790s, and other societies did likewise. In time the New York legislature permitted a public lottery for the benefit of the Widows' Society. Incorporation was one way to reduce the normal limitations on women's legal right to act, and permitted them to do things otherwise forbidden to married women such as acquiring, holding, and conveying property.[53] The speed with which the San Francisco society asked for state money as well as a state charter suggests that by mid-century both had come to be standard procedure for benevolent societies.[54]

It has become a truism that organizational experience played a significant part in the changing self-concepts of the women involved. Nancy Cott, in *Bonds of Womanhood,* suggested that on the one hand benevolent societies reinforced the prevailing cultural definition of womanly behavior, but on the other hand helped make women conscious of themselves as women—a necessary first step, she argued, to the development of what would many years later be labeled a feminist consciousness. Nancy Hewitt took issue with this view saying that, at least among the elite charitable societies in Rochester, class and kin relations were far more likely to be reinforced than feelings of sisterhood. These observations are not mutually exclusive, nor do they encompass all the possibilities.[55] Members of benevolent societies might empathize particularly with women—thus establishing bonds of sisterhood—while at the same time exhibiting the class prejudices common to both sexes among their own friends and family. They certainly saw poor women as more vulnerable than poor men, and concentrated their resources on helping them.

And in any case, whether feeling bonds of sisterhood or those of class, active benevolent society members were inevitably changing themselves. Especially for the leaders, the voluntary association offered a chance to establish an identity independent of husbands and a chance to exercise competence or achieve ambition. When these things happened, even if only to a handful of women in a given place, but multiplied by hundreds and hundreds of communities, the aggregate effect was surely to begin to change the social definition of women's roles. These effects would be more visible in the next phase of associational life, which began to develop in the 1820s.

A Century of Benevolence:
The Case of the Boston Fragment Society

The Boston Fragment Society may be unique in the continuity of its records from the first meeting to the present decade. The minutes of this association provide an illuminating case study of a society created by white women who were already part of an established elite, one destined to be extraordinarily durable. Their experience illuminates many of the points made in this chapter.

When six single and five married women of Boston's leading families met in October 1812 to form what they decided to call the Fragment Society, it is doubtful that they saw themselves as part of a great national movement bringing women into public life, and still more doubtful that they thought of themselves as beginning to influence the social history of their community.[56] Many decades later members of the society would begin to see their own history as an important part of Boston's history, but in the beginning their conscious concern was to meet the needs of the widows and orphans whose numbers were being multiplied by the War of 1812. They saw themselves as doing God's work, and a kind of work appropriate for women.

When the founders met in 1812 Boston had thirty-two thousand inhabitants and was still, in Sam Bass Warner's phrase, "a walking city."[57] The parable of the loaves and fishes provided the name (John 6:11, "Gather up the fragments that nothing be lost"). From the first a secretary kept careful records, a habit that has continued to the present day. Manuscript minutes, especially those in which a chatty secretary wrote down everything she observed, along with printed annual reports and occasional newspaper clippings allow us to see how this group began, how its members defined their responsibilities, how it responded to or held out against changes in the community and the nation over more than 170 years. Fragment Society members clung to tradition, especially their own, but the world changed and the organization reluctantly reflected some of those changes.

The early records reveal a material and domestic world very different from our own. In a remarkably short time, the eleven founders had recruited four hundred others whose names were a roll call of Boston's leading families: Cabots, Dudleys, Greenleafs, Higginsons, Belknaps, Lorings, Lymans, Otises, Bullfinches, and so on, joined as family groups.[58] Forty-two members shared a surname with at least one other, in some cases with five or six others. The copperplate handwriting of many signatures to the constitution testified to a level of education unusual among women in 1812.

Early minutes recorded with great precision every gift to a "destitute and worthy" person. Thus a Mrs. Bethel got one sheet, one frock, one petticoat, one pair of hose, and two shifts; a Mr. Tyler received one pair of pantaloons, and so on. The Prudential Committee was empowered to "attend such wants as may offer between meetings of the Board"; otherwise the board heard a detailed report on each applicant and voted on each donation.

The four hundred (and more, over time) subscribers who gave money and were called members of the society met annually, while the ongoing work was done in neighborhood sewing circles and by the board itself, which met frequently, summer and winter, to allocate resources and do its share of sewing the layettes for which the society became famous.[59] Fines were imposed on any member who missed a meeting without an acceptable excuse. Chests of linens and baby clothes were collected to be lent to expectant mothers with the injunction that they were to be returned clean after they had fulfilled their purpose. In the same manner sheets and blankets were lent to sick people—neither the germ theory nor the throwaway society was yet dreamed of. In 1818 eighty-seven people borrowed bedding; sixty-seven returned it "clean and in good order." Members seemed to think this a reasonable proportion.

In the first year, at least 506 calls for aid were answered, and in one meeting, in January 1813, the board authorized gifts of garments (usually four or five) to each of 75 persons, mostly women. In that year there were 584 subscribers—clearly a significant number of Boston women had access to some money which they could allocate as they chose. Already the society was trying to find work for its clients; unemployment was then, and would continue to be, a constant problem for people who had little possibility of saving for such exigencies. Over and over members were exhorted to raise more money. "As widows and orphans are fast multiplying around us in consequence of our present calamities, it is earnestly recommended that every member of the Society use her influence to obtain subscriptions and donations." Winter was always hard for poor people; the number of recipients regularly rose as the weather turned colder.

Pregnant women were a special concern. Fragment Society layettes—which members took the utmost pleasure in making and delivering—were of the best quality flannel, of a peculiarly recognizable yellow. No one appears to have asked how the recipients might feel about being thus identified as the receivers of charity.[60] By 1815 some members had joined the Massachusetts Female Bible Society and undertook to deliver Bibles along with clothing. They reported many promises to read the sacred book.

Class lines were not yet firmly drawn; members of the same family might be found on different rungs of the social ladder. Mobility was downward as well as upward. Minutes and annual reports repeatedly reminded members that they themselves might someday be in need. Occasionally note was taken of a subscriber who had fallen on hard times whom the society was called upon to help, or of a recipient who had been restored to prosperity and become a subscriber. Despite constant complaints that its resources were not enough to meet the growing need, the society began to invest some of its money in notes of the Second Bank of the United States. In 1818, of $1,126 received only $776 was spent: the rest went into the Permanent Fund. Though they sought financial advice from men, these women showed no reluctance to manage money.

The depression of 1819 was writ large in the minutes. Donations dropped and needs rose, and in 1822 the annual report spoke again of the fragility of prosperity: "In this chequered life the cup of sorrow is often filled. We know not how soon it may be proffered to each of us."[61] And indeed, many well-to-do Bostonians had "suffered reverses," as the phrase went, in the preceding three years.

In the beginning, names of subscribers and recipients had been interchangeable, and were nearly all English, Scottish, or Welsh. Over the first decade a few Irish names began to appear among the recipients, and, in time, Italian names as well. As the number of immigrants multiplied, women of the Fragment Society emphasized their feeling of responsibility for "our own poor," and by 1827 adopted a rule that no one who had lived in the city for less than three years could receive aid. Even with three years' residence, foreigners had to be "well known to the directors or to some subscriber who recommends them" before they could expect help. The changes wrought by immigration would become a constant theme in the minutes.

As newcomers began to compete with native Bostonians for jobs, so an increasing number of benevolent societies competed for resources. The Fragment Society secretary noted, somewhat defiantly: "The streams of benevolence have been diverted into many new channels, but this is far from disheartening to us."[62] Meanwhile, board members persuaded some of their clients, whether wives of alcoholic men or women who were themselves given to drinking is not entirely clear, to form a "Female Union Temperate Society" and promised to make these women "the special objects of our attention." Alcohol loomed large in their analysis of the causes of poverty.

Decades before Social Darwinism was thought of, the Fragment Society had to defend itself against the charge that extending alms discouraged poor people from exertion in their own behalf. Not so, the secretary wrote, as she provided touching stories of helpless children and beleaguered widows, who could not possibly have helped themselves. She also commented vehemently upon the inadequate wages paid to females, and wondered how self-supporting women could survive at all. Elsewhere in Boston by this time the Seaman's Aid Society had set up projects intended to improve the wages of seamstresses; there is no evidence that the Fragment Society had heard of this experiment.[63] By 1834 it was providing clothing so children could go to Sunday school and had begun to talk about breaking the cycle of poverty. By making it possible for young children to get schooling, the women believed, "present suffering is not only alleviated but something is done to prevent its recurrence in the next generation.... The child who enjoys constantly the advantage of these schools we cannot expect to see, in after life, among the degraded poor—especially if it was early brought under moral and religious influence in the Infant School.... *To give education to the young children and lucrative employment to the parents is undoubtedly the best charity*" (italics mine).

In 1838 came another serious depression. One board member of long experience reported: "I find I have assisted fifty families, eighteen of whom were respectable widows. I have distributed among them one hundred and eleven garments and forty-five pairs of shoes, and I think I can of truth say I have never witnessed so much suffering among the respectable poor for the twenty-five years I have visited." She went on to describe a washerwoman who was begging for work, an aged woman and her daughter sewing sheets for eight cents apiece, and two cases of "intemperance reclaimed." With such examples before them, the women again reminded themselves of the "instability of all earthly blessings" and the ever-present danger of a "reverse of fortunes." Clearly they could imagine themselves remanded to respectable poverty. More Irish names appeared among the subscribers. In 1841, in the midst of the Washingtonian temperance revival, the minutes announced, with somewhat premature optimism, that the rapid growth of the temperance movement, together with the work of the Sunday schools, would soon make the society's work unnecessary.[64]

After thirty years, the founding generation began disappearing from the scene, but the society had developed a powerful social cachet, and daughters and granddaughters, as well as other women from the expanding upper middle class, filled their places. Membership marked a woman as a member of the elite. Despite the advent of a new generation and the rapidly changing milieu of mid-century Boston, the spirit of the minutes and reports was remarkably unchanged. It was as if Fragment Society members, having created a comfortable niche outside their homes, were determined to preserve it, come what might.

Each annual report reiterated that winter had been hard on the poor and urged members to be willing to visit as well as to give money. Actually going into the homes of poor people was seen as valuable to the visitor who would otherwise "lose the lesson and influence which the various strata of society are designed to teach us." People in need, the officers insisted, must be helped to believe in themselves, and "whole and decent clothing" built self-confidence. Self-confidence, in turn, would prevent a poor person from "sinking into beggary." From the first the society had insisted on providing new clothes and shoes, not hand-me-downs.[65] Members were enjoined to be on the lookout for those in need, since experience showed that many people waited until they were absolutely desperate to ask for help.

At mid-century, Fragment Society members still saw themselves as doing God's work and still reminded themselves constantly that *they*, in contrast to their clients, had been blessed by Providence and must show their gratitude by doing good for others. But Boston was changing, and some adaptation could no longer be avoided. For example, so many members had moved to the suburbs that long afternoon meetings followed by supper and more work had to give way. The women could no longer walk home. Movement of such families to the suburbs sharpened the distinction between classes which had been growing since the society began.

In 1854 the secretary returned to the vexed subject of women's inadequate wages—they were, she wrote feelingly, quite out of proportion to the cost of living. Even a healthy working woman, working as hard as she was able, could barely support herself, much less any children. Yet her only conclusion was that such women should not be ashamed to ask for assistance when they were ill. Perhaps for the wives and daughters of Boston's business community an effort to deal seriously with the issue of women's wages might raise anxiety-producing questions about the sources of their own good fortune.

From time to time they did perceive social change. In 1859 the secretary wrote at length: " . . . we cannot look from our windows, we cannot take our daily walk, without meeting want and degradation at every step. The tide of emigration which breaks upon our coast rolls inland the strong, the vigorous, the enterprising to the distant prairies, while the feeble, the idle, and the unthrifty like tangled masses of sea weed, are left by the waters limit. . . . Daily the cry grows more and more urgent. . . . "

The Civil War brought new problems. Inflation taxed the society's resources, and in time cotton flannel for layettes disappeared. Shoes were expensive and hard to get; contributions flowed less freely; and most difficult of all, war work diverted the energies of members. Recognizing the inevitability of war-created demands, the leaders worried about time once given to the poor being devoted entirely to soldiers. Recognizing, too, that nearly every family had sons or brothers in the army, they nevertheless hoped that members would not cease to attend to the suffering around them.

In 1864 the society's president suggested that feelings battered by the horrors of the war and the revelations from Libby and Andersonville prisons were less likely to respond to the "simple account of destitution." She warned members against sinking into inaction when vast numbers of artisans were out of work, when state aid for soldiers' families had ended, when many veterans were invalids and increasing numbers of women widowed. High prices were adding to the burdens of working people. "Each of us without the slightest sacrifice might double our subscription," she noted sternly.

In 1867 postwar weariness crept into the record: "Let us take up our work then, not with the feeling of sameness and wearisomeness, but glad we are permitted to do something for Him who has done so much for us." In the following year discouragement was even stronger: the secretary wrote that the society must keep on doing good even if members could not see any impressive results from their charity.

The minutes described the business depression of 1873 as a "great calamity"; demands for help multiplied. Although the Permanent Fund had now reached nine thousand dollars, no one suggested dipping into capital. Problems came from another quarter as well: The society's annual social event had gradually become expensive, exclusive, and highly visible (the group regularly sent a carriage to bring the society editor of the *Boston Evening Transcript* to these parties), and in the midst of the depression, criticism began to reach the members' ears. People were saying pointedly that the money required for such affairs could better be spent for the poor. Within the society, debate on the subject was inconclusive. Five years later euphemistic discussions of this issue were still going on—the members did not want their good works harmed by "evil speaking" but obviously did not want, either, to give up their elegant parties which had come to identify them as a special kind of elite. In the end the parties continued.

In the eighties and nineties, annual reports became more matter-of-fact. Except from the hand of an occasional very pious secretary, religious imagery declined, and fewer discussions of the providence of God were recorded. Members observed what they took to be a decrease in the amount of beggary in Boston, along with other social changes. The annual meeting had to be shifted from October to November to accommodate officers who were now in the habit of staying on in their summer homes until late fall. The long-established custom of reading from the Scripture before tea was served at sewing circles had been abandoned; the change called forth some criticism. The secretary observed that the character of these meetings had changed: "If we contrast the quiet room of former days, with the small number reverently laying aside all occupation to listen, with subdued demeanor, to the holy words, with the crowded parlors of the present day, often so spacious that many of those assembled cannot catch the sound, and some even continuing to ply the busy needle in ignorance of what is going on, we cannot but feel that its continuance under such circumstances is no longer desirable." Scripture or no, she reminded her readers, "We do not wish our friends to forget" that sewing was the real object of these sociable meetings.

For nearly twenty-five years private charity in American cities had been developing toward systematic organization and cooperation, but the women of the Fragment Society were reluctant to risk losing their identity or diluting their prestige by joining with other groups. Their habits of functioning were deeply fixed, and after much discussion they agreed to go their independent way.[66] Members continued to sew layettes, including hand-made diapers, and to distribute cash, goods, and shoes, the latter bought year after year from the same company.

By 1894 a minister giving the traditional lecture at the annual meeting spoke of the progressive reform in city government then going on in many American cities, and implied that the work of the Fragment Society could be seen as part of this movement. Two years later the annual report noted that the women had been hearing a good deal about class hatred, "which has been termed the greatest curse of European nations." Bostonians, they said, could "point with pride to noble charities," which they perceived as over-coming the regrettable chasm between the social classes. The minutes suggest that they were aware of the progressive attack on municipal corruption:

Our municipal politics rule and govern the poorer constituency by the opening up of the liquor traffic each year to a greater degree; [and through] promising petty office or ill-paid city labour for the sake of a vote, and the consequent degradation of not only the respectable foreign population, but also of the native born American citizen causes us to pause and wonder sometimes, if the trouble that our Society [goes to] to clothe Mrs. Shankey and her seven children or [to coax] Mrs. Brown and her three hungry growing boys into an effort of decent living, and thorough respectability can ever make any headway in the great social reform which even a Society like ours is trying to push forward. . . .

Three years later the secretary noted uneasily: "Thinking men and women are unable to predict what the results will be of the active discussion now going on by all classes regarding the social and economic questions which confront us." The security of the social order was no longer to be taken for granted.

The striking stability of the society's values and its determination to preserve them were reinforced by frequent reference to its own history. Year after year the minutes of an 1815 meeting were reprinted to remind members of their origins. Social affairs featured women wearing clothing in the style of 1812, and each year's records were carefully preserved.

By 1902 the president felt called to comment: "As we near the end of a century of usefulness we try to broaden our field and meet the demands of an ever increasing and complicated population...." As she wrote, the number of recipients was rising—there were more than a thousand in 1904, twice the number of 1813. The population of Boston, of course, had multiplied by fifteen since the society began.

Two years later, for the first time, some members expressed concern that the distinctive color of their excellent layettes placed a stigma of charity on recipients. A compromise ensued: If a member wished to sew her share in white flannel instead of the traditional yellow, she might do so. The annual report suggested the existence of other challenges: "The past six months has been one of awakening and reform in many parts of our country. In the changes that may come in our methods may we be guided by clear insight and calm judgment."

The society was still struggling to come to terms with the challenges of the twentieth century when the World War began. It sent some help to the Belgians, "but we feel our principal duty is to encourage our own citizens who come to us from all nations of the world for freedom and growth, and who through no fault of their own, will be called upon to suffer hunger and privation during the coming winter." This was a broader vision of "our own poor" than that of the early years—but the emphasis was still on "respectable" people who were too proud to ask for help. The war ended, and the president wrote: "We hope the lessons taught us by our forebears may help us solve the many problems that will surely face us in the new world, when the New Democracy and the Christian ideal of brotherhood will I believe sink deeper into our hearts."

Exactly how "the lessons of our forebears" helped the society get through the 1920s, the record does not reveal. In the 1930s, the Great Depression brought problems on a scale hitherto unknown, while at the same time the society had to come to terms with an increasingly bureaucratized system of private and public welfare. While urging its members to support President Roosevelt's efforts to deal with the Depression (surprising in view of the general response of Boston's elite to the New Deal), the Fragment Society still dealt in highly personal charity. For example, a poor girl lost her glasses, the society bought new ones so she could go to work, and her letter of gratitude was read aloud at the next meeting.[67] At the same time they were slowly adopting new ways: A paid buyer shopped for the society—she was instructed to make sure that Filene's knew for whom she bought and gave the best possible price—and people referred by government agencies as well as those identified by its own members were among the recipients. The society gave lump sums to various city missions.

World War II brought more changes. Dutch Treat luncheons, first at the College Club and then at the more democratic Women's Educational and Industrial Union, replaced lavish entertainment in a member's home. Sometimes two hundred women turned out. Only in 1949, after 137 years, did the younger members finally hoot out of existence once and for all the handmade diapers (euphemistically called "Art Squares" all those years), to the great relief of everyone concerned. By that year, a new problem had arisen: Too many of the older members were spending winters in Florida. For the work to continue, the group must attract young women. The board wisely judged that this meant finding interesting work for new members to do.

Thus the Fragment Society continued on its way. In 1812 dues had been set at two dollars a year or thirty dollars for a life membership, and so they remained for 150 years. The work was financed in part by wealthy men, and, as time passed, by an ever-increasing number of legacies from members. The Permanent Fund, though affected by the vicissitudes of the economy, was carefully invested, until it became a substantial capital that provided regular income.

In the beginning, members of the board had sewed faithfully at every meeting and distributed their own handiwork to the poor. But as the urban economy became more dependent upon cash, so did the society. Though sewing continued, it provided only a small part of the goods to be distributed.

Beginning at a time when the elite often shared family ties with the poor, and the elite could imagine themselves cast into respectable poverty, the Fragment Society had become part of the established order. Poor people, however "respectable," were pitied—and patronized. Members, on the other hand, were confirmed in their social standing, and the very existence of their exclusive group emphasized the widening gap between the haves and the have-nots.[68]

The society changed with the times, but very slowly, and in many ways not at all. Members clung to the simple idea that good-quality shoes and clothing in themselves would put a poor child on the road to self-improvement. There were winters when a thousand Boston children wore Fragment Society shoes. However much members worried about not having enough money to provide every barefoot child with shoes, they never threw caution to the winds and withdrew capital from the Permanent Fund.[69] The minutes create a curious sense of insularity, almost of unreality, as one watches these women of Boston's best educated, most elite families go through decades of social conflict over slavery, of social disruption following the massive Irish immigration, of debate about public schools, discussion of woman's rights, industrial conflict, workingmen's parties, strikes and lockouts, the ferment of Progressivism, the Red scare, without, seemingly, recognizing any of it. They continually deplored the existence of poverty (though sometimes arguing, paradoxically, that the poor existed to educate their betters), but rarely attempted any careful analysis of its causes, though by the late nineties there were occasional uneasy recognitions that such analyses did exist and contained implications threatening to their peace of mind. Through it all, the women of the Fragment Society moved along their accustomed channel, adapting when they absolutely had to, but most of the time hardly recognizing—if the minutes accurately reflect the prevailing mindset—the existence of profound moral or political issues. After the Civil War, some Boston women had become immersed in the temperance and suffrage movements, but these concerns did not appear to touch the Fragment Society, except insofar as the members always saw alcohol as the chief cause of poverty.[70]

It was as if they had marked out once and for all their particular public responsibility, and anything else was somebody else's business. Few societies anywhere have kept such complete records or managed to maintain so much continuity. The president, in 1962, was descended from the first president of 1812. The society still functions as I write.

2

To Overleap the Modesty of Nature: The Emergence of Female Activism

While the Fragment Society and its ever-increasing number of counter-parts continued on a quiet and well-marked path, women and men alike were trying to adjust to rapid change and increasing social complexity. The Second Great Awakening was in full swing, and the idea that people could choose to be saved, could by act of will give up sin and approach perfection, provided much of the energy for "freedom's ferment"—the proliferation of reform movements ranging from utopian communities to diet and temperance, from moral reform to antislavery, and, increasingly, to women's rights.[1]

Many women were content to remain in the safe confines of the benevolent society; others responded to the electric atmosphere of the antebellum years with daring forays into public activism. The ideology of "true womanhood" convinced some women that they should exercise the moral power, said to be peculiarly theirs, only at home, but others were beginning to argue that their responsibility extended to the larger society. Though reformers often ventured forth in company with men, they exhibited a strong propensity to form all-women organizations, which they could run to suit themselves. Prostitution, the double standard, alcohol, and slavery were the social issues that first brought women into public notice. In undertaking to deal with such explosive questions they began to behave in ways hitherto considered not entirely proper and to invade territory long reserved for men. The opposition they encountered stimulated some women to think about their own restricted legal and social status.

Whatever combination of forces was attracting more men to active involvement in public life and making them less and less willing to defer to traditional leaders affected at least a minority of women as well. In the face of social developments that they saw as threatening to their families women began speaking in public, circulating petitions, and in other ways practicing active citizenship. One Rochester woman, after years of trying to deal with the most disadvantaged people in town through traditional benevolence, decided that charity was never going to change their—to her—deplorable behavior and proposed that women should go in a body to the city council demanding a workhouse "where idle and drunken mothers and fathers must go and work." She was, more than she could know, foreshadowing the future.[2]

For years historians have argued that rapid economic development and social change bred a pervasive anxiety and a strong desire on the part of comfortable citizens to control the behavior of the growing working class. While it is certainly true that well-established white Protestants often exhibited disdain for immigrants, black people, and almost anybody different from themselves, as well as distaste for the life of crowded slums, personal and literary documents do not support any easy generalization as to what men or women hoped to accomplish through their voluntary organizations.

The chronology varied considerably from place to place; as the population moved west women in new settlements tended to recapitulate the history of earlier communities in compressed form, combining older forms of activity with the new. In Cleveland, for example, the Female Charitable Society and the Female Moral Reform Society appeared simultaneously in 1837 when the town had barely two thousand inhabitants. Nearly two decades later San Francisco women, as we saw in the first chapter, combined practices developed in Boston and New York half a century before and adapted them to the peculiar needs of a gold rush city. While women in the longer-settled areas were developing new forms of organization, benevolent societies continued to appear on the frontier.

By the 1830s change was visible in many places as women's moral reform, temperance, and antislavery societies took shape, and women factory workers organized short-lived but vigorous efforts to improve their wages and conditions of labor. Here and there, middle-class women also took up the cause of working women's poor wages and difficulty in finding work. Black women, in a context of discrimination and deprivation, strove urgently to help themselves. All these groups had in common the desire to change behavior. There was considerable crossover in membership among organizations, nearly all had a high degree of religious commitment, and most encountered a greater or lesser degree of community opposition. Few escaped a degree of internal conflict.

Moral Reform

The first involvement of women in collective efforts to reform prostitutes, discourage their clients, and prevent young women from being drawn into a life of prostitution is hard to pinpoint; sometime early in the century Isabella Graham, the leading benevolent woman in New York, had joined a group of men in the city to form a short-lived Magdalene Society.[3] Graham died in 1814 and so did the society. In Boston by the 1820s there were said to be fifty-seven thousand prostitutes, and a Female Missionary Society founded a Penitent Females Refuge in an effort to reform a few of them.[4]

By the 1830s the term "moral reform" was coming into use. In New York City an eager young minister named John McDowall had attracted a good deal of attention when he "discovered" the evil of prostitution and set out with great enthusiasm to rescue its victims. Responding to McDowall's revelations, a group of wealthy men had organized a second Magdalene Society but speedily retreated when public opposition to open discussion of the subject exploded. Meanwhile, a group of evangelical women who had ventured into the slums bearing religious tracts were appalled by what they saw. Seizing upon the prostitute as epitomizing the degradation of urban life, and symbolizing the profoundly resented double standard so blatantly practiced in their own social circle, these women organized what would come, after various permutations, to be called the New York Female Moral Reform Society (FMRS). In the beginning this society set out to offer an alternative life to "fallen women," and at the same time to shame, and thus reform, the men who were their clients.[5] This small, seemingly intrepid group of women took over a journal McDowall had started. Renamed *The Advocate of Moral Reform* and staffed almost entirely with women, this journal carried the war against "licentiousness" into small towns and large and became an important tool for recruiting new supporters.

At first the New York women sought counsel from ministers and other men, some of whom presided over the early meetings; it was not long, however, before the women were taking full responsibility for their organization and turning to men only for advice on financial questions or, occasionally, for help in visiting dangerous neighborhoods.

In its first year the New York FMRS circulated two thousand pamphlets describing its aims and inviting other women, no matter where they lived, to join. Members visited houses of prostitution to pray for (or with) the startled inmates, and noted for later publication the names of men they saw coming and going. When clergymen and laymen joined in vituperative attacks on the society, castigating members for unladylike behavior, the women were unmoved, reminding their critics that since men were in the habit of holding women responsible for improving the moral tone of society they could hardly complain when they assumed that responsibility.[6]

An experiment with a house of refuge for prostitutes who might want to find a new way to earn a living proved disappointing. Despite the best efforts of the reformers, the handful of prostitutes who were persuaded to

seek rescue showed a strong tendency to backslide; warnings of the consequences of "deliberately preferring eternal misery to a life of virtue" had
little effect.[7]

While this experiment was limping along, so many satellite groups were
forming upstate, in New England, and in the Middle West that the New
York FMRS laid claim to two hundred auxiliary societies.[8] In three years
this number doubled, and by 1839 the numbers had grown to the point
that the name of the parent body was changed to American Female Moral
Reform Society.

Meanwhile, in New York City, the refuge idea having proved unworkable,
members of the society, who were beginning to think that prevention might
be more effective than cure, set up an Office of Registry to provide
employment services. Commercial agencies, they were convinced, often
simply directed job-seeking women to houses of prostitution. The employment service, unlike the house of refuge, attracted large numbers of
women, but the initiators soon discovered how difficult it was to help
self-supporting women find jobs of any sort, much less jobs that paid
enough to live on. Gradually the moral reformers began to perceive
something more than willful sin in an unwillingness to be rescued from a
life that at least for young women paid a living wage.

As they tackled practical problems, members' confidence and willingness to experiment grew. Observing deplorable prison conditions during
visits to their clients, they began to urge the city government to appoint
women matrons. One by-product of that campaign was the formation of a
Female Department of the New York Prison Association, which in its turn
established a home for discharged female convicts.[9] When the city council
agreed to put matrons in the prisons, the women were emboldened to turn
their attention to the state legislature, where they began lobbying for a law
against seduction. Moral reform societies in smaller cities and towns joined
enthusiastically in petitioning for such a law and in 1848 the New York
legislature gave in.[10] Though the law itself was virtually meaningless, the
power of concerted lobbying would not be forgotten.

There were other learning experiences along the way. In 1841, finding that
a male business agent had mishandled its money, the New York FMRS, after
consulting "business friends" who gave a considered opinion that "a lady of
good education, vigorous health, and accustomed to the details of business
could discharge the duties of office," appointed a woman treasurer. Before
long it appeared that she had failed to report a large contribution. Pressed,
the woman said she had been keeping the money to send to missionaries in
the Sandwich Islands and refused to turn over her books. After consulting
"several legal gentlemen," the board expelled her; she publicly questioned
the society's motives. Women, it seemed, could be as troublesome as men.

By the mid-1840s moral reformers' attention began shifting from prostitutes to children. Experience had shown that the absence of child care was a major obstacle to women's self-support. An initial experiment with day care failed because the nursery was too far from the homes and workplaces of the women in need of help, but a Temporary Home for Friendless and Destitute Females and Children of Good Character was far more popular and in time developed into a major refuge for orphans and abandoned children. As they set out to raise money for this house, members were warned that the name "moral reform" put off some potential donors, and that it might also prevent the legislature from issuing a charter. Thus, in 1849, the society was incorporated as The American Female Guardian Society, and the journal became *The Advocate and Family Guardian*. In this form it was destined to continue for years, but with a focus that had changed considerably from the early days.[11]

Unlike the benevolent societies that took on what would be their permanent form very early, the New York Female Moral Reform Society went through a rapid evolution. Beginning with the notion that they could reform both prostitutes and the men who visited them, the women had quickly discovered that neither group was inclined to change its ways. In the process of making this discovery, however, members of the society learned something about the problems of wage-earning women and began to experiment with institutions that might begin to ameliorate some of them.

Carroll Smith-Rosenberg summed up the change that had taken place in less than twenty years:

> The Moral Reform Society . . . had been founded . . . as a zealous . . . and in some ways feminist . . . movement to end sexual transgressions and hasten the millennium; by the 1860s, the Society, renamed the American Female Guardian Society, had become a shelter for indigent women, an employment agency, and an educator of slum women and children. Instead of filling its publications with exhortations to moral and spiritual perfection, it now published analyses of city inspectors' reports on health and housing, articles concerning milk adulteration, and discussions of the proper diet for the working poor. Increasingly knowledgeable in regard to the problems of slum life, the Society's managers embarked upon a highly eclectic "social service" program: they rented sewing machines to unemployed seamstresses; they even encouraged working women to organize and raise wages.[12]

In its early days the New York society had defied public opinion to insist on women's right to deal with such a sensitive topic as prostitution. Later, members lobbied successfully in city councils and state legislatures. By mid-century, Smith-Rosenberg suggests, the New York society was a prototype for the civic improvement associations which women would establish in large numbers toward the end of the nineteenth century.[13]

While this impressive evolution was going on in the city, moral reform societies in smaller towns kept a narrower focus. The constitution of one small society, for example, after denouncing the "onward march of licentiousness . . . with all its attendant evils . . . destroying the foundations of domestic happiness and threatening our cities with the fate of Sodom and Gomorrah," pledged its members to "cultivate purity of morals in thought and deed," and announced that members would not go to balls or theaters or entertain company at unreasonable hours.[14]

The Female Moral Reform Society of Grafton, Massachusetts, organized in 1838 as an auxiliary of the larger Boston Society, is a good example of the five hundred or more local societies whose members were endeavoring to cope with the perceived wave of "licentiousness." Called together by a minister's wife who would be president for many years, fifty-five women signed the constitution, and agreed to pay one dollar a year. They met once every three months, to study scripture, pray, and read *Friend of Virtue,* the publication of the Boston society. At one meeting members discussed the "fatal tendency of indulgence in wandering thoughts . . . the pathway to every degrading vice." Many meetings concentrated on the complexities of trying to raise moral children. The name of a "fallen member" was brought before the society; she was suspended and a committee appointed to "converse with her."[15] After due examination of the evidence, the committee recommended that the suspension continue until the society was convinced of her genuine repentance.

Despite the hundred paid members, the minutes bemoaned the small attendance at meetings, blaming this apathy on the absence of "stimulating speakers." The society did, however, secure three or four hundred signatures to the petition calling for a law against seduction. Meantime it collected clothing for the Temporary Home for Penitent Women, and for the Boston Asylum. By June 1857 the minutes recorded a meeting when only five women attended, yet somehow the group survived and was still meeting ten years later.

Both *Friend of Virtue* and the *Advocate of Moral Reform* regularly printed reports of real-life cases of fallen men and women. The innocent woman seduced and abandoned was the most common theme, but there were also stories of respectable married persons, male and female, meeting for illicit purposes, and of young men gone to the bad with both alcohol and sex. These reports about actual incidents along with moral tales about prostitution or adultery allowed women to write about (and read) titillating material under the guise of moral purpose. Copies of McDowall's *Memoirs,* filled with shocking revelations, circulated widely, and members of one society gave him all the credit for having opened their eyes to the "extraordinary extent of wickedness" in their own town.[16] Many reform movements have benefited from the human tendency to be curious about ways of life different from one's own.

Between New York City on the one hand and towns and villages on the other lay many rapidly growing small cities. In both Utica and Rochester the moral reform societies were structured like benevolent societies. Based on kin networks, for a time they attracted large numbers of members, some of whom were veterans of benevolence. In Utica, a rapidly growing commercial and manufacturing town, members began, in emulation of the New York City society, by visiting slums and brothels and reporting on the many varieties of vice they encountered. Next they fixed attention on the young, single men living in boardinghouses, whose behavior they attempted to monitor—an effort that led to a publicity war between the women and the young men. In 1841 the women circulated petitions calling for a law against prostitution, and went to court on behalf of a young woman whose employer had demanded sex as a condition of employment. As far as Mary Ryan was able to discover, the organization simply died in the 1840s at about the time that the New York City group was undergoing a metamorphosis.[17]

In Rochester the pattern was somewhat similar and the enthusiasm was such that for a while the society claimed five hundred members. It went through something of the same change of focus as had occurred in New York, but in the end disappeared, probably to merge with the Rochester Home for Friendless and Virtuous Females, while some members went on to temperance or antislavery, or returned their energy to benevolence.[18]

Temperance

Moral reformers were not the only women who, fortified by organization and catching the spirit of the times, began to behave in what their detractors would call "strong-minded" ways. Temperance, the largest and most all-encompassing of antebellum reform movements, also attracted women who were willing to defy public opinion.

Agitation on the subject had begun sometime around 1810 when a group of elite Boston men aspired to set an example to the masses by their moderate use of alcohol. The masses did not appear to be particularly interested. Ten years later the American Temperance Society, also beginning as an elite group, followed the example of the American Tract Society by sending out lecturers and publishing instructive literature.[19] Artisans and small proprietors took to the cause with enthusiasm and men "of the middling sort" who were not content to preach dignified moderation came to dominate the organization. They called for pledges of total abstinence and soon claimed to have organized six thousand local groups, containing in all a million members.[20]

Women were natural recruits to the temperance cause. Beginning with their earliest efforts at benevolence, they had perceived three major causes of poverty: age, illness, and intemperance. For the first two, only palliatives were possible, but if poor people could be persuaded to give up drinking, benevolent women thought, fundamental improvement in their economic situation would surely follow.

Excessive drinking, furthermore, was not confined to the objects of charity. Many women who rushed to join the temperance movement had firsthand experience with alcoholic husbands, brothers, or fathers, and occasionally with an alcoholic woman as well. An organized movement provided reinforcement for their individual efforts to change drinking behavior among friends and relatives as well as among the poor.[21]

From the point of view of the male leaders of the rapidly democratizing movement, women—whose power as mothers was so constantly extolled—could be a great help. But those who joined the male-dominated temperance societies soon found that they were expected to work but not to have opinions. It was not long before they began to organize all-female societies in which they could speak their minds.

As the movement developed through a series of phases, women continued to prefer to work separately. When, in the 1840s, mostly working-class men initiated the enthusiastic Washingtonian movement, a kind of temperance revival, women, many also from the working class, formed Martha Washington societies.[22] The Washingtonians built their emotional impact by parading persuasive lecturers who told stories of their personal salvation from alcohol. Though the peak of enthusiasm quickly passed, the short-term effects were spectacular. W. J. Rorabaugh has calculated that between 1830 and 1845 alcohol consumption dropped from 7.1 gallons to 1.8 gallons annually for every citizen over the age of fifteen.[23] Evidently the hopeful view—expressed by the Boston Fragment Society in 1841 and hinted by the Cambridge Female Humane Society a year later—that people were drinking less had some basis in fact. In Rochester, in December 1841 alone, women reported one thousand signatures to the total-abstinence pledge and in the following month thirteen hundred more. One Rochester woman wrote her husband: "I have no doubt that the great & universal disposition & effort to forsake this vice is a distinct harbinger of the millennium. . . . "[24]

After the Washingtonians came a new organization, the Sons of Temperance, which, taking a leaf from the book of the Independent Order of Odd Fellows, tried to bring a measure of order and ritual to the movement. The Daughters of Temperance, in addition to proselytizing for total abstinence, engaged in traditional charity, offering the familiar argument that clean clothes and decent food were necessary for any permanent reformation of character. In Cincinnati the Daughters set up an employment bureau to help destitute women find work.[25]

Susan B. Anthony first entered public life as a Daughter of Temperance and was converted to women's rights when the men in a Sons of Temperance Convention announced that the women were there to learn, not to talk. In 1852 and again the following year, women made a considerable stir by demanding to be heard in various temperance conventions and, when their demands got nowhere, by organizing an all-female national convention.[26]

Meanwhile, the temperance movement turned in a new direction when Maine enacted the first statewide prohibition law. Persuasion, temperance leaders thought, was not discouraging alcohol consumption fast enough. In fact, if Rorabaugh is right, it had been remarkably effective for a time, but reform movements are characteristically cyclical and by the 1850s drinking may have been again on the rise.[27] In any case, the Maine law inaugurated a trend toward legal coercion. With this turn of events women were ready to draw on their experience in petitioning state legislatures. In at least one community, women organized a Maine Law Society for the purpose of promoting the election of men who supported prohibition. By 1860 thirteen states and territories had adopted prohibition statutes.

More dramatic than traditional political activity, and even more out of character for proper women, was the rather sudden appearance of civil disobedience as a weapon against the saloon. In the early 1850s women in dozens of communities took to the streets with axes and hatchets, and at least temporarily put a good many saloons out of business. The participants in these vigilante raids were described in the temperance press as women of the "greatest respectability," and in some communities they had considerable support from the male establishment. In one striking example, nine women in Marion, Illinois, were brought to trial and Abraham Lincoln, one of their lawyers, defended them with analogies to the Boston Tea Party.

From 1850 on, the closest student of this phase of temperance agitation concludes, a "distinctly female approach to temperance reform" dominated the whole movement. The Civil War accelerated the increase in alcohol consumption that appears to have begun in the fifties, and the women's temperance movement, which became rather quiet during the war, would come back to life with unprecedented energy in 1873.[28]

Antislavery

Nowhere did women defy traditional norms of female behavior more vigorously than in their antislavery societies.[29] Black women led the way in

1832, when they established female antislavery societies in Salem, Massachusetts, and in Rochester, setting a pattern that was soon followed by white women. The black societies' methods of fundraising and agitation were very similar to those of the mixed groups, but their spirit had a different ring to it, exemplified by the constitution of a group of Philadelphia black women, organized to support Frederick Douglass's weekly, *The North Star:*

> Whereas, the necessity of an efficient organization for the support of our cause has long been apparent and its absence deplored; and Whereas, believing Self-Elevation to be the only true issue upon which to base our efforts as an oppressed portion of the American people, and believing the success of our cause depends mainly upon Self-Exertion and the Press and the Public Lecturer are the most powerful means by which an end so desirable can be attained: Therefore we do agree to form ourselves in an Association to be known as the Woman's Association of Philadelphia.[30]

Black women's associations would continue to put as much emphasis on the prevailing race prejudice as on the abolition of slavery.

The roots of white antislavery agitation went back at least to eighteenth-century Quakerism and the writings of John Woolman. When, early in the nineteenth century, the American Colonization Society proposed to free slaves and send them to Africa, some of its most active members were women, southern as well as northern. The movement took a dramatic turn in 1831 when William Lloyd Garrison published the first issue of *The Liberator,* calling for immediate, uncompensated emancipation of all slaves. A few women attended the first meeting of the Massachusetts Anti-Slavery Society, and when Garrison soon afterward organized a New England Anti-Slavery Society, Maria Weston Chapman and three of her sisters set up the Boston Female Anti-Slavery Society as an auxiliary. In 1833 the American Anti-Slavery Society was organized in Philadelphia, and though Lucretia Mott offered what all agreed was an apt modification of the draft Declaration of Sentiments and Purposes, neither she nor any of the women there were permitted to vote or to sign the declaration. Almost immediately Mott responded to the urging of some of her Quaker friends by initiating a Female Anti-Slavery Society in Philadelphia. A decade later she reflected on these beginnings: " . . . at the time I had no idea of the meaning of preambles and resolutions and votings. Women had never been in any assemblies of this kind. I had only attended one Convention—a Convention of colored people in this State—before that. . . . "[31]

In very short order, separate female societies began to appear all over New England and in the Middle West, many of them in places where a male-dominated society already admitted women to its deliberations. By 1836 10 percent of the 527 antislavery societies were all-female; a year later the total had reached 1,006 of which 77 were women's groups.[32] The spirit of the latter was reflected in the annual report of the Boston Female Society: "They found for their encouragement abundance of 'abstract principles.' They also found a strong opposition to acting in accordance with those principles. . . . One of the principles which, when they acted upon it, brought criticism was that which led them to admit black women to equal membership."[33]

The report went on to note that though antislavery women had been called mad, their influence had begun to be felt in the churches, and their numbers had increased along with the conviction that the work was in accord with the gospel. They said bitterly that every effort had been made to suppress them, while benevolent societies "basked in the sunshine of popular favor."

When the Boston Female Society announced a meeting to be addressed by George Thompson, a radical English abolitionist, opponents threatened a riot, and even though Thompson's appearance was called off to protect him, the mob came anyway. Garrison, who had come to show support, was carried off with a rope around his neck, and only the intervention of the mayor of Boston saved him from further indignity. Although all antislavery activity aroused opposition, women, defying popular opinion both by calling for an end to slavery and by speaking out in public, seem to have aroused particular violence. In Philadelphia, a mob burned down a hall in which the Female Anti-Slavery Society was conducting a meeting.

Nothing in the record suggests that antislavery women felt themselves to be subordinate to the male societies. In Boston, indeed, the popular perception ran quite the other way: Maria Weston Chapman was thought to wield great power over the men.[34] The correspondence of the Weston sisters shows that as new societies were formed in New England they generally asked to be auxiliary to the Boston Female Society rather than to the societies run by men.[35] Their letters asked the Boston women for detailed advice. The support for separate women's work exhibited in one may stand for many: "It has seemed to us that such a measure [the formation of a national women's executive committee for antislavery objects] if not absolutely needed, is at least, highly expedient, in the best sense at a crisis like the present, when there is so much to be undertaken for the cause, for which woman and she alone is fitted. . . . We have adverted to the fact that the cause stands in present need of just such assistance as we can appropriately render. . . . "[36] She went on to say that women must be heard by their senators giving "one united expression of shame and grief."

The best-known women's societies were those in Boston, Philadelphia, and New York. Each had its own idiosyncratic history. In Boston, Debra Gold Hansen argues, two somewhat incompatible groups of women had joined together—one group headed by the Weston sisters she describes as elite and radical, and the other she sees as "middle class" and moderate, much influenced by the clergy. This incompatibility, exacerbated by the conflict within the Massachusetts Anti-Slavery Society to which it was at least technically auxiliary, led to a split in 1839, after which the more assertive Weston faction worked closely with men, and the moderate group turned to traditional benevolence.[37] Despite the bitter internal conflict members of the Boston society played a vital role in the petition campaign that was a major accomplishment of antislavery women in the 1830s and 1840s. Boston women also helped organize two national conventions, and developed the familiar benevolent money-raising "fair" into a fine art.[38]

The Philadelphia society, by contrast, had an exceptionally long life. It survived both the Civil War and the Thirteenth Amendment and was still active in 1871. Made up principally of black and Quaker women, it taught many Pennsylvanians about the movement, tried to promote education and social opportunity for black people, took part in the petition campaign, and energetically promoted the use of "free produce" (goods produced without slave labor). As early as 1839 it led a petition drive urging the state legislature to provide jury trial to all persons arrested within the state as fugitives from slavery.[39] The society also resolved to give help to "colored people" in their trades and business. The minutes suggest that members were given to envisioning large projects and then discovering that they had neither the necessary womanpower nor the skill to carry them out. For example, in the 1840s committees set up to visit schools for black children found the task overwhelming, and though they complained that the teachers in some of the schools were not adequately trained, the society found no solution to the problem.

In the early forties the Philadelphia women began sewing for an annual sale, and, when they succeeded in raising money beyond their expectations, such sales became more and more one of their central activities. However, the society continued to proselyte and to hire lawyers for runaway slaves. In 1849 they asked the Pennsylvania legislature to grant citizenship to colored inhabitants, and continued regularly to petition for a variety of causes.

During the war, the Philadelphia FASS garnered a thousand signatures to the petition of the Women's Loyal National League calling for a constitutional amendment to abolish slavery. In 1865 the society began agitating to permit "colored persons" to use the public transport system of Philadelphia from which they were barred, sometimes by force. In April of that year a black minister boarded a street railway car and several Irishmen insisted that he should be removed, while his fellow African Americans insisted that he stand firm. The conductor finally took out a warrant against the man for assault and incitement to riot, and he was hauled off to court.[40] A year later one of the black members of the FASS was still speaking bitterly about the exclusion of colored people from the street railways, and accusing the society of withholding comment for fear of hurting the chances of the Republican party in the coming election. Perhaps it was this issue that had inspired the discussion on 11 October 1865 of "the course of the Republican party and the degree of their faithfulness in applying the principles of justice." Three years later the Philadelphia women petitioned the Congress, asking it to take steps to assure a republican form of government in each state. In March, as Congress was engaged in passing the Reconstruction Acts, the minutes reflect dismay: "A feeling of quiet sadness seeming to pervade the meeting, Mary Grew represented the importance of patient acquiescence in the changes which time brings to us all. . . . "

In contrast to the radical wing of Boston women, neither Philadelphia nor New York antislavery women as a group showed any great interest in promoting women's rights, though individual members were active in that movement.[41]

A single surviving minute book provides a close-up view of the spirit of antislavery women in one small town. The Lynn, Massachusetts, Female Anti-Slavery Society was formed in 1835 and held its first annual meeting in May 1836. The minutes, written in the best seminary-trained handwriting, noted that the year had brought "unparalleled opposition and violence against the Anti-Slavery cause," but that "thanks to the blessing of God" the opposition had not succeeded in destroying the movement.

The secretary urged members to ignore the frequent suggestion "that it is a subject with which women should have nothing to do because it has a political aspect. Its brightest and most distinctive aspect is a moral and a benevolent one, and in this sphere it is not denied that women may operate with propriety and efficiency. It is woman's woes that call most loudly for our effort to free them, and their children, from the most cruel oppression, from degradation and outrage in every form. . . . "[42]

Antislavery is generally viewed as a movement so controversial that only the most courageous women took part in it. In Lynn, however, the number of women in the Anti-Slavery Society was about the same as in the benevolent societies, and many belonged to both. It is also interesting that two women who were active in the shoebinders' protest movement belonged to the Anti-Slavery Society.[43]

The Lynn society enrolled more than fifty women in the town of four thousand.[44] It had raised $109.25, circulated hundreds of tracts and books, given some money to the Samaritan Society, and contributed goods of its own manufacture to the Boston Female Anti-Slavery Society fair. As in the benevolent societies, officers were about equally divided between married and single women, and many members were related by blood or marriage.

The group met in the Universalist Church, the denomination that, next to the Quakers, was most accepting of activist women. Any woman could become a member by signing the constitution and paying eight cents a month dues. Programs included both scripture and antislavery literature and the women not only supported emancipation but also "removing the obstructions to the improvement of the free colored population."

In August 1836 a committee including such well-known abolitionists as Sarah and Mary Buffum and Abby Kelley was appointed to seek signatures to a petition calling for the immediate abolition of slavery in the District of Columbia. In 1837 the Lynn society appointed five delegates to a "convention of ladies to be held in New York on the 9th day of May."[45] To pay for the trip the women sewed articles for sale. Sixteen to twenty members attended regularly, but by 1837 paid memberships had declined to thirty-three.

At the next annual meeting, Angelina Grimké (rather than a male minister, as had been the case before) offered prayers. Members discussed the apparently increasing difficulty of persuading people to sign their petitions and pledged themselves to "untiring perseverance." A lively discussion of the value of the petition campaign followed. The women argued that it brought them in direct contact with the pro-slavery people, as well as with the indifferent and with those who continually raised objections, not about the goal but about the women's methods. "In fine, with all, whatsoever may be their sentiments, so that many who would not otherwise think at all about it are induced to give it a little place in their minds, and we hope some are by this means led to examine thoroughly, with a desire for the truth."

At about the same time the male antislavery society in Lynn agreed to hire an agent to seek signatures to the same petition. Men, of course, were occupied with business and professional affairs, and perhaps felt themselves to be too busy to carry petitions from house to house as the women did. It is possible to doubt that their responsibilities were heavier than those of most housewives, and to wonder whether they were simply less inclined to face their neighbors in an unpopular cause.[46]

Whatever the reason for the difference, the women saw their direct approach as a two-way street, educating the petitioners as well as those being importuned to sign. They urged each other not to "shrink before scorn and ridicule," and reminded themselves that simply joining a society did not relieve the individual of responsibility for "instilling correct principles and awakening Christian feeling for the crushed and withering slave in the parlor, in the kitchen, in the school, in the walk, in the ride, and in every other situation where opportunity presents." In short, no opportunity for preaching antislavery was to be missed.

The minutes go on:

We trust that what woman is doing in the present struggles will accelerate the approach of that time when, instead of contumely and scorn which are now heaped upon her who enlists in a moral conflict against wrong with a determination to do her whole duty, even should that duty require her to overstep the bounds "prescribed by a corrupt public sentiment" she shall be hailed as a Minister of Heaven, sent on an errand of mercy to the erring. . . . When it shall be practically acknowledged that man and woman are both one in Christ.

In a ponderously worded resolution, the women of the Lynn society called upon each other to overcome "any diffidence that may withhold us from coming forward and communicating our thoughts unreservedly." After a strong statement from Angelina Grimké, the resolution was adopted.

Another resolution suggested that as long as two-and-a-half million of "our countrymen" were held in slavery, it was inconsistent to support foreign missions. It was, the society announced, "like washing the outside of the platter while the inside is full of ravening and wickedness." A third resolution suggested that people were most likely to be interested in causes in which they had invested money, and called on those "who have cause to lament their own indifference" to reduce their indifference by liberal giving.[47]

In 1838 Lynn women raised enough money to give three hundred dollars to the Massachusetts Anti-Slavery Society and to subscribe for a hundred copies of *The Liberator.* They also appointed delegates to a female convention in Philadelphia. There is no record of their reaction to the fact that when the Lynn Anti-Slavery Society despaired of raising the money it had promised to contribute to the parent body, the men, as a last resort, turned to the Female Society, suggesting that perhaps a young woman could do it for them![48]

If Lynn is in any way typical, small-town female antislavery societies presented a mix of religious concern, benevolent-society experience, and willingness to take the consequences of speaking out on one of the most controversial subjects of the time.[49]

Moral reform, temperance, and antislavery were all broad social movements encompassing much of the country, and in all of them all-female societies played a somewhat different role from that of their male colleagues. Women in moral reform and temperance undertook activities that had no parallel in the male associations. Although the evidence is scanty, antislavery women seem to have been more inclined than men to carry their own petitions, raise their own money, and welcome black members. Quaker women particularly stressed the importance of everyday interaction with black people. Women in all three associations, arguing for woman's special responsibility for morality and compassion, found themselves propelled into politics; petitions, lobbying, and sometimes going into court became steadily more common female activities.

There were other new kinds of women's associations in these same years, including some directed at particular community problems. In Jacksonville, Illinois, for example, a newly settled town with aspirations to greatness, a group of women teachers joined with ministers' and professors' wives in 1833 to establish the Ladies Association for Educating Females. Noting that parents on the frontier were often too busy to teach their children, the Jacksonville group invited women from all over their new state to join in an effort to make sure that the next generation did not grow up in ignorance. The society proposed to provide help for "interesting females" in small communities who had the potential to become schoolteachers but no resources for their own education.

Declaring themselves to be Christian but nonsectarian and entirely independent of any other organization, Jacksonville women raised money by the traditional methods (sewing, bazaars, collections in church) and by appeals to eastern friends. During its first ten years the society provided 180 scholarships, and by the end of its second decade had helped 532 young women prepare themselves to be teachers. The organization was destined to continue well into the twentieth century, adapting to changing educational needs as it went along.[50]

Reflecting a similar concern in older states, Emma Willard crisscrossed New York and Connecticut organizing women into associations for the common schools which, she assured them, were essential if teachers were to be encouraged and children properly taught.

In Providence, Rhode Island, a group of highly respectable, well-to-do women initiated a society for the specific purpose of helping poor seamstresses to raise their wages and providing vocational education to improve their employability.[51] How they came to try this line of activity or what made them sensitive much earlier than most women of their class to the serious problem of starvation wages, the record does not show.[52] Like Sarah Josepha Hale in the Boston Seaman's Aid Society, the Providence women set up their own business, paid above-market wages, and took what Susan Porter Benson calls a "self-assured and confident stance" before the community. The first president of the society tartly denied that women were out of their sphere in dealing with such issues: "[women] if any understand what female labor is worth and what female suffering means. If either sex is disqualified to judge of these matters it is not our own."

While middle-class women like those in Providence tried to help poorly paid women workers, some sewing women and factory women set out to help themselves. The best-known such effort is the Lowell Female Reform Association, which led a series of all-women strikes and circulated petitions calling upon the legislature to establish a ten-hour day. In 1831 women shoe binders in Essex County, Massachusetts, formed a society to press for higher wages. Only by cooperation, the leaders said, could individual women be protected from exploitation by the men who gave out work to be done. Two years later a Female Society of Lynn and Vicinity for the Protection and Promotion of Female Industry organized to protest a wage cut. The local newspaper reported that a thousand women had met in the Friends' Meetinghouse. Stirring statements of demands and rights notwithstanding, the society did not survive.[53] Similar efforts of the United Tailoresses of New York City, who went on strike in 1831, and a Female Union Society of Tailoresses and Seamstresses in Baltimore in 1833 were similarly short lived. The odds were against these early industrial women even when, as in Lynn, they had male support.[54]

In other places sewing women, sometimes with benevolent-society help, established Female Protective Unions and tried to develop cooperative workshops as protection against the exploitive wages.[55] They, too, despite vigorous beginnings and some support from middle-class women, encountered strong opposition from employers and soon disappeared from the record.[56]

No group faced more difficulties in associating for self-help than the free black women in northern cities. Despite meager resources and very little help from white contemporaries, they continued to set up their own independent, segregated associations devoted to the needs of their own community. There were African American temperance, moral reform, Bible, and missionary societies, as well as mutual aid and literary societies. The former sought to provide a measure of insurance against the ordinary vicissitudes of life and the latter were a way for black women—who had little access to formal schooling—to achieve some measure of education through their own efforts.[57] The literary societies are particularly noteworthy, since here, as in the case of antislavery, black women led the way. Of the forty-six African American literary societies Dorothy Porter was able to document, at least eight were made up solely of women; others may well have been (such as the Edgeworth Society, for example, doubtless named for the redoubtable Maria). Even more than their white counterparts, black women found voluntary associations to be practically their only avenue to social and educational reform.

In retrospect it is easy to believe that all this disparate activity was bound to culminate in a women's rights movement. For a long time, indeed, students of women's rights have located its roots in antislavery, or in moral reform, and to some extent in temperance. The traditional view is that in working for the rights of the slave, women were made conscious of their own "slavery of sex," and forthwith began to take issue with their place in the society. Ellen DuBois has made a more plausible argument: that what women learned in all these reform associations was not that they were circumscribed (they knew that already) but how to go about doing something about it.[58]

The ideology of women's rights had been developing at least since Mary Wollstonecraft, and had gotten its most systematic statement from Sarah Grimké in 1838.[59] A constituency for the movement gradually emerged and in 1848 the Seneca Falls Convention codified the principles of the cause. The calling of that convention has acquired the status of a legend: In 1840, the story goes, Elizabeth Cady Stanton, then twenty-six years old, found herself seated behind a curtain at the World's Anti-Slavery Convention in London in company with the forty-two-year-old Lucretia Mott. The unwillingness of the convention to seat women delegates led the two to an animated discussion about the discrimination they were experiencing. Stanton would testify that Mott told her things she had never before heard spoken about the natural rights of women. (Asked, upon her return, what had been the most interesting thing she had seen in England, Stanton is said to have replied: "Lucretia Mott.")

Eight years and several children later, Stanton, restless and yearning for intellectual stimulation in the isolated town of Seneca Falls, New York, met Mott again. Continuing their interrupted conversation of eight years earlier, they drew up a Declaration of Sentiments, carefully modeled on the Declaration of Independence, listing women's grievances. They then sent out a call inviting interested men and women to discuss the subject of women's rights. More than three hundred showed up, and most signed the declaration. Appealing to the political theory of the American Revolution, the declaration announced that women should have the right to control their own property and to have a voice in the government under which they lived. Other issues clustered around these two central ones: woman's right to an education, to enter a profession, to speak in public, to have a voice in the church, to control the destiny of her minor children, to set standards for sexual morality—in short, the rights men took for granted.[60]

Public discussion of the Seneca Falls Declaration made many women aware of grievances they had never before articulated and the virulence of press attacks brought the whole matter to public attention as forcefully as did the arguments of the proponents. The result was a surge of interest in the "woman question" and the launching of a vigorous debate that was destined to increase in scope and volume through the next seventy-two years, and beyond.[61]

Summing up nearly half a century of women's organizational and political experience, the convention announced: "we shall use every instrumentality within our power to effect our object. We shall employ agents, circulate tracts, petition the State and National legislatures and endeavor to enlist the pulpit and the press in our behalf. We hope this Convention will be followed by a series of Conventions embracing every part of the country." Looming behind this statement we can see tract societies, antislavery petitions, the politicking of moral reformers, and hundreds of conventions held in good various causes in the preceding forty years. A few women were prepared to begin at once to carry out this ambitious program. Instead of setting up a new organization, they relied on the American Anti-Slavery Society and its newspaper, *The Anti-Slavery Standard*, to disseminate information. Ad hoc conventions open to all were called into being by individuals or small groups as they felt inspired to do so. Only two weeks after Seneca Falls the first of these took place in Rochester. Numerous local and state conventions followed, without any central direction or planning, and one or another group of women called a national convention each year.

In the first burst of enthusiasm individual women created societies in their hometowns. One Emily Collins, for example, of South Bristol, Ontario County, an out-of-the-way corner of upstate New York, inspired by what she had just witnessed at Seneca Falls, summoned a few neighbors to form an Equal Suffrage Society. Fifteen or twenty women met twice a month for discussion, and shortly submitted to the legislature a petition bearing sixty-two signatures asking that women be granted the right to vote. The society met faithfully for about a year, and then, during a spell of bad weather, fell out of the habit of regular meetings, but continued to send off petitions from time to time.[62]

Other enthusiastic women initiated state societies. In 1853, after three conventions in Ohio, for example, Josephine Griffing, an antislavery activist, and Hannah Tracy Cutler set up an Ohio Woman's Rights Association.[63] In the same year a resolution supporting a woman suffrage amendment was introduced in the Ohio legislature and lost only on a tie vote. A Woman's Rights Association appeared in Kansas while it was still a territory and woman suffrage narrowly missed being adopted by the first legislature in Washington Territory.[64] In 1855 Amelia Bloomer, then living in Iowa, went to Nebraska in an effort to persuade its territorial legislature to put suffrage in the state constitution.

Even before 1848 women had lectured as paid agents of antislavery societies. Some, like Lucy Stone, had often spent more time on woman's rights than on abolition. Now lecturers whose focus was on women's rights began to multiply, and other women began in various ways to make a name as advocates of the cause. Among these were Lucretia Mott, by now in her fifties, and her feisty thirty-five-year-old collaborator, Elizabeth Cady Stanton. Stanton, though somewhat hampered by unremitting childbearing, published vigorous letters to the *New York Herald* and sent stirring appeals to any gathering of woman's rights enthusiasts that solicited her views. Susan B. Anthony and Lucy Stone, still in their early thirties, lectured and organized constantly and were increasingly identified as "strong-minded women." Their slightly older colleagues, Frances Dana Gage, Caroline Severance, Clarina I. Nichols, and Hannah Tracy Cutler, were busy in Iowa and Ohio, where woman's rights sentiment seemed to abound. In the East, Elizabeth Buffum Chace and Paulina Wright Davis, both residents of Providence, called a convention in Worcester, Massachusetts, from which enthusiasm flowed into the far corners of New England. Periodicals such as Amelia Bloomer's *The Lily* and Paulina Davis's *The Una* spread the word. Thanks to the efforts of some of these women several states and territories adopted married women's property laws.

By the end of the 1850s women's rights had taken on all the elements of a social movement. There was discussion and debate in lyceums, in young men's literary societies, in many parlors and social halls, and in an increasing number of newspapers. College students debated the question. A few adventurous editors were beginning to offer support. A shared ideology which combined, however tenuously, elements of natural rights philosophy with the notion of woman's moral superiority was taking shape, and leaders, local and national, were meeting each other and developing habits of communication. If modern techniques of opinion polling had been available in 1860, it seems likely that the number of people who knew something about woman's rights issues would have shown a sharp increase in twelve years.

Opponents, who announced that women were getting out of their place and predicted the imminent demise of the family, did as much or more than supporters to make nearly every literate American aware that something was going on. The very bitterness of those who scoffed in print, or drew cartoons depicting advocates of woman's rights in most unflattering ways, made the subject interesting.

Optimism among the committed was running high when the Civil War brought agitation to an abrupt halt. In the twelve years between Seneca Falls and the firing on Fort Sumter, the movement spread, attained a degree of respectability, and could point to several married women's property acts as accomplishments. While many members of moral reform, temperance, and antislavery groups were unwilling to join the women's rights movement, it is also true that nearly every leader in that movement had previous experience in one, two, or three of the other major voluntary associations.[65]

The nature of these movements and the kinds of people who were responsive to them combined to create a new kind of woman activist, one who was less concerned than the average member of a benevolent society about proper womanly behavior and more concerned with bringing about some significant change in social behavior. The handful of studies that have been done so far tends to suggest that the activists were generally from somewhat different parts of the social structure than were the typical members of benevolent societies, but a good many women belonged to both groups. It is perhaps emblematic that one of the earliest efforts at moral reform in New York City was led by none other than Isabella Graham and that the editors of *Friend of Virtue* were antislavery activists. By 1860 black and white, Catholic and Protestant, working-class and middle-class women had all experimented with separatism as strategy.[66] With the experience of more than sixty years to draw upon, women north and south were prepared to pick up the responsibilities thrust upon them by war.

3

We Are Now Very Busy: Women and War

When sectional conflict reached the point of no return in April 1861 neither side was well prepared to wage a modern war, and few things about the early days were as remarkable as the speed with which women on both sides organized to respond to the need for such basic things as food, clothing, and medical supplies. An economy which in peacetime relied heavily on household production needed women's labor even more in wartime. Soldiers' aid societies transferred to the community the production women had always carried out for their own families. Some of the details remind us of the enormous difference between the nineteenth-century world and our own. A generation accustomed to an army equipped with K-rations, vitamin C, and the PX, not to mention an efficient and highly professional medical corps, may find it hard to realize, for example, that scurvy was still a threat to soldiers so that the strenuous effort to provide fresh vegetables and fruit juices was literally a matter of life and death. We must think ourselves into an earlier time to comprehend the economic and military significance of women sewing shirts and tents, preserving fruit, bottling wine, making "comfort bags," rolling bandages, collecting herbs for medicinal use, or engaging in the unrelenting search for substitutes for goods the war had banished that preoccupied southern women. Brought into the limelight, and endowed with national purpose by wartime exigency, the contributions of women's organizations were clearly visible to contemporaries. Many men expressed wonder at skills of which they had been unaware as long as they had been confined to benevolent societies and reform organizations. Though women's labor was essential to the maintenance of both armies, no economic historian has tried to assess its importance for the overall conduct of the war.

The question of war aims provided new opportunities for public political activity as well. As the North felt its way toward a clear goal for the fighting, the Women's Loyal National League brought together women from many northern and midwestern states with the overt purpose of securing a constitutional amendment to end slavery, and the covert purpose of keeping the women's rights movement alive.

As women took public roles, leaders emerged and the war began to have its heroines who were almost as well known as its heroes. In the North especially, and to a lesser degree in the South, wartime experience prepared a generation of women for the great leap forward they were to make in the postwar decades. Feeling themselves to be part of a vital national cause, women created records of their experience that reveal a good deal about how they functioned under pressure and about their fundamental view of the world. Despite the vast difference in the situation each confronted, women on both sides of the conflict approached their work in ways that were remarkably similar.

The sequence of events in Cleveland in the first weeks of the war showed just how well prepared women were to recognize and respond to national needs. On 20 April 1861—five days after Lincoln called for seventy-five thousand volunteers—Chapin Hall was filled to overflowing with women, eager for concrete opportunity to take part in the great wave of patriotic enthusiasm aroused by the firing on Fort Sumter. Rebecca Cromwell Rouse was called to the chair, and a special committee appointed to confer with male civic leaders about the best use of funds already being collected for the benefit of soldiers' families; three days later the Ladies Aid and Sanitary Society began preparing medical supplies for the army. The war was not yet in its third week.[1]

Very shortly a thousand volunteers arrived in Cleveland without blankets. The Aid Society divided the city into districts, staffed eight carriages with two women each, and set out to provide each soldier with a blanket. Two days later the job was done. In the process, however, many "farm boys" among the volunteers were discovered to be badly in need of clothing. After another sweep through the city for materials, the women sewed a thousand shirts. Before the last stitch was set, illness broke out in nearby Camp Taylor, and they turned to recruiting nurses and supplying hospital stores.

Pausing for breath, the leaders decided that efficiency demanded an Aid Society for all of northern Ohio. Once again Mrs. Rouse took charge, and another organization was created, which began immediately both to coordinate the work of the existing local societies and to promote the formation of new ones.

Sixty-two-year-old Rebecca Rouse was an appropriate choice to lead the women of northern Ohio in this war-inspired endeavor. Her life history encapsulated the history of women's associations in Cleveland. Born in

New England in 1799, at twenty-two she had married Benjamin Rouse, stonemason, veteran of the War of 1812, and one of the organizers of the first Sunday school in Boston. In a memoir written late in life Benjamin noted that in his youth he had prayed to be guided to a right choice of wife. He wanted to find one with "an unconquerable desire to do good.... adequate to impart right council [*sic*] when asked." He thought Rebecca filled the bill. In search of wider opportunities, the Rouses moved to New York and there met the Tappan brothers, who put them to work distributing tracts in the city slums. What they saw reinforced their evangelical commitment and in 1830 the American Tract Society hired both Rouses to carry the gospel to Ohio. There Benjamin organized two hundred Sunday schools, distributing books and tracts as he went, while Rebecca initiated a Female Baptist Sewing Society in the new village of Cleveland "to combat the moral destitution and to recognize that it is more blessed to give than to receive." Members sewed to raise money for the Home Missionary Society and for the poorhouse. In 1842 Mrs. Rouse combined her commitments to temperance and to charity by organizing a Martha Washington and Dorcas Society (incorporating the Moral Reform Society as she went), which in turn created the Protestant Orphan Asylum. In 1850 she became a charter member of the Cleveland Ladies Temperance Society and in 1851 briefly supported an effort on the part of the underpaid sewing women of the city to organize a "Protective Union" and a cooperative store. Described as a small, slight woman with energy in inverse ratio to her size, she had long been the person Cleveland women looked to for leadership. Now the war gave her opportunities commensurate with her administrative talent. In the fifties she had often complained of ill-health; after 1861 she was indefatigable.[2]

With Mrs. Rouse in command, the Northern Ohio Soldiers' Aid swung into action on many fronts. Letters went to postmasters all over the state asking that the society's circulars be put "in the hand of some active, benevolent woman," and that he send back names of six women who might be able to form a local organization. Notices to be read from the pulpit went to every church, articles to every newspaper. Names and addresses culled from hotel registers provided further leads to people who might be put to work. Women who came to Camp Taylor to visit relatives found themselves being recruited to go home and organize. "Home mission societies, church sociables, sewing societies and various benevolent organizations were converted into Soldiers' Aid Societies without change of organization...."[3]

Soon Mrs. Rouse was traveling the state drumming up support and refuting rumors that donated supplies were not reaching the soldiers. The railroads and Western Union were induced to provide free services. Keeping organizations going in small towns required constant vigilance; after the first enthusiasm wore off women tended to drift away from the insistant demands of the dedicated leaders. Letters from grateful soldiers were industriously circulated to renew their enthusiasm.

The northern Ohio society got hold of a printing press; women taught themselves to set type and began to publish and distribute regular circulars. Circular 2, for example, gave detailed specifications for medical supplies and precise measurements for preparing garments. Circular 3 instructed little girls as to what they could do to help; Circular 6 vehemently denied a rumor that the women who ran the organization were being paid; only the draymen and porters, the circular asserted, got any wages at all. Other circulars emphasized the need for useful materials. Thousands of such circulars were printed and distributed. A regular column in the *Cleveland Leader* thanked people by name, and thereby—it was hoped—encouraged generosity. Very soon the Northern Ohio Society could claim 525 affiliated groups, all more or less committed to providing not simply amenities but vital supplies to the Union army.

Meantime an office was set up in Cleveland where a man instructed the women in the approved methods of keeping books and writing invoices. Mrs. Rouse and her deputies constantly emphasized the need for "system" and "order" in the handling of the increasing volume of supplies passing through their hands, and surviving account books bear witness that the lesson was well learned. The volunteer bookkeeper, Ellen F. Terry, "did her whole work with a neatness, accuracy and dispatch that would have done honor to any business man in the country."[4] By the time the society formally affiliated with the United States Sanitary Commission in October 1861 it had already pioneered many of the methods of work which the commission would soon recommend to local societies everywhere.[5]

Spring found Mrs. Rouse on a military transport headed for Paducah, Kentucky, preparing to deliver supplies and set up a hospital. She wrote calmly to her husband (who was taking care of the house and children) that the scenery was lovely and her appetite "a caution to the cook." She was rather pleased to find herself in the line of fire. One purpose of her trip was to make sure that the supplies went to their intended destination; through the war some aid societies were wary of turning over their hard-won collections of goods without safeguards to make sure they would not be siphoned off by corrupt officials for private gain. She warned Benjamin that there would be no letters on the return voyage since she would be busy taking care of wounded soldiers.[6]

In August 1863 the women who ran the Northwestern Sanitary Commission in Chicago put on a great Sanitary Fair which raised $80,000—nearly three times as much as anyone had thought possible. Officers of the Northern Ohio society went to Chicago to observe and came back inspired to do likewise; they thought the fair "opened a new era in benevolent effort."[7] Benevolent societies had long organized fairs to raise money and in the 1830s antislavery women had adopted the idea for the dual purpose of raising money and building membership. Now, on a grander scale, fairs became a favorite device for financing soldiers' aid. The Ohio women, inspired by what they saw in Chicago, organized their own fair in Cleveland and raised $100,000. At the war's end the Northern Ohio Society recorded that over the years of its existence it collected and spent precisely $130,405.09 in cash and $1,000,003.00 in goods.

Even before the war ended the society became aware that returning soldiers needed help in finding work, claiming their pensions, or restoring their health. In 1863 the Cleveland women organized a soldiers' home; more than fifty-six thousand men passed through its portals before it wound down in 1866. At least four women worked there full time and many others gave large amounts of time and energy to the enterprise. In May 1865 an employment agency for veterans was added to help returning soldiers claim their pensions and find jobs. An enthusiastic friend, paying tribute to Mrs. Rouse with typical nineteenth-century hyperbole, evokes the self-images and values which lay behind this extraordinary effort: "She is of tireless energy and exhaustless sympathy for every form of human suffering. For forty years she has been the foremost in all benevolent movements among the ladies of Cleveland, spending most of her time and income in the relief of the unfortunate; yet she is entirely free from personal ambition and love of power or notoriety.... Though plain and polite in person, she possessed the rare ability of influencing those whom she addressed."[8]

It might have been said of many of these women, as it was of one, that she "put on her hat and shawl the instant Sumter was fired upon, and scarce took them off until the Rebellion was subdued...."[9] And the Ohio society, as its historian would proudly note, "early dropped its mendicant character and took rank as a business establishment."[10]

Troy, New York, also responded almost instantly to news of war. Before the end of April 1861 the venerable Emma Willard—the best-known educator of women in the country—called for the immediate establishment of a soldiers' aid society. Even then she predicted a long war. "Gentlemen will say they have no time," she wrote, but added that women would do the work. Indeed, she went on, with a touch of sarcasm, perhaps the men had not noticed that educated women were quite capable of running societies, "not excepting such as require regular accounting in monetary concerns."[11] An aid society was organized with Willard as president and immediately applied for a government contract to make army clothing as a way of providing employment for the soldier's wives in the community. Cleveland

and Troy were only two of hundreds of villages, towns, and cities all over the North and Middle West, where—without waiting for direction from anybody—women convened meetings, drew up constitutions, and began to do their self-appointed work.

Meantime, the United States Sanitary Commission (USSC), one of the most innovative of wartime inventions, owed its existence in part to the early mobilization of New York women.[12] In April 1861 a well-known, able, and somewhat self-important Unitarian clergyman, Henry Whitney Bellows, watching the spontaneous organization of soldiers' aid societies, concluded that "without concert of effort and a clear idea of common goals these devoted women might waste their zeal and produce as much harm as good from their excitement."[13] With his friend Elisha Harris, a medical doctor interested in what was then called "sanitary reform"—we would call it public health—Bellows took it upon himself to attend a meeting of fifty or so New York women who had been summoned by Dr. Elizabeth Blackwell to consider what women might do to help meet the medical needs of the army. Bellows took the chair and did most of the talking. With his help the group wrote an "Appeal to the Women of New York," signed by a large number of women well known in the city, calling for a mass meeting at the Cooper Union. The women (there were also some men) who came to that meeting agreed to establish a Women's Central Relief Association (WCRA), which, despite its name, had equal numbers of men and women on its board. Twenty-three-year-old Louisa Lee Schuyler, daughter of one of the signers of the appeal, was chosen president.[14]

The women—who from the beginning seem to have done most of the work of the WCRA—decided that if the organization was to be effective a formal relationship with the War Department would be required and sent Bellows off to look into the possibility of establishing such a tie. Rebuffed by army men and civilians in the War Department, Bellows returned "considerably flattened" to say that, after all, a citizen effort of the kind the WCRA had undertaken would do more harm than good. The women insisted that he had given up too easily, and urged him to try again. Thus prodded, Bellows and Harris proceeded to Washington. On the way they talked at length about the recent experience of the British army in the Crimea where more men had been lost to disease than to enemy gunfire, and where Florence Nightingale had demonstrated that a rigorous attention to the health and welfare of the soldiers and to the sanitary condition of camps could dramatically reduce mortality.[15] She had induced the British War Office to establish a sanitary commission with power to change army practices in these matters. Bellows and Harris were convinced that the Medical Department of the United States Army had not absorbed the lesson of the Crimea, and that a civilian sanitary commission modeled on the British one was essential if the soldiers of the rapidly growing volunteer army were to be fit to fight. After a lengthy and discouraging encounter with the bureaucracy they finally persuaded the Secretary of War to accept a limited version of their plan and in due course President Lincoln, somewhat reluctantly, signed an executive order creating the United States Sanitary Commission.[16]

Bellows was appointed president of the commission, with Frederick Law Olmsted, the polymath creator of Central Park, as secretary general. The commission was made up of about a dozen men: ministers, medical doctors, and military officers, many of whom had a strong interest in the development of measures to promote and protect public health. Their principal announced concern was the maintenance of the health, morale, discipline, and welfare of the volunteer soldiers, a concern that the army seemed hardly to recognize as an essential part of its task. Nobody at the outset envisioned the major role the commission—despite constant discouragement and ongoing battles with the military and with various rivals—was destined to play.[17]

More than twenty years ago George Fredrickson in his pathbreaking book *The Inner Civil War* adumbrated the proposition that Bellows, Olmsted, and several other members of the commission had a significant covert agenda. They were of course committed to the public purposes for which the commission had been established, but in addition they hoped to carry out its work in a way that would convert wartime patriotism into a national consciousness that they felt to be woefully lacking in the United States with its long history of state and local loyalties. In Europe nationalism was simply happening; in the United States, in this view, it had to be brought into being. In the end, Fredrickson concluded, Bellows and Olmsted felt that they had failed in this, to them, great purpose.[18] On the practical side, however, the commission's work must be seen as a considerable success. Its significant accomplishments in improving conditions in army camps are well documented. Only very recently, however, have historians even begun to examine the essential contribution to this success of the seven thousand or more soldier's aid societies.[19]

Two major aspects of the commission's work were carried out largely by women. The first—which has received some attention from historians—involved the recruiting and training of nurses, an enterprise initially undertaken by the Women's Central Relief Association but later turned over to an army nurses corps headed by Dorothea Dix. In the afterglow of Nightingale's work in the Crimea it was not difficult to find eager young American women, caught up in the passionate patriotism of the war, who were willing to take on backbreaking responsibilities in military hospitals and hospital transports.[20] While the history of the military nurses on both sides has yet to be fully written, their work is ensconced in our folklore.[21] The work of the soldiers' aid societies, by contrast, is almost unknown.[22]

While Bellows and Harris were trying to convince the administration of the need for civilian involvement in the care of the army, women all over the country continued to organize themselves without waiting for official guidance. Then the commission began its work. Olmsted, who was one of the first of that new breed of administrators who were beginning to appear in response to the increasing scale and complexity of American institutions, had strong views as to how the commission should conduct its affairs.[23] He also had a compulsive desire to be on top of every detail. To promote efficiency he decided to put the WCRA in charge of coordinating the work of the far-flung soldiers' aid societies, whose contribution he realized would be essential but whose independence he found disconcerting. In addition to providing advice and guidance to such existing societies as were willing to come under its direction, the WCRA was to encourage the formation of new ones in places where none had yet appeared.[24] Louisa Schuyler, like Olmsted a born administrator, tried to establish rules for the local societies. She wrote thousands of letters, established close ties with trusted women in various places and preached the gospel of nationalism and efficiency with all the fervor of a convert. The commission hired a number of men to travel the country making speeches and encouraging women to organize.[25]

Schuyler's task was not an easy one. Despite the initial enthusiasm and the example of places like Cleveland, Newport, Chicago, and Boston, in many towns and villages it was an uphill task to keep work going. In many towns aid societies were quickly born and as quickly died, only to be re-created following some crisis in military affairs or when an enthusiastic emissary of the Sanitary Commission came to town. In larger places the problem was just the opposite: the aid societies were healthy and growing but hardheaded about protecting their own power and very slow to take direction from New York. They were confident that they knew how to run their own affairs. The WCRA wanted all supplies to go through central warehouses for deployment where they were most needed. Local societies were sensitive to community pressure to send the contributions to "our boys"—soldiers from their own town or village—rather than to central depots from whence they would be impersonally distributed. The disinclination to use central distribution points was reinforced by the omnipresent rumors about what was happening to "comforts" women had worked so hard to gather. One perennial anecdote was of the young soldier who gave his last dollar for a pot of jam only to find his mother's name on the bottom of the pot.

Still the Sanitary Commission, represented by Schuyler, persisted in trying to bring all the disparate societies under its umbrella and to order their behavior. Some simply refused and went their own independent way; others did as they pleased despite their presumed relationship with the USSC, while innundating the WCRA with complaints; still others affiliated with the rival Christian Commission or the semi-independent Western Commission in St. Louis.

In 1862 the commissioners decided that the coordination of effort might be improved if each region had a group of Associate Managers—men respected in their communities who would represent the commission on the spot. What happened next is instructive. In Boston, according to the commission's official historian, "the Associates . . . transferred their work, at an early day, to the New England Women's Auxiliary Association, an organization conspicuous during the whole war for its vigor and energy. . . . " In New York the Women's Central Relief Association was already functioning as the direct representative of the commission. "Following the example of Boston and New York," the official history continues, "it was determined to transfer the whole business of collecting supplies in Pennsylvania, Delaware, and Western New Jersey to a number of ladies who afterwards took the name of the 'Women's Pennsylvania Branch.'" In Chicago the Associates, as one woman caustically wrote, found that there was work involved, and speedily turned the responsibility over to women.[26]

Chicago, where the Northwestern Branch of the Sanitary Commission had headquarters, provides an excellent example of the way things developed. Mary A. Livermore, associate editor of a Universalist paper, had met Jane Hoge when both were engaged in establishing the Home for Aged Women in Chicago. At the beginning of the war Hoge went to nurse sick soldiers in her son's regiment, which was stationed nearby. Observing needs there, she and Livermore began collecting supplies and recruiting nurses. In the process they visited military hospitals in Cairo and Mound City, Illinois, to find out whether they, too, were inadequately supplied. In November 1862 the Sanitary Commission summoned a number of local leaders to take part in the Women's Council which the commissioners had designed as a channel for getting across their message of the virtues of central control. Hoge and Livermore were among those called to hear the message; they returned to Chicago having somehow acquired full responsibility for the Northwestern Branch, which they then proceeded to run their own way. Together they supervised day-to-day work in the city, and in their spare time encouraged the founding of new societies in towns and villages in five states, seeking out "efficient and executive" women to take charge of each new group. They also put on the Northwestern Sanitary Fair, which—despite initial opposition and even scorn from members of the commission—became a model of successful money raising for the rest of the country.[27]

Through the war, tension continued between the Sanitary Commission and many of the local associations. Even the aid society in Hartford, Connecticut, of which Olmsted's stepmother was secretary, insisted upon reserving part of the goods and money it had collected for Connecticut soldiers, and no amount of guidance from the top convinced the members to do otherwise.[28] Partly the women were responding to local sentiment; partly they simply wanted to run their own show.

In the North, black women were inspired to wartime organization by the needs of former slaves as well as by those of the black soldiers who were eventually permitted to enlist in the Union army. Susan Paul Vashon, an 1850 graduate of a seminary in Somerville, Massachusetts, ran a sanitary fair in Pittsburgh for the benefit of black refugees in the Ohio Valley, and in Lawrence, Kansas, the Ladies Refugee Aid Society came to the rescue of former slaves who were coming to Kansas in large numbers.[29] The existence of all-black units in the Union army inspired African American women in liberated areas to undertake soldiers' aid societies. In November 1864 the Colored Ladies' Soldiers Aid Society in Louisville, Kentucky, provided Thanksgiving dinner for the "colored soldiers in the hospitals" and for those in Taylor Barracks. In January 1865 these women were recognized in the *Louisville Daily Union Press* for help they had provided black soldiers sick and well, and for a silk flag they had made for the 123rd U.S. Colored Infantry. A woman presented the flag along with a stirring speech in which she linked the Union cause with that of freedom for black people throughout the world. The evidence suggests that, in the following month, the society was participating in the creation of a school for freed children, and once the war was over it took part in an effort to build a hospital for freed people.[30] At the same time other recently freed black women began organizing societies to take care of the health and welfare of recently emancipated slaves.[31]

The Sanitary Commission and local leaders alike faced a constant problem of keeping people involved as the war—once expected to be short—dragged on without much prospect of resolution. In places like Cleveland where leaders were experienced and committed, work went on steadily, but this was not the case everywhere. In Buffalo, for example, where the aid society had followed rather preceded the formation of the Sanitary Commission, 120 women joined over the three and a half years of its existence but only 50 stayed the whole course.[32] When, at the end, the commissioners asked for reports from the aid societies, they were bombarded with detailed descriptions of the difficulties women had had to overcome when they added war work to home duties.[33]

With all the problems incident to large-scale efforts in wartime, especially efforts based on voluntary labor, it was generally agreed that the soldiers' aid societies had contributed a very large part of the fifteen or twenty million dollars in goods and money which undergirded the commission's accomplishments. This figure did not take into account the many millions more represented by voluntary labor. From time to time Olmsted, though he continued to wish for cooperation in his dream of central management, admitted that without the women's unceasing effort, the work could not have gone on. In 1868 Bellows, who once had spoken of women doing more harm than good, sang quite a different tune: "No words are adequate to describe the systematic, persistent, faithfulness of the women who organized and led the Branches of the United States Sanitary Commission. Their volunteer labor had all the regularity of paid service. . . . Hundreds of women evinced talents there, which, in other spheres and in the other sex, would have made them merchant-princes, or great administrators of public affairs. . . . They became instructors of whole townships in the methods of government business. . . . "[34]

More impressive, because evidently deeply felt, was a letter written in 1866 by Alfred Bloor, who had worked as Olmsted's assistant. Writing to Senator Charles Sumner he detailed in elaborate sentences his favorable observations on women's work, summed up in the statement that "the chief work in the practice of the Sanitary Commission . . . that of providing the means for ministering to the physical needs of the soldiers . . . was exceedingly well done by women and comparatively ill done by men." The conclusion Bloor drew from his observations startled the senator: "The signs of the times . . . plainly indicate . . . that the question of the enfranchisement of women will soon emerge from the distant domain of speculation and prediction . . . into the more immediately practical field of politics and legislation, and as you are likely to be active in whatever movement may stir the van of national progress, I give you, for whatever you may think it worth, the testimony of one who has been, he hopes, an appreciative observer of a certain class of *a propos* facts. . . . "[35]

Confederate Women Organize

Meantime, on the other side of the Mason-Dixon Line, Confederate women were behaving very much like their northern sisters.[36] In Charleston the first women's society began rolling bandages in January 1861, more than three months before the first shots were fired. By May the same women were making cartridges and preparing sandbags to be used for fortifications. In July the newspapers reported that the Soldiers' Relief Society had organized by wards and that the women were working every day. A day or two after the first battle of Bull Run, 192 women showed up for a meeting of the Ladies Charleston Volunteer Aid Society, subscribed a thousand dollars, and, according to a young woman who was there, "all seemed to enjoy seeing their friends as well as the purpose for which they came."[37]

In North Carolina, Catherine Edmonston noted in her journal: "One thing has struck me throughout the whole progress of the summer: the universality and the eagerness with which women entered the struggle. They worked as many of them had never worked before, steadily and faithfully, to supply the soldiers with clothing and the hospital with comforts of various kinds."[38] In Augusta, Georgia, as men were recruited their wives began sewing. One made a note in her journal: "Some of our women are emulating the example of our Revolutionary mothers. . . . the order is given for sandbags, uniforms &c and the busy fingers of our women are engaged in the task of love and in an incredibly short space of time the order is filled. Sunday is not excepted but they are busy on that day too."[39]

Lest we assume that human nature was on holiday, however, it is well to record that as early as September 1861 Mary Chesnut noted, "Small war in the Ladies Aid Society . . . and already secession in the air—a row all the time in full blast."[40] Still the work got done.

In two or three months, more than 150 aid associations had been created in South Carolina alone. A sewing group met in Petersburg, Virginia, every day including Sunday. Thirty women brought their sewing machines to one house in Dougherty County, Georgia, and sewed companionably, practicing division of labor, and in Sandersville virtually the whole adult female population joined the Soldiers' Aid Society.[41] In Canton, Mississippi, a "big mansion was turned into a factory for supplying Confederate needs" as a Mrs. Johnstone and her daughter organized a "busy body of working women."[42] Before long nearly every town and village in the Confederacy had its society with the result that, in proportion to population, there were at least as many women's groups at work as in the North.

The problem of outfitting the Confederate army was challenging since there were few factories prepared to produce cloth, clothing, or matériel, and there was no stockpile of regular army supplies. Well-to-do women gave their jewelry and family plate to raise money for gunboats. Others provided materials to outfit whole units of volunteers, while those who had principally labor to contribute made uniforms, tents, cartridges, and bandages.

As in the North, Sunday schools, benevolent societies, and missionary societies converted themselves into soldiers' aid societies, while denominational exclusiveness gave way and women from all the churches were urged to join together. In Montgomery, a Hebrew Ladies Soldiers' Aid Society was established in the synagogue. A letter written by a Virginia woman on 18 August 1861 could have been written almost anywhere in the South by that day: "We are now very busy making clothes, knitting socks for the soldiers. Each lady proposes making one hundred garments—some are making mattresses, preparing bandages and knit nightshirts and comforts for the wounded—all are doing the most they can to add to the comforts of the soldiers."[43]

Other letters described churches being turned into depots for materials and sewing machines, as the women's societies experimented with division of labor and small-scale mass production. Alabama women were said to have created a structure of organizations that "approximated a minuscule government."[44] One small society reported making 2,320 garments in three months, besides spinning yarn and knitting great numbers of socks. A Montgomery group offered to knit up as much wool as the public would supply. The records do not show how much of this labor was performed by slave women, though it may have been considerable. Here and there one encounters a comment to the effect that the members of the society prepared materials while slave women spun, wove, and sewed, for the benefit of an army fighting to keep them enslaved.

The governor of Alabama set up a rough system of coordination, appointing probate judges to act as receiving agents for the materials women created and holding them responsible for making sure that the supplies reached their destination.[45] Loyalty to locality and state ran strong in the South, and southern women, even more than those in the North, were intent on providing for the men from home. Like the Confederate government itself, southern women's aid societies paid a high price in efficiency for their insistence on local control.[46] They could have benefitted from the proddings of an Olmsted!

The societies paid close attention to the needs of soldier's wives and children, while they also supplied hospitals and recruited nurses. Fairs, bazaars, tableaux, and concerts raised money—and provided the principal community recreation in some towns where social life had been drastically curtailed by wartime shortages.[47]

Every war has its scoundrels, and in Coosa County, Alabama, it was reported that a member took all the uniforms the Antioch Ladies' Aid Society had produced, sold them for $241.15, and sent the money to her son. Though the law enforcement officers tried to find her, members of the society were forced to conclude that she had "flown the coop for good."[48] And, as in the North, there were always problems of failing commitment. A young woman in Orange County, North Carolina, wrote to her uncle in January 1862: "Now that our soldiers have received some clothes I hope we will have a little time to read and study. Some of the folks about here were much concerned because the men complained of the size of the pants we sent. They were too large and the soldiers did not like them, and those people said if they were so particular and tasty, let them go without. . . . There is a great deal of human nature in woman, as well as in man. . . ."[49]

Women's societies established, supplied, and administered what were called "wayside hospitals" along the railways to take care of wounded soldiers who were being sent home by whatever means of transportation could be found. Several places claimed credit for inventing this particular institution, but whoever created the first one, their numbers increased rapidly as the war became bloodier. Some of these hospitals cared for large numbers of soldiers who otherwise would have had a difficult time getting food or rest as they made their way home. Additional wayside hospitals continued to be created until almost the end of the war, and functioned as long as supplies held out. One woman remembered her experience in Pendleton, South Carolina: "This little hospital was kept up until poverty closed its door, for we had at last not so much as a pot of cowpeas to send down. . . . "[50]

In keeping with what was generally considered to be the essentially compassionate nature of women, even northern soldiers had a share of southern women's attention. At one time the government was hard put to feed a large contingent of prisoners who had been brought to Florence, South Carolina, many of whom had typhoid fever. The soldiers' aid society reported that "five thousand starving men, dying of disease, though they were the enemy, appealed strongly to the hearts of our women. . . . " Food was prepared and transported to the barracks.[51]

Though women functioned in similar ways North and South, the situation faced by Confederate women was in many ways more complex than that confronted by their sisters in the North. The most fundamental difference was that as many parts of the South were invaded, women witnessed the physical destruction of hospitals they had created or supplies they had gathered. Gunboats for which women had given their treasured possessions were burned before their eyes when invasion threatened. The blockade and the meagerness of certain resources combined to create a demand for ingenuity which became a part of the folklore of the postwar South. Forty years later, aging women still described in precise and concrete detail the substitutes they had invented for almost every necessity of life. Carpets had become blankets; wool from mattresses and rabbits became knitting yarn; old garments were reconstructed for new purposes; every sort of bean was roasted in the search for a drinkable coffee substitute; wild plants were sought for medicines and dyes; salt was recovered from the dirt floors of smokehouses; and so it went.[52] Ingenuity took many forms. One southern woman reported her dismay when an old farmer brought as his contribution two giant slippery elm trees. However after some effort a method was devised to retrieve the inner substance, prized for its healing value, and it was sent off to an army hospital.

Though there was no overarching organization to match the Sanitary

Commission in the North, in many places soldiers' aid societies had some formal link with local or state government, often one that included cooperation in procurement. As resources became ever more scarce, women often found themselves working for the government, which supplied the raw materials while they provided the labor. In Athens, Georgia, for example, the Ladies Aid Society, which had devised individual patterns for each Clarke County soldier, made up cloth bought by the county.[53] But for the meticulous nature of their accounts the amount of material southern women transformed into uniforms, shirts, hospital supplies, and the like would defy belief.

On both sides as the war dragged on, as casualties mounted, and, in the South, food and medical supplies disappeared in some places, women's zeal and initial patriotic fervor gave way to stoic endurance and in some cases to outright despair. In some places as material to be made up became scarce and family needs more pressing, the women's organizations gave up. In others they continued doggedly to the end; some then transformed themselves into memorial societies obsessed with commemorating the Confederate dead.[54]

Neither side in the Civil War had a monopoly on sentimental talk about women, and as one would expect "the Confederate woman" came in for a large share of extravagant praise.[55] Yet there was a bitter irony in the history of Confederate women's war work: many people, including a number of northern generals, thought their assiduous labor had prolonged the war. Indeed there may be an even larger irony: if women on both sides had kept closer to their assigned sphere and let the two governments muddle on without their labor, the short war which so many had predicted might indeed have occurred, and nearly everybody would have been better off.

War Aims and Women's Rights

While large numbers of women were working to supply the armies with food, clothing, nursing care, and help for soldiers and their families, some northern women also organized to lobby for their definition of war aims. In the spring of 1863 a number of women concerned that freedom for the slaves should be a central goal answered a call to a convention issued by Elizabeth Cady Stanton and Susan B. Anthony to the "loyal women of America."

In 1861 leading advocates of women's rights had agreed, despite Anthony's dissent, that agitation would cease for the duration of the war. The Emancipation Proclamation, which freed only the slaves in rebel hands, and hence, in practice, none, gave Stanton and Anthony a reason to call a meeting to consider what they called "the solemn lessons of the war: liberty to all; national protection for every citizen under our flag; universal suffrage and universal amnesty." Emancipation of all slaves was, they believed, the key to a quick end to the rebellion, but women's need for liberty was also much on their minds.[56]

In many communities Ladies Loyal Leagues or Ladies Union societies already existed, though the extent to which they also functioned as soldiers' aid societies varied from one community to another. One, in Madison, Wisconsin, which claimed to be the first such group in the country, stated its purposes as 1) to encourage retrenchment in household expenses, 2) to strengthen loyal sentiment and instill love of the national flag, and 3) to write to the soldiers.[57] Another, in Connecticut, included among its purposes a careful study of "the great principles of civil liberty."

Representatives from these and numerous other women's groups converged in May 1863 to debate vigorously whether organized and vocal "loyal women" should support women's rights as well as the emancipation of slaves.[58] The final decision was embodied in a resolution that included support for woman suffrage, but the concrete work of the Woman's National Loyal League was almost entirely that of gathering, with the help of all kinds of local women's organizations, 400,000 signatures to petitions calling for a constitutional amendment to end slavery. By May 1864 the Women's Loyal National League claimed 5,000 members and employed two women as traveling lecturers. These lecturers were able to combine discussions of women's rights with those of freeing the slaves, preaching that once the slaves were freed, both black men and all women should be enfranchised.

While women may have enjoyed the war's challenge, they also found it a great burden, and in some times and places almost an intolerable one. Farmers or planters went off to fight and left women to run the farms or plantations. Money was scarce and prices ever-rising. Beloved husbands or sons died in battle or from disease. In the South toward the end of the war numerous women begged governors and even Jefferson Davis to send their husbands home lest the children starve. Such experiences could hardly have been seen as in any way liberating. But even the intolerably burdened, if they survived, had a new sense of themselves afterward.

On both sides the war allowed women to hone organizational and political skills which had been a long time in the making. Women who persevered to the end were often reluctant to give up the satisfactions their wartime experience had brought. As Katharine Wormeley, a worker for the Sanitary Commission, put it in a letter: "You are right; it is worth five years of any other life. . . ."[59] Rebecca Rouse was so reluctant to return to a more restricted sphere that she continued to work at the soldiers' home she and the aid society had created, remaining as long as it lasted. On 30 July 1865 Benjamin Rouse wrote to his daughter: "Mother is just as busy as she can be feeding soldiers on their [way to] return home to different western states and taking care of the sick and wounded at the Soldier's home. . . . during the month of June they fed 1,900 soldiers. . . . Mother wishes me to say she works so hard at the home days she's too tired to write you at night. . . . "[60]

The desperation that pervaded southern society by the winter of 1865 was such that there was probably no southern woman who felt sorry that the war was over, though many would grieve for the rest of their days that the Confederacy had been defeated. Yet women who had shared the experiences of the war, like their northern counterparts, would never be quite the same again—as their reminiscences written years later suggest.[61]

On Memorial Day in 1881 Oliver Wendell Holmes, Jr., spoke to and for his fellow veterans when he said: " . . . the generation that carried on the war has been set apart by its experience. Through our great good fortune, in our youth our hearts were touched with fire. It was given to us to learn at the outset that life is a profound and passionate thing. . . . "[62]

Few women had Holmes's eloquence, but many might have said much the same thing about their Civil War experiences. Women often noted that those years had marked a turning point. In a Memorial Day address in 1888 Clara Barton told her audience that when the Civil War was over "woman was at least fifty years in advance of the normal position which continued peace . . . would have assigned her."[63] Frequently in the ensuing years women in various positions of leadership spoke of what they had learned in wartime as having laid the foundation for the greater postwar efflorescence of women's activism.

So far no one has collected systematic data to test these statements. The vast array of Sanitary Commission papers has only recently begun to be used to illuminate women's experience in that organization. None of the surviving records of soldiers' aid societies have, so far as I can discover, been examined with an eye to tracing the postwar careers of the women who ran them, though such an examination would be illuminating.

Even without systematic evidence as to what happened to thousands of women war workers afterward, evidence drawn from the few who, having inhabited for a time what they described as "a larger sphere of usefulness," went on to become "notable" in their day and generation suggests something of what may have happened on a much larger scale in local communities.[64]

Jane Hoge, whose work in the Northwestern Sanitary Commission had been so impressive, was fifty-four when the war ended. The network of women she had developed through her war work provided the basis for her postwar career. In six years she had become president of the Women's Educational Association of Evanston, Illinois, where she directed a difficult and ultimately successful fund drive to create the Evanston College for

Ladies, of which Frances Willard would become president. A year later Hoge was also head of the Women's Presbyterian Board of Foreign Missions for the whole northwest.

Her colleague and friend Mary Livermore, in her forties in 1865, had a long and active life ahead. Her experience with the Sanitary Commission had convinced her of women's need for the vote. She organized the first Illinois Woman Suffrage Association, established a women's rights newspaper, *The Agitator,* and became vice president of the American Woman Suffrage Association. She went on to merge her paper with the *Woman's Journal,* which she edited briefly, became president of the Massachusetts Women's Christian Temperance Union, worked with the Women's Educational and Industrial Union, and made her living lecturing all over the country on subjects having mostly to do with women.

Helen Louise Gilson, age thirty in 1865, had organized soldiers' aid in Chelsea, Massachusetts, and then had become an army nurse. She went south after the war to work in an orphanage for black children.

Abby Hopper Gibbons, a Quaker who had had a long career as a reformer before the war, was in her mid-sixties in 1865. With her daughter Sarah she served for three and a half years as a Civil War nurse, and afterward returned to work in voluntary associations of several kinds. One of these was the Labor and Aid Society, which she organized to help returned soldiers find work and to provide employment to widows and orphans.[65] Rebecca Rouse was also of the older generation, but she continued until old age to be a leading member of almost every women's organization in Cleveland. At eighty-five she finally retired from the board of the Protestant Orphan Asylum which she had helped to found, urging those who remained to pray for the orphans *and* for the women who ran the institution!

Louisa Schuyler's postwar career was a natural outgrowth of her wartime service. After a considerable hiatus during which she traveled in Europe to recover her health, in May 1872 she organized the State Charities Aid Association, an elite group dedicated to bringing her notions of system and order into the charitable world of New York. She was joined by her friend Josephine Shaw Lowell, another veteran of the Women's Central Relief Association, who would later organize the original Consumers' League.

Abigail May, of the New England Women's Auxiliary Association of the United States Sanitary Commission, was in her thirties when the war ended. She went on to work with the Freedmen's Aid Society and to take part in founding the New England Hospital, as well as the New England Woman's Club, of which she was one of the most effective members. She became president of the School Suffrage League and with three other women broke tradition by winning election to the Boston School Committee in 1873 and again in 1874. Annie Wittenmyer, also in her thirties at the end of the war, and already a veteran of several associations, had worked first with the Sanitary Commission and then with its rival, the Christian Commission. In 1873 she was one of the founders of the Woman's Christian Temperance Union (WCTU) and became its first president.

Katherine Wormeley, a thirty-five-year-old nurse at the end of the war, wrote books to document the role women had played in the Sanitary Commission's work, and in 1874 became the principal founder of the Newport, Rhode Island, Charity Organization Society.

Tracing the postwar experience of southern women is more difficult. There were few opportunities for women to rise to more than local leadership, and records of their war work are as scarce as biographical data covering their future lives.[66] Sallie Chapin of Charleston is an exception; born in 1830, she was president of the Soldiers' Relief Society and of the Ladies' Auxiliary Christian Association of Charleston. She continued her interest in Christian associations after the war, and in 1879, attending a national temperance convention, she discovered that she could sway an audience. (It was said, later, that she could "hold unflagging interest for an hour and a half.") She became a major lecturer and organizer for the Woman's Christian Temperance Union and one of the best-known women in the South. By 1891 she was an avowed suffragist, and had embarked on what would be a successful campaign to create an industrial college for women in South Carolina.

The few like Sallie Chapin aside, however, southern women who emerge in the biographical compendia of the late nineteenth century were generally those born in the 1850s and 1860s, daughters of women who had lived through the war. When A. D. Mayo went south in the 1880s to study southern women's education he was struck by the enthusiastic support mothers of the war generation were giving young women in search of higher education and careers as teachers. These young women were, he wrote, "everywhere encouraged by the sympathy, support, sacrifice, toils and prayers of the superior women of the elder generation at home."[67] It may be that the "elder generation" was so busy with the need for recovery that it was only their daughters who could exhibit the consequences of wartime experience.

The situation of black women was, of course, transformed by the war and its aftermath. Leaders began to emerge even before the Thirteenth Amendment was ratified, and in the ensuing decades they appeared in ever increasing numbers, both in the churches and in secular organizations.

Taking it all in all, the war gave thousands of women, north and south, opportunities for involvement in important work and a sense of participation in the central activity of the time. One consequence was a redefinition in their own minds, and in the minds of some men, of "woman's sphere." It also gave numerous women not only an opportunity to develop administrative skills, but provided impressive evidence that they could function as administrators, record keepers, policy makers—in short, as people who could achieve results in a sphere often denominated "male." The pressing need for their labor removed for the time being various restraints on what was "proper" for a woman to do, and all experience shows that when such restraints are once removed it is very difficult to reimpose them.

Men developed different relationships with women in wartime. The southern men who, as life became ever more difficult, began saying "Use your own judgment, it is as good as mine," might be taken as emblematic of a generation.[68] Men who had long believed that women required masculine direction discovered their mistake through sometimes bitter experience. The effusive praise of women's war work on the part of men like Bellows and many others, South and North, requires complex psychological analysis, but it does suggest that at least for the time being a new estimate of women's capacities was beginning to take shape. One thing is certain: in the following decades women in unprecedented numbers created or joined organizations. For many of them, war work had been the first step.

PART II

A New World—to Some Extent

At ten o'clock of a July night...the Adams family and the Motley family clambered down the side of their Cunard steamer into the government tugboat, which set them ashore in black darkness at the end of some North River pier. Had they been Tyrian traders of the year B.C. 1000, landing from a galley fresh from Gibraltar, they could hardly have been stranger on the shore of a world, so changed from what it had been ten years before....

How much its character had changed or was changing, they could not wholly know, and they could but partly feel....

—*The Education of Henry Adams*

Although any moment in the past may be defined from some perspective as a transition, a turning point, some are more visibly so than others. In order to cope with the flood of events, historians devise "periods" (the early national period, the age of Jackson, the Progressive era) which then take on lives of their own. We give special meaning to certain decades—though they, too, are a human construct.

Realizing how much periodization may be a function of the historian's need to organize the flow of events so that they can be grasped, we may still see the Civil War decade as a significant turning point, one that marked change in the life experience of many people. The industrial-urban development that had begun in England in the eighteenth century was now rapidly becoming the dominant economic structure and the primary source of cultural change. It represented something new in human experience. There were few precedents to guide people who lived through this mammoth change. There was continuity with the past, of course, but there was also change on a scale that was not easy to assimilate.

For the women who are the subject of this book, horizons expanded in soldiers' aid societies or the Loyal League did not contract just because peace had come. And while much that would happen in the world of voluntary associations for the next three or four decades had visible connection with societies of the antebellum period, for them as for many other segments of American society, what we call the modern world began in the late 1860s.

By 1880 there were roughly fourteen million adult women in the United States. Two-thirds of them lived in the country and were, as farm women had always been, producers in what was still partly a household economy.[1] Many freedwomen were hoeing corn and chopping cotton in the fields in the South much as they had done in slavery, although now, with any luck, some part of the output belonged to them.[2] Among the urban third, more than a million worked for wages as domestic servants, a growing number of young single women worked in shops and factories, and the wives of men who labored in mines, steel mills, factories, construction, and transportation helped support families in any way they could devise, whether by "home work" or by taking in boarders.[3] From the perspective of the late twentieth century, most of the fourteen million led hard and difficult lives, though we do not know how many perceived themselves as downtrodden; material circumstances have less to do with happiness than we sometimes imagine. Whatever their self-perceptions, one thing is clear: most women were too much occupied taking care of families or earning a living to do much else.

Among all these late-nineteenth-century women, the ones most visible in the pages that follow were drawn for the most part from a small minority of the prosperous, usually wives or daughters of substantial farmers, or of white-collar and professional men. Thanks to the increasing availability of factory-made goods and of poorly paid black and white household servants, these women were relieved of much domestic responsibility and were finding, or making for themselves, steadily widening opportunities in the new urban-industrial world. Some such women, to be sure, were content to become part of Thorstein Veblen's leisure class: those who spent their time shopping, entertaining lavishly, paying calls, exhibiting the latest fashions, and complaining about their servants. Their principal function, Veblen argued, was to draw attention to a husband's material success by practicing conspicuous consumption.[4] Some of the young women, not content with unproductive leisure, were going off to the new women's colleges or the newly coeducational universities. The new college graduates played a major role in increasing the effectiveness of women's associations. Many young women were choosing to remain single in order to become teachers, social workers, doctors, lawyers, or ministers. Some were beginning to talk about the right to vote.

From this small group of the unusually favored came the growing numbers of women who emerged from their homes in the 1880s to join associations, to plunge into politics, to help build new communities and reshape old ones, to think about the meaning of the emerging urban-industrial society and about their own place in it. Together they created a new phase in the history of women's voluntary associations.

New as the postwar world was, the past was not dead. As these women went about their collective activities the habits and patterns formed in benevolent and reform associations and sharpened during the war were all still visible. They began with traditional forms of organization and ways of expression. Every group, however small, had its constitution and by-laws, and hewed to the line of *Robert's Rules of Order.*[5] Like those who had preceded them, most of the first generation of postwar women (including many whose principal activity was in secular associations) held strong religious convictions and, again like their predecessors, some were gifted politicians. Many demonstrated skill in what they called "business methods" which they exhibited over and over in the creation of community institutions. The most striking continuity of all was that most of them clung—at least in their public statements—to the notion of woman as moral being whose special public responsibility was to bring the principles of the well-run Christian home into community life.

European travel was increasingly possible for women of their class, and for some, at least, the encounter with other cultures raised new intellectual and moral issues. A few women, mostly drawn from the first generation of college graduates, were eager to grapple with the emerging social thought of their time (Jane Addams reading Carlyle and Comte, Florence Kelley translating Engels, members of the Chicago Woman's Club studying *Das Kapital* were unusual, but not unique).[6]

In the last thirty-five years of the nineteenth century, women's organizations increased so rapidly in number and variety that by 1900 no one had any idea how many or how many different kinds of associations there were. Local, state, regional, and national as well as international federations increased communication among them. The largest number of organized women were still to be found in religious societies, but secular organizations developed very rapidly, and many women belonged to both kinds.

The exhilaration and spirit that characterized so many of these late-nineteenth-century women's associations should not conceal the fact that human beings are inevitably, though perhaps to different degrees at different times, culture-bound. The occasional woman who stepped decisively beyond the recognized cultural definitions of women's role (an Emma Goldman or a Victoria Woodhull) was generally a loner; the vast majority who joined organizations, even socialist women, stayed within the accepted cultural definitions or tested the boundaries without actually breeching them. Carrie Chapman, for example, negotiated a premarital agreement with George Catt which guaranteed her a certain number of weeks each year for suffrage work, but it was only as a widow that she made suffrage a full-time career. The women who began the settlement movement, to take another example, despite their often radical commitment to establishing a society in which justice was possible, created a "home" as their base of operations. At this distance it is impossible to distinguish clearly between those for whom Victorian rhetoric and ladylike behavior were convenient masks for innovation, or possibly even for subversive ideas, and those who had so internalized the ideology of domesticity that they took for granted and operated within its framework.[7]

A sudden challenge could bring a woman to question values she had accepted for half a lifetime. A Raleigh, North Carolina, woman provided a typical case in point. She had quarreled with her husband over the issue of supporting their daughter's desire to go to Bryn Mawr (she wanted to do so, he didn't). In defiance she sold the only family property that was in her name, waved the daughter off to college, and recorded for posterity the fact that from that point on she no longer accepted the view the home should be the center of her life.[8] Others like her, raised in the bonds of "true womanhood," slipped those bonds and found that the heavens did not fall.

Like motherhood, racism was deeply imbedded in the culture, North and West as well as in the South. Behavior on the part of northern and western women that has sometimes been seen as an undue deference to southern opinion in fact represented simply their own—and most of their contemporaries'—view of the world.

The making of a middle class proceeded rapidly in the postwar decades, though few things are as much disputed among historians as the meaning of that phrase. Do we define "middle class" by income, by "relation to the means of production"? Or is it defined by a certain set of values, especially the drive for self-improvement, the high regard for work, and the concept of respectability?[9] Did the middle class construct itself, as Mary Ryan and John Gilkeson have argued, in the 1830s and 1840s? Or did it begin to make itself visible in the late eighteenth century as Stuart Blumin implies? And, in any case, the part women's voluntary associations played in its creation is barely beginning to be understood. Blumin, for example, writes that " . . . events in the 'separate sphere' of domestic womanhood were influential, perhaps even crucial, in generating new social identities. To this extent, middle-class formation was woman's work." But his chapter on voluntary associations, after a page or so on women's organizations, devotes thirty pages to those of men.[10]

Many characteristics: income, values, concepts of respectability and propriety, education, behavior, self-definition, even clothing and patterns of church going, distinguish the middle class from the emerging working class on the one hand and the handful of homegrown, self-defined aristocrats on the other.[11] By such an eclectic standard, most of the women, white and black, who peopled the numerous voluntary associations were part of that class, and by their activities and behavior contributed to its creation. Inevitably their collective work fed into their own and society's notion of what "class" meant.

The drama of women's continued emergence into public life is complex, as were the individuals who peopled the stage. Within the minority of privileged, educated, middle-class, or upwardly mobile women who joined associations or forged careers, not all were equally committed or equally adventurous. As we will see, many women joined societies for reasons that had little to do with self-improvement or reform, but simply for sociability or the opportunity to associate with the kinds of people who belonged. In so doing they contributed to the male stereotype which saw women's societies as an excuse for gossip. Leaders often left rank-and-file members far behind in their conception of what women could and should do, yet it is they who created the records upon which we must rely for reconstructing the history of associations.

With all these cautions, it is nevertheless true that the organization of women into literally thousands of voluntary associations created one of the central social movements of the years after 1865. What had begun in the first half of the century with the multiplication of local groups now became a whole series of national organizations in which we can see mirrored much of the social history of the time.

4

Onward Christian Women

In the pivotal years of the 1860s and 1870s American women black and white built on the past and foreshadowed the future in three major clusters of religious associations: the home and foreign missionary societies of the Protestant churches, the Woman's Christian Temperance Union, and the Young Women's Christian Association.[1] All three drew members from the same pool of church women, and each had what it perceived as a mission. They cooperated with each other, and in some communities were so interrelated that an outsider might have had trouble keeping them separate.[2] These rapidly growing organizations operated on several levels: in a religious context not only could women do things otherwise forbidden, they could also begin to grapple with social and political issues that could have seemed alarmingly radical in a secular political setting. In so doing they began to develop a grass-roots version of what would come to be called the social gospel. As local societies began to coalesce into regional and national organizations, a gap developed between leaders and followers, between what the most articulate leaders wanted to accomplish and what timid members of local groups were willing to undertake. The leaders polished their skills in organization, management, and public persuasion and many joined the cadre of "notable" women who more and more began to dot the landscape of the late nineteenth century. In the missionary societies women in nearly every denomination began demanding the right to run their own organizations and handle their own money; male opposition to this drive for independence inaugurated an ongoing struggle between the sexes, most visibly perhaps in the black and white Baptist church and the Methodist Episcopal Church, South. The WCTU was attacked by indignant male clergy who thought its members were presuming to preach the gospel, and the YWCA encountered opposition from men who thought the Young Men's Christian Association deserved the community's resources more. Opposition bred further demands for independence and stimulated the beginning of what we would now label a feminist consciousness.

Home and Foreign Missions

Missionary societies, though they took on greater significance in the postwar years, were not a new phenomenon. The concept of mission had long been integral to New World culture and women had begun forming their own societies for the benefit of those they defined as heathen as early as 1800. For many nineteenth-century American women, indeed, missionary work became a "grand passion."[3] Under the banner of "women working for women" they raised money, supported missionaries, fought for the right of single women to serve abroad, tried to promote intercultural understanding, and built hospitals in Burma or schools in China. Many early missionary societies doubled as benevolent societies, caring for the needs of women and children in their own communities as well as of those in far-off places. Until the Civil War these societies had always been local; the power to make decisions beyond the local community had rested with various all-male missionary boards. Most of the money the women raised was handed over to male boards to spend.

In 1861 Sarah Doremus, a versatile leader in the Dutch Reformed Church in New York, undertook to organize an interdenominational Woman's Missionary Union Society of America, with auxiliaries in major cities. Although the timing was bad—war was just beginning—this enterprise survived and marked the moment when some women began to assert the right to direct their own missionary enterprises.[4]

The end of the war brought a new wave of enthusiasm and a rapid increase in the number of missionary societies in all the churches. Here, as in so much else, wartime experience had provided an impetus. As one missionary society member wrote: "the efforts of our sex during our late war exhibited, as never before, [woman's] latent and unemployed power to labor for great and noble ends."[5]

Women in the Congregational church were the first to ask for a board of their own, but since Methodists and Baptists together encompassed the vast majority of Protestant church members, it was particularly significant that women in both began soon after the war to negotiate for the right to direct their own affairs. By 1872 Methodist women in the North had persuaded the all-male General Conference to recognize a denomination-wide Women's Foreign Missionary Society. But the conflict as to what the women could do without male approval did not end, and only after twelve years of ever-expanding work did the conference recognize the Women's Society as an official organ of the church. Male attitudes were highlighted at a General Conference in 1888 when five women, duly elected by their home churches, appeared as delegates. After a special committee recommended against seating them there was a strenuous debate. In the end the men voted not to seat the women, though they generously offered to reimburse them for their travel![6]

Some Baptist men were, if anything, more opposed than Methodist men to sharing power. Baptist women found it expedient to organize first in regional associations in which they were soon taking on responsibilities that had hitherto been those of all-male boards. In the black Baptist church some (not all) men were as opposed as their white counterparts to granting women autonomy. In the face of considerable opposition, during the 1880s black Baptist women began forming separate conventions, and finally in 1900 the National Baptist Convention permitted the formation of an auxiliary national woman's convention. Independence was never achieved without a struggle, but in one form or another most of the smaller denominations followed the Methodist and Baptist examples.[7]

The work of the foreign missionary societies is a story in itself and one that has been well told by able historians. In such groups women practiced management skills on large scale. They raised money for and built schools and hospitals. By supporting the right of single women to serve as foreign missionaries they helped create new careers for women.[8] The first medical missionary ever to go abroad was sent by a woman's missionary society.[9]

Members of foreign missionary societies, intent upon self-education, studied geography and history, listened to returned missionaries, and made extraordinary efforts to understand cultures different from their own.[10] Joan Jacobs Brumberg has argued persuasively that the ethnography perceived by missionary women not only represented a good deal of projection (as they described the awful oppression of women in "heathen lands," far from their normal experience), but also that the lessons taught in women's societies shaped much of nineteenth-century American popular understanding of foreign cultures.[11]

Foreign missionary work, for all its complex significance at home and abroad, was open to the charge that had been levied by the Lynn Anti-Slavery Society in an earlier day: that it was a way of avoiding serious issues close to home. Home missionary work, by contrast, brought churchwomen face to face with conditions in their own communities from which they might otherwise have been shielded and about which they could, if they chose, do something direct and consequential.

"Home missions" was not a new term. For years benevolent societies and moral reform societies had hired or appointed "city missionaries" to work with poor people, prostitutes, and other outcasts; "home missions" had also been used to designate the work of missionaries on the frontier or with Native Americans.[12] Sending help and teachers to newly freed black people in the South, as northern churches did soon after the war, was still another area defined as home missionary work. In the seventies and eighties, however, foreign missionary societies in local communities began to add "home" to their titles or to organize separate "home missionary societies" for work with needy people in their own vicinity. When Laura Askew Haygood, a Methodist schoolteacher, created the Trinity Home Mission in Atlanta in 1882, she set a pattern for much that would follow.[13] The work proved so compelling that some women who had educated themselves to become foreign missionaries decided that there was plenty to do at home and became full-time social workers in their own towns.

As they were doing in foreign missions, women began to create institutions (schools, hospitals, social settlements), and to manage considerable sums of money. Responding to perceived needs, they undertook to establish low-cost boarding homes for working women, kindergartens and day-care centers for the children of wage-earning mothers, settlement houses in black as well as white neighborhoods, well-baby clinics—indeed the whole panoply of community institutions created by one nineteenth-century women's voluntary association after another as members surveyed the new industrial cities and found them wanting. Some churches re-established the ancient office of deaconess in order to train church women as social workers.[14] The historian of a small society in Macon, Georgia, described the self-image typical of many local groups: "There arises in the community a need, eyes are opened to it, hearts are touched by it—a proposition rises to meet it, and God's children respond to it. A movement is set on foot, plans are projected, people go to work and a need has been met. . . . "[15]

The process by which women began thinking of going beyond benevolence to social reform is delineated in John Patrick McDowell's detailed study of women seeking autonomy and inaugurating social programs in the Methodist Episcopal Church, South.[16] By the 1870s southern Methodist women, following the example of their northern counterparts, achieved a denomination-wide foreign missionary board, and then in the eighties, working slowly and tactfully, step by step gained approval for a home missionary board as well.

In 1886, as the result of diplomatic but intensive lobbying, the General Conference of the southern church agreed to establish the Woman's Department of Church Extension to be responsible for building and repairing parsonages for ministers in the West. Lucinda Helm, one of a group of remarkable leaders who transformed women's work in the southern Methodist church, was named secretary of this new department. Helm's vision, which she was careful not to share with the churchmen, was of a Woman's Home Missionary Board with a broad mandate and a great deal of autonomy. Taking care of parsonages was an acceptably traditional kind of activity for women; for her it was the camel's nose. By 1888 there were enough home mission societies to bring more pressure on the General Conference. In

1890 the men agreed to change the name to Woman's Parsonage and Home Mission Society, and to give it responsibility not only for parsonages but for "otherwise aiding the cause of Christ."[17] Despite the opposition of many ministers and some women who feared that foreign missions would suffer if home missions became a central concern, social work at home began to develop rapidly.[18]

Pressed as to their motivation many leaders and most members would have spoken of a desire to "bring the masses to Christ." Faced with the realities of life among poor people, however, a handful of women began to realize that converting hungry, discouraged people was not easy. As Lucinda Helm put it: "the poor have naturally gained the impression that she [the church] is not concerned with what they consider real life, that her province is the spiritual and the future, which do not appeal strongly to men whose wants are mostly physical and altogether present."[19]

By emphasizing their Christian responsibility for the quality of home life, whether that of poor people or black people, this little group of leaders was able to bring a considerable number of conservative southern women to think and talk about such issues as the regulation of child labor, minimum-wage laws, improvement of working conditions in factories, better educational opportunity for poor children, education and opportunity for black people—all subjects generally considered radical in the South.

The historian in Macon, Georgia, cited above, described her society's support for female autonomy: "The women who were doing the work demanded recognition by the brethren. . . . the patronizing spirit manifest in the term 'the good women' or 'the elect ladies' was very offensive to some of the women. They resented the insinuation that the women were unequal to the responsibility of conducting our own work." She then described what was going on in south Georgia in the 1890s: The women were studying, she said, "slums, child criminals and how they are made, infant mortality and its chief causes, fallen women . . . civic righteousness, the laws of sanitation as related to housing the poor, disease, crime and poverty. . . . the information thus gained was printed . . . and scattered broadcast. Rescue homes, Doors of Hope and modern missionary institutions, with all their varied social and industrial activities in the cities and towns and trained deaconesses became an integral part of church life."[20]

Though Macon was not a major city, the home missionary society had organized three settlement houses with 115 volunteer workers. Members had come to share the view suggested by one of the regional leaders when she wrote: "The most sinister thing in connection with our rapid growth as a manufacturing nation is the increasing employment of women and children, and the utter lack, in nearly all the states, of any safeguarding of these workers by law."[21]

As early as 1894 the women's board had outlined a course of reading for members of the home mission societies which included the works of Washington Gladden, Josiah Strong, Walter Rauschenbush, Richard Ely, and other well-known proponents of the social gospel. Meanwhile the home mission magazine, significantly named *Our Homes*, carried articles on a variety of such topics for those who were unlikely to read the books. In the 1920s, looking back, one Methodist woman wrote that her coworkers had strongly emphasized education, child welfare, sanitation, housing, health, recreation, and the improvement of social and economic conditions. This work, she said, "has been carried on in remote rural areas, mountain coves, mining camps, industrial communities and city neighborhoods where overcrowding, disease, ignorance, poverty and vice make the condition of the underprivileged a lamentable commentary on our vaunted Christian civilization and shows us the long way we must travel before our democracy has made good its connotation of well being. . . . " She described missionary women as studying, among many other things, democracy in industry and the problems of rural tenancy.[22]

By the 1890s, as race conflict escalated and lynchings increased, a profound gloom descended upon black people, as well as upon a handful of white people who were concerned for the future of the New South. State after state disfranchised blacks and enacted Jim Crow laws. Segregation tightened. Black women constantly heard themselves described as immoral, irresponsible, careless mothers.[23] Examples are so numerous that one will have to stand for them all. A distinguished historian of the South, whose books were widely read and cited, wrote: "The average [black] father and mother are morally obtuse and indifferent and at times even openly and unreservedly licentious. Their character is such . . . that they have no just conception of the parental obligation."[24]

It is no wonder that the years after 1890, described in white textbooks as "the progressive era," appear in the work of black historians as "the nadir." Though some white people were beginning to recognize the injustice of racial discrimination, the president of the University of Georgia complained that it was impossible to talk about the issue, since there was no freedom of speech to be found anywhere in the region. The whole South appeared to be in an uproar when President Theodore Roosevelt invited Booker T. Washington to dine at the White House, and the state of North Carolina was similarly aroused when a respected southern-born history professor at Trinity College wrote that except for Robert E. Lee, Booker T. Washington was the greatest southerner of the century.[25]

In the midst of this crisis, black women, who had been organized for many decades to deal with the social needs of their own people, redoubled their efforts, often with missionary societies as the principal vehicle for action. Disfranchised like all women, discriminated against like all African Americans, and, in addition, subjected to the myth of their natural immorality, they responded vigorously to the deteriorating situation. In the 1870s women in the African Methodist church began their own home and foreign missionary societies. Like the white women, their history of small local missionary societies went back to the early part of the century, and when, in 1874, a bishop of the AME church sent out a call for women to organize he met an enthusiastic response. The work grew rapidly.[26] Despite the generally limited resources available in black communities, these women accomplished impressive feats of fund raising and institution building.

In the black Baptist church, home and foreign missionary societies were also extremely active. Relying to some extent on resources provided by white Baptist missionary societies in the north, who believed that the best hope for improving the lot of freed people lay in educating the women, they worked diligently to provide educational opportunity. Spelman College was one result. The National Training School for Women and Girls, headed by Nannie Burroughs and supported by the Woman's Convention of the black Baptist church, was another. There a young black woman could get a liberal education, training for a vocation, and a strong dose of black pride.[27] Missionary societies in other northern white churches, Presbyterian, Lutheran, Disciples of Christ, Congregational, and Dutch Reformed, as well as various Quaker congregations, helped southern black women found and support many schools and some colleges. Occasionally similar help came from southern white women. Scattered about the South these schools sent out a generation of women prepared for leadership in the church and community.

In the southern Methodist church a handful of unusual white women were appalled by the discrimination and suffering they had witnessed in their welfare work in black neighborhoods. In 1897 Belle Bennett, president of the Parsonage and Home Mission Society, exhorted its members to take up special work among black people. Bennett had developed a deep concern about white women's responsibility for what she called "this great race of people" and she now called upon Methodist women to recognize their plain duty and begin to deal with the deprivations of black citizens.[28]

The beginnings were small. In 1901 the Methodist Home Missionary Society at its annual meeting agreed to help raise money for a vocational department for women at Paine College—a black school in Augusta, Georgia, which had been established by cooperative efforts of black and white Methodists. The next major step came ten years later with the appointment of Mary DeBardeleben to work full time in a black community, also in Augusta. In the face of apathy or outright hostility among the white people she established a settlement house, and began what would become her life work. In eight other southern cities Methodist women followed her example. In 1912 the Women's Missionary Council of the southern Methodist church, said to represent 200,000 women, voted unanimously for an antilynching resolution.[29]

The fruit of these beginnings would hardly be visible for twenty years, but what began as a small, tentative effort became in time a far-reaching program, based on cooperation between black and white women. What began as an expression of *noblesse oblige* led in time to mutual respect and a growing interracial movement in which men as well as women took part.[30] Jessie Daniel Ames, who in 1930 would organize the Association of Southern Women for the Prevention of Lynching, had been raised in the southern Methodist church. It would be rash to exaggerate the amount of rank-and-file support for this interracial work, for racism would continue to be rampant, north as well as south, for years to come, but these early pioneers have hardly been recognized, partly because they have been judged by late-twentieth-century standards rather than by those of their own time.

By 1916 an interdenominational Home Mission Study course included an array of books dealing with pressing social and political problems written specifically for the use of missionary women. Among others, there was a book about American Indian life, one on the problems of Spanish-speaking citizens, and one about the adjustment to industrialization. In 1918 the annual report of the Council of Women for Home Missions called for a social awakening, saying, "There is an ever-widening gulf between the women of the church and the women in industry, working women are drifting away from the church.... [we] must enter upon ... education for social justice and righteousness. The Christianizing of America in no small way depends upon getting in touch with industrial workers." The council organized and ran summer schools on these topics, which sometimes attracted a thousand women.[31]

The existence of this interdenominational Council of Women for Home Missions bore witness to the strong ecumenical spirit among missionary women, a spirit that does not appear to have been much shared by their male counterparts. As early as 1888 representatives from the United States, Canada, and Great Britain had created a World's Missionary Commission of Christian Women which reached not only across denominational lines but also across national boundaries. This commission took part in setting up a Women's Congress of Missions as part of the larger Parliament of Religions at the Columbian Exposition of 1893.[32]

Since the record has generally been created by the leaders, it is hard to know how far ideas of social reform or racial justice reached into the mass of membership. Clearly many faithful members had only the vaguest idea of the larger issues comprehended by the term "social gospel." For those who did understand, however, the home missionary society provided a safe place in which to work for social change.

The struggle of church women to attain some autonomy of action as they pursued their missionary objectives had an ironical side. By opposing what might easily have been interpreted as the natural right of women members who, after all, had founded many churches and supported the practical side of church life from the beginning, church men created the very thing they feared. In the face of condescension and opposition, women began to reassess their position and one group after another began demanding an expansion of their rights within the churches. Over and over the men voted them down. These campaigns came to mirror, in language and spirit, the secular drive for woman suffrage. Though couched in religious terms, church women's struggles raised issues and inspired responses similar to those that suffragists encountered as they tried to persuade male politicians that they were entitled to the franchise. As late as 1914 the bishops of the southern Methodist church replied to women's demand for full laity rights by saying: "We have reason to believe that the demand for this kind of equality is not in harmony with the general sentiment of the women of our Church who, in the main, look upon their relation to the work of the Church in the light of duties to be performed rather than of rights to be claimed. We believe, furthermore, that the spirit of this movement is against the view which our people at large have held and still hold in regard to woman's place in the Church and in society. . . ."[33]

In such exchanges the churches became one arena in which the ideology of women's rights developed.[34] The opposition to women's activism within the churches may have been one reason so many turned their energies to the WCTU and the YWCA where there were no men to hamper them.

Woman's Christian Temperance Union

Women had, of course, been deeply involved with temperance agitation since the 1820s, and even before the war a few had begun to experiment with political action as well as with direct confrontation of saloons and liquor dealers. While army life was teaching many young men to drink, women's temperance activism had been all but submerged under wartime demands, especially those of the soldiers' aid societies. Then, at the end of 1873, reacting to a speech by Dr. Dio Lewis on the subject of what women could do to promote temperance (a lecture he had delivered many times before without any spectacular consequences), women in Fredonia, New York, suddenly took to the streets, marched to a local saloon, knelt in prayer, and demanded that the saloon keeper close his doors. Three days later the same thing happened in Jamestown, New York. Through the agency of newspapers, private letters, travelers, and circulars the movement spread across the country so that, in less than a week, by the time Dr. Lewis, who was on a lecture tour, reached Hillsboro, Ohio, women there were already prepared to follow his advice. Soon whole states were afire with temperance enthusiasm. Television, had it existed, could hardly have brought more rapid diffusion of an idea.[35]

Before the Crusade, as it came to be called, burned itself out, women in at least nine hundred towns had inaugurated daily mass prayer meetings aimed at arousing public sentiment against alcohol. In at least half these places they also organized repeated visits to saloons where the crusaders stood outside noting the names of those who entered in order to publish them, or went inside to pray with the sometimes infuriated owners.[36] Temperance women staffed coffeehouses in which various kinds of "wholesome entertainment" offered a substitute for the sociability of the saloon. In many towns crusaders went door to door urging people to sign pledges of total abstinence.

For a time, the exhilaration (and fear) that accompanied daily prayer meetings and marches foreshadowed the emotional state of the suffrage marchers in the second decade of the twentieth century or the civil rights marchers in the 1960s. For some the Crusade became virtually a full-time occupation. Many women testified that they felt called by God to engage in this unladylike behavior, and recounted in detail the conversion experiences which had emboldened them to take to the streets. One observer in Missouri wrote to a relative: "the women are in desperate earnest and say it is the Lord's work. . . . the time for freedom from alcohol has come just as the time to end slavery came—and he has chosen them—the weak vessel—to do his work."[37]

Historians and sociologists have tried to understand what triggered such an extraordinary outpouring of zeal at this particular moment. The causes were certainly complex, but one thing is clear: whenever women were dependent upon men for support, persistent male drinking was an ever-present threat to their well being. When most people lived on farms a woman with an alcoholic husband, while she certainly had a problem, could feed herself and her children from garden and barnyard. A family dependent on cash wages was more vulnerable: if the breadwinner drank up his pay there was no food. In middle-class families with other resources the problem of drinking men might be as much psychological as economic, but it was disruptive all the same. Impressionistic evidence suggests that many families of all classes had experience with the devastating consequences of alcohol abuse. The fervent fears mothers so often expressed for their sons were put in terms of "ending up in a drunkard's grave." Mary Austin, writing in the 1930s, remembered how she had perceived the problem as a child:

> It [the saloon] was a place from which might issue at any moment people you knew, other girls' fathers, forcible ejections of sodden and bleary men who proceeded to be violently sick on the sidewalk. . . . Sooner or later you might meet the mother of one of your schoolmates, shamefacedly steering her tipsy and abusive lord to the home where your mother wouldn't let you visit, lest you might see some such spectacle as you actually did meet occasionally on your way to school. . . . Thus you get the substance of what [my] mother's generation could express only in the quality of shocked sensibility, deal with only under the figures of iniquity. . . . [38]

But why 1873? During the decades just preceding the Crusade the liquor business had expanded rapidly. The number of dealers paying federal tax increased 154 percent between 1864 and 1873. Retail outlets increased much faster than the population and overall consumption was increasing as well. In Ohio there was said to be one saloon for every twenty inhabitants. Many women thought drinking, and indeed wickedness of all kinds, was on the upswing, and with respect to the first, at least, the evidence bore them out.[39]

Finally, it is important to recall that spells of highly emotional religious enthusiasm had appeared over and over since the days of the Great Awakening; the temperance crusade was a variation of this familiar phenomenon.

For a time the Crusade may have relieved pent-up anxiety, but the experience was too intense to be sustained for long. While it lasted, however, it was, according to one recent historian, "a true grass roots movement which attained a combination of size and intensity unprecedented for women, with no planning, minimal coordination, and no central control. . . ."[40]

By the time the daily marches and prayer meetings had settled down to weekly or monthly gatherings a national temperance organization had come into being which would in time develop interests far beyond alcohol abuse and would affect American women in ways that had little to do with temperance.

The organization of a national Woman's Christian Temperance Union grew out of a gathering of temperance-minded church women at Lake Chautauqua, New York, in August 1874. The leading spirit in this enterprise— Jennie Willing—was a college professor and a veteran of the Women's Foreign Missionary Society of the Methodist church. From Chautauqua a call went out for representatives of each congressional district to meet in

Cleveland in November. In due course that meeting was held, a new organization was created, and a renewed temperance movement was launched.

The president, Annie Wittenmyer, whose previous experience had included founding a Methodist home missionary society, and Frances Willard, corresponding secretary, also a Methodist, set out on a cross-country tour, organizing local unions and initiating petitions to Congress calling for an investigation of the liquor traffic and for national prohibition. By 1879 they had created or encouraged a thousand local unions with a total of twenty-six thousand members. In that year Willard, a woman of immense ambition and organizational genius to match, after a bitter struggle in the national convention, defeated Wittenmyer for the presidency of the union. Under her leadership thirty-nine "departments" would ultimately be required to oversee its numerous reform programs.[41] A concern for alcohol abuse led in many directions. In Michigan, for example, the WCTU drew up and lobbied for a bill to establish a girls' reformatory, which the legislature adopted in 1879. The law stipulated that women should constitute a majority on the Board of Control and by this means the first women came to public office in that state.[42]

Justifying all their activities on the grounds of woman's responsibility for home life, various local or state WCTU groups built, among other things, kindergartens, schools, medical dispensaries, low-cost restaurants, and homes for the homeless. They supported prison reform, sex education in the schools, minimum wage laws, and—finally—woman suffrage. The phrase "Home Protection ballot" made suffrage acceptable to many conservative members. In several southern states the WCTU led the fight for state-supported higher education for women and for an end to the notorious convict lease system.[43] A newspaper, *The Union Signal,* linked women from many parts of the country and many walks of life, and helped build the movement. Cooperation with the Knights of Labor both nationally and locally brought conservative middle-class women into alliance with working-class men and women. Black locals and unions designed to attract working women broadened the membership. In the 1890s Willard, who by that time had spoken in every town in the country of more than ten thousand inhabitants, recruiting organizers and setting up new unions as she went, would stand before a convention in Buffalo, New York, and proclaim herself a Christian socialist. Civilization, she told her audience, was the common property of all the people, and therefore all had to work with their hands, as well as share alike in the benefits of education and refinement. She believed, she said, that "competition is doomed."[44] In 1893 she joined the British Fabian Society, and that year called her presidential address "Gospel Socialism."

Willard's most recent biographer sums up what might be called the view from the top: "she rode the crest of women's rising ambitions in the nineteenth century. . . . at the same time she recognized women's need for the security of woman's place in the domestic sphere. . . . She preached and personally exemplified a womanliness . . . that did not challenge existing cultural values, but through the vehicle of a militant temperance organization designed as a protection for the home and children she permitted women to do whatever they wished in the public sphere. . . . "[45]

But there were other angles of vision. Although few of their records have yet been examined, it is clear that the degree to which local unions shared Willard's enthusiasm for a larger reform agenda varied enormously. At one extreme were the big-city unions—Chicago was an example—which, as Willard urged, tried to "do everything" and became a major player in that city's complicated reform network. At the other extreme a tiny group in Wellfleet, Massachusetts, whose minutes have by chance survived, barely managed to stay alive, and was reduced to such innocuous activities as taking flowers to sick people and distributing tracts to sailors.[46]

The Ladies Temperance League of Oberlin, Ohio, is a good example of a local union somewhere in the middle of the spectrum, one that provides a detailed picture of the way a local group moved from the frenzy of the Crusade to routine work that continued for many years. Oberlin, in 1874, was a somewhat sleepy college town (population 2,880) with a reputation for plain living and high thinking, and a tradition of enthusiasm for utopian reform. The evangelist Charles Grandison Finney, a long-time supporter of temperance, had lived there since 1835, first as professor, then president of the college, and then as minister of the First Congregational church. When the Crusade came to Oberlin, the first meeting was held in this church and Finney's wife was among the women there.[47]

Word had come from many directions about what was going on in other Ohio towns and in cities on the East Coast. On 12 March virtually the entire adult female population of the town met to adopt a constitution and elect officers as preliminary to marching. The women prayed, sang hymns, and approved a letter written by one of their number which assured women in neighboring towns who had already begun to march that Oberlin was about to join the fray.

For the next six weeks they met virtually every day. They prayed constantly for guidance, made a systematic sweep of the town in search of signatures to a total-abstinence pledge, and visited the one local saloon in an attempt to persuade the saloon keeper to go out of business. The whole group gathered at the railroad station to sing hymns as delegations were sent off to proselyte or learn from other towns. Letters from crusaders elsewhere circulated, and mass prayer meetings, which included much testimony about alcohol-related family tragedies, were convened every weekend. Various local offenders found themselves the subject of public prayer. For so small a town Oberlin provided an astonishing array of horrendous examples of the evils of drink.

The first weeks were intense. On 14 March, for example, the secretary noted: "The hour was altogether too short for the prayers and remarks which the ladies had it in their hearts to make." And two weeks later: "So numerous and interesting were the subjects brought before us that the meeting continued until nearly 5 o'clock."

If the prayers, hymns, and discussions were exhilarating, so too were the canvass in search of signatures to the pledge and visits to the saloon. The saloon keeper refused to sign the pledge, but somewhat forlornly remarked that he would cease to sell liquor if he knew any other way to make a living. The women attacked and temporarily got rid of the town billiard parlor, and confronted a grocer who was known to sell hard drink, though he claimed to purvey only cider. When it was reported that certain "German and Irish girls who were Catholics, declined to sign," the women enlisted the aid of the Catholic priest.

Small groups continued to travel over the state, sometimes to offer help, sometimes to receive it. Delegates to county and state temperance conventions, and—in time—to national conventions, returned to give detailed reports of what was going on in other places. In the process, of course, they were seeing something of the world, meeting new people, and expanding their horizons. Daily meetings of members continued while mass meetings for prayer and exhortation filled local churches on weekends. The president discussed at length an article "concerning the conflict between our home and public duties." The minutes are obscure, but apparently she was warning her comrades not to neglect their homes lest they undermine support for their public activities.

On 23 April the minutes read, "The League met as usual and though we were few in number the meeting was of interest to all." From this point forward, intervals between meetings began to lengthen, and attendance waxed and waned. The disturbing news that liquor was again being sold by people who had agreed to give it up brought a large turnout, as did the announcement that delegates who had been to Cincinnati for a convention would report. From Cleveland came hints as to how women might obtain evidence of bad faith on the part of those who had agreed to give up selling liquor. Apparently the method was akin to spying, and the Oberlin women remarked, uneasily, "The enemy is cunning and skillful and cunning and skill may be used to defeat him." During the summer of 1874 members of the league worked diligently to persuade voters to turn down a clause in a proposed new state constitution providing for licensing saloons. Along with the rest of the Ohio temperance movement they were triumphant when this campaign succeeded.

A certain letdown followed, but by November, as the weather cooled, the league was again in full swing and delegates to a convention in Cleveland reported: "Never before has it been our privilege to be present at so soul-inspiring a meeting as this. That God should give such inspiration to woman as we witnessed there, that He should so develop her for doing His great work and in so short a time, and all through this blessed cause of temperance is conclusive proof that the cause is His and that He will bless our efforts so we will work on to Victory. We feel much encouraged in the fact that our meetings are more and more largely attended...." Attendance did indeed pick up, and people at the mass meetings had so much to say that it was often difficult to bring them to a close.

By the spring of 1875 the militant phase of the Crusade was over. Liquor was still being sold in Oberlin, the billiard parlor was once again in business, and the temperance organization settled into a pattern of prayer and anecdotes. Members made valiant efforts to monitor the saloon and the liquor-selling grocery, but to little effect. From 1875 to 1877 there is an unexplained gap in the record. Perhaps a different secretary used a different book which has not survived. The minutes pick up in October 1877 with the notation: "It being election day the few present prayed for the election of temperance men." This was a far cry from the diligent political canvassing in 1874.

In the following year the league began to pay special attention to schoolchildren. Like the benevolent and moral reform women before them, they had found adults recalcitrant, and so were now determined to begin with the young; children, they argued, should be persuaded to sign the pledge before they had learned to like the taste of cider or beer.

The first reference to a national organization only appeared in 1878 when members agreed to pay dues to the national WCTU, and ordered copies of Frances Willard's manuals of instruction on the organization of local unions. Attendance continued to rise and fall, depending on the community mood. By 1879 Oberlin was experiencing a religious revival that evidently preoccupied people who otherwise might have given their attention to temperance. Still the league persisted and regularly sent delegates to county and state conventions where they were impressed, as one put it, "by the delightfully earnest and inspiring character of these meetings." Frances Willard's election as national president, with its implications for the future of the organization, caused not even a ripple. No reference to this change appears in the Oberlin minutes.

November brought the first open recognition that women, too, could be drinkers. Members were considerably shocked as they listened to a visitor from Chicago tell various anecdotes on the subject. They discussed reviving the techniques of the Crusade in an effort to get rid of the "evil influence of the tobacco store," but some members argued persuasively that militant measures would not work as long as "prominent business men are so indifferent." As militance continued to decline, the tamest of all forms of agitation—the ancient custom of distributing tracts—became a regular part of their repertoire: members offered temperance literature, bought from the national office, to the people from whom they sought pledges of abstinence.

In 1880 several women suggested that the league support a "city missionary" to work with the local black population. The ministers, when consulted, thought such activity fell in their bailiwick, and were cool to the idea, but the women held their ground and went on to organize a mothers' group among black women. Hearing that a new saloon was about to be opened they embarked upon "the most earnest prayer" that it would fail.

In March of 1882 the Oberlin league agreed to change its name to conform to that of the state and national organizations. Thus the group became the Oberlin Woman's Christian Temperance Union. In spite of the name change, the record does not suggest that the national organization had much effect on concerns in Oberlin, though since they subscribed to the *Union Signal* we must assume that the women had plenty of opportunity to learn about the "do everything" national program. Perhaps a good deal of that program was simply irrelevant in a small, homogeneous community.

At this point the manuscript record ends. Partial and incomplete though it is, it provides a revealing counterpoint to the history written from national records, and suggests the gap between the ambitions of the national leaders and the realities of small unions in country towns. Oberlin women, mostly wives of college professors and ministers, and all church members, were convinced—as moral reformers had been a half century before—that the world was being engulfed in a tide of wickedness. Alcohol and tobacco were symbols of this tide but were also a concrete and, in their view, real threat to the well-being of their children. The Crusade was a dramatic expression of this anxiety, and—no doubt—it also provided a welcome change from the ordinary routine of life, in a town where generally there was little excitement. The local union provided opportunities for women to exert leadership, to travel, to meet people from other places, to find interests beyond their normal routine, as well as to attempt to bring about social changes which they very much wanted to achieve.

Surviving records of two local unions in Massachusetts add a little to the picture we can gain from Oberlin. In Cambridge, where the union had been organized in the wake of the Crusade, the women had taken to political action with enthusiasm and were proud of their part in persuading the mayor and town council to adopt a "no license" ordinance. In nearby Cambridgeport the 1884 annual report gives some sense of the satisfactions temperance work might bring: "Such active, busy lives we temperance women have come to live that we can scarcely tarry long enough for the New Year's greetings ere we go on in the bustle and labor which is ever before us on every hand."

There had been twenty-two meetings in the previous twelve months with an average attendance of twenty-five members. From the beginning this union paid attention to children, noting: "It is so much better to save the children than to reform them after they have been wasted." Seventy-five dues-paying members had raised more than two hundred dollars, though the treasurer suggested that twice that amount could have been "wisely expended."[48]

Unions would continue to be founded decades after the Crusade had wound down. In Berea, Kentucky—another small, isolated academic community with a long history of radicalism—the WCTU began in 1890 when thirty-four women took the pledge and embarked upon a temperance program.[49] They welcomed men as honorary members, if they signed a total abstinence pledge and paid a dollar a year. Occasionally, in a reverse of the traditional "ladies night" common among male societies, the Berea WCTU allowed itself a "social evening" to which men were invited.

Several things stand out in the Berea minutes: first, the significance of state and national conventions as sources of inspiration to local women; second, the tendency to combine traditional social welfare work with temperance agitation; and finally, a tendency to move from temperance into general community reform. The group had a special interest in Berea College, which had been founded as an interracial school but which by the 1890s was concentrating on the education of young white people from poor mountain communities.

Even in the smaller towns the WCTU experience could have profound meaning. Listen again to Mary Austin:

> How the women of our town, an important minority of them, loved that organization! With what sacred pride they wore its inconspicuous white ribbon; with what pure and single-minded ardor they gave themselves to learn to serve it, legal technicalities, statistics, Robert's Rules of Order, the whole ritual of public procedure. . . . During those first years there was scarcely a meeting in which they did not more or less come to grief over parliamentary procedure. . . . And then they would hold hands and sing a hymn and begin all over again with the result that for precision and directness in the conduct of public meetings, American women finally reduced our Senate and Houses of Representatives to shame.[50]

Or listen to Belle Kearney, a Mississippi woman who met Frances Willard when the latter made one of her sweeps through the South, and then spent the rest of her life working for temperance and suffrage: "The W.C.T.U. was the generous liberator, the joyous iconoclast, the discoverer, the developer of southern women. . . . "[51]

The situation in Georgia was a good illustration of Kearney's point. The dramatic rise and spread of the WCTU in the South was bound to cause concern among the men who had so strongly opposed women's activity within the denominations. In the 1890s influential ministers in the Methodist and Baptist churches in Georgia began to attack the national organization because it supported woman suffrage, and to demand that the Georgia union should secede. Frances Willard, the men said, was attempting to "revolutionize the social system" and subvert the relations of women and marriage. The attack from, among others, a leading Methodist bishop, brought an immediate decrease in the number of local unions, but the president of the Georgia WCTU held firm:

> As to 'dissolving' connection with our Northern sisters who have so long been our comrades in arms, it is not to be thought of for a moment. The organization that was born of suffering and baptized with tears, that has stood together in unbroken ranks through years of trial, difficulties, opposition, persecution, discouragement and numerous defeats will neither be intimidated or coerced into dissolution; neither will it fall to pieces voluntarily, unless something more threatening and less hopeful than woman suffrage presents itself.[52]

Then, as a clincher, she pointed out that the Georgia union had never mentioned the subject of woman suffrage, but now "the question is thrust upon us for discussion and decision, let us pray God to direct bearing ourselves in a way worthy of our high calling in Christ Jesus." In the event, the Georgia union did not endorse suffrage but neither did the state board bow its head to the clerical opposition, and by 1895 membership began to regain the lost ground. In July 1907, thanks at least in part to its efforts, the state legislature passed a prohibition law.

In North Carolina temperance women took a position even more controversial than woman suffrage. The first permanent temperance unions appeared there in the early eighties, after a visit from Frances Willard. By the late nineties there were fifteen hundred active members in fifty-seven local auxiliaries. White leaders actively encouraged the organization of black units, and by 1890 black women had set up a statewide organization which they called WCTU #2. The word "colored" was not used, they said, because they did not want to be exclusive: "we believe all men [*sic*] are equal."[53] Black and white groups alike were extremely active, and apparently black representatives attended white conventions. The North Carolina women in addition to the usual range of temperance activities tried to reform prostitutes, assist unwed mothers, protect young girls, and do away with the double standard. A resolution adopted as early as 1889 sounded like moral reformers all over again: "That we as women will use our utmost efforts to encourage and strengthen our sisters of every name and profession— that their sorrows shall be our sorrows. If they have strayed we shall try to reclaim them; if they are oppressed we will seek redress, and whenever we find the law of the State unjust towards any, we will by petition and agitation endeavor to change the same."[54]

The range of WCTU interests was wide, and depending on location and leadership local groups might do as little as Wellfleet or as much as Chicago or Boston, Georgia or Texas. Across the country, thousands of local unions could have been placed somewhere along a spectrum from most active to least active but there is no way to estimate how many belonged in each category. The union was unusual not only for size, but for the range of women it encompassed: rich and poor, women wage earners and immigrants as well as middle-class women, blacks and whites. In many places the actual institutions it created were indistinguishable from those of the missionary societies, or later of the YWCA.

A Louisiana member summed up a point of view that was increasingly common among her colleagues. Men, she noted, were full of advice to women as to how they should conduct themselves, and "have decided that brain work is detrimental to the full development of the organization of the female," but, she went on, "they do not worry over the effects of tobacco, whiskey, and certain vile habits upon the congenital vigor of both boys and girls. Fathers and medical men ought to look well to the hygienic duties of their own sex. . . . "[55]

In looking back many women described the Crusade as an unforgettable watershed experience: the "richest and noblest year of their lives." It "startled me into an active thinking life," or gave one "a broader view of woman's sphere and responsibility." There is plenty of evidence to support Frances Willard's own statement that "the WCTU is doing no more important work than reconstructing the ideal of womanhood."[56]

Politically active from the very beginning, local unions were organized by congressional district. Women learned the techniques of lobbying and pioneered in voter education. The WCTU probably contained more suffragists than did the two suffrage organizations put together, and many members became leaders in other organizations.[57] Women never succeeded in putting an end to alcohol abuse, but as all these examples indicate, and as they would go on to demonstrate in the years ahead, the changes wrought in themselves were lasting.

The Young Women's Christian Association

Like the missionary societies and the WCTU, what would become the YWCA came into existence independently in several different places.[58] The original idea is sometimes traced to a prayer society established in England in 1855 for the purpose of praying for the souls of many categories of women, beginning with "our princesses and all who are in the glitter of fashionable life . . . " and going on (in descending order, apparently) to "daughters at home of the middle classes . . . young wives and mothers . . . governesses . . . shop women . . . domestic servants . . . factory girls . . . the criminal and fallen," and ending with "those who are enchained by Judaism, Popery and Heathenism."

In 1858, perhaps inspired by the English example, a Prayer Circle and Ladies Christian Association in New York declared itself prepared to labor for the "temporal, moral, and religious welfare of young women who are dependent on their own exertions for support," and set out to establish a boardinghouse for such women. In 1866 at the home of Pauline Fowle Durant (whose husband would later found Wellesley College) a group of Boston women followed suit. The idea spread rapidly, and by 1875 there were twenty-eight such associations, most but not all in cities. Together they could point to thirteen boarding homes, three-quarters of a million dollars in assets, and eight thousand members. Clearly the idea responded to a felt need, and though the early members dwelt on saving souls for Christ, they went about the task in practical ways with a focus on women who worked for wages. In addition to inexpensive boardinghouses, the associations established libraries, classes of various kinds aimed at improving women's job options, placement bureaus to help them find jobs, gymnasia (because working women needed to be strong and healthy), low-cost restaurants, rooms for recreation, and anything else they could think of that might improve the lot of the growing number of women working in shops and factories.[59] It would be a while before they began to realize that minimum-wage legislation might accomplish as much as all their ameliorative measures put together.

The ideology was familiar. One way members of the YWCA described their work was "providing the influence and protection of a Christian home" for the women—perceived as poor, lonely, and isolated—who had left their own homes to come to the city for work. The middle-class women who worked to set up the associations also recognized, and talked about, their own search for meaningful work. For many of them, the YWCA was a particularly satisfactory way of meeting this need.

The New York City association was open about its method of attracting young women who were not likely to come seeking salvation: " . . . we must take human nature as we find it, adapting our work to its needs. The hard-working person seldom desires to be instructed . . . but seeks to be amused. . . . Thus the entertainment becomes the door by which a woman enters upon the enjoyment of all other benefits of the Association, chief among which we rank the Bible class and the religious training which is given there. . . . "[60]

Benevolent habits were strong. In Pittsburgh, for example, the YWCA created homes for aged women, and for unmarried mothers, a hospital for incurables, and an industrial school. In other cities there were day nurseries, night schools, and mothers' meetings.

There was the usual opposition—from ministers who were suspicious of nondenominational Christian work, and from men who wanted resources concentrated in the Young Men's Christian Association. As in the churches, such arguments seem principally to have inspired the women to work harder. Mary Sims, who wrote two in-house histories of the Y, and was not a particularly sentimental person, noted her reaction to the records of the early years: "the outstanding characteristics of these women . . . were their courage and resourcefulness and their tremendous energy. They were fired with a missionary zeal. . . . "[61]

When representatives of several associations met in 1873 they struck a note that would come to be a dominant theme in women's work in the ensuing decades: "We are helping to solve the problem in social science, as to how to bridge the gulf that divides the favored from the less fortunate." Members also saw themselves as part of the movement for "betterment of woman's condition."[62] Along with the Home Missionary Society of the Methodist church, the YWCA was among the first women's associations to establish training schools for its workers.

Begun as it was with a focus on working women, the Y prided itself on crossing class lines. Cultural biases ran deep, however, and for a long time it was not certain that the well-to-do women who founded and financed the organization would—despite their rhetoric—build the bridge they dreamed of. Nevertheless they continued to strive for diversity. Mary Sims candidly recorded:

> Left to itself any local Association tends to become homogeneous and slough off the most different parts. Years ago it was recognized that if the really different groups of the community, such as women and girls in industry, the foreign-born who do not speak English and the Negro girls, were to be a part of any Young Women's Christian Association it was necessary to make special provision for them. The careful plans developed for access to these groups have brought them into the fellowship of the organization nationally and to a considerable extent locally. Nevertheless, experience seems to show that it is necessary to be constantly vigilant if these more different elements are to

continue to be an integral part of the whole and function naturally within the voting members.[63]

Like the women in the home mission societies and in the WCTU, those who became deeply engaged in the day-to-day work of the YWCA in industrial towns began to observe the lives of "working girls" at first hand and were often profoundly shocked by what they saw and heard. The president of the Louisville, Kentucky, association expressed the ideal when she confidently asserted that "the crowning glory of the Women's Christian Association is that it lives 'down among the people.'" At first the response was principally ameliorative—cheap boardinghouses, low-cost restaurants, and job training—but in time the leaders of the growing organization would come to support factory inspection and minimum-wage laws. In the Y, as in the missionary societies and the WCTU, the beginning of what would become the woman's agenda in the Progressive movement was already visible in the 1870s and 1880s.[64]

As was true in the WCTU, manuscript records of local units reveal complexities that are not always visible from the national records. The history of the Cambridge, Massachusetts, YWCA, for example, illustrates the paradoxes that often attend efforts of the privileged to do good among the less privileged.[65]

In 1891 the local WCTU had called a community meeting to discuss the needs of working girls in the area. One speaker asserted that it was a disgrace for the city to be spending eight thousand dollars a year for the Young Men's Christian Association and doing nothing for the young women. A committee of women from various churches was appointed to raise money to establish a YWCA. The WCTU women who had set the plan in motion turned over the responsibility with a sigh of relief, observing that their own part "has called for no little of nerve force and physical exertion. We hope we have been led by the Lord, for certainly we had no wisdom of our own. . . . " They agreed that they would "cherish and guard" the new association in the days of its youth.

Once established, the Cambridge Y grew rapidly. Any young woman who was a church member could join for a dollar. Those of "good moral character" who did not belong to a church could become associate members for fifty cents with all privileges except that of voting. Any "gentleman" could become an honorary member by paying five dollars.

The organizers (referred to in the minutes as "the ladies" in distinction from the working women who were regularly referred to as "girls") rented rooms to which working women could come for recreation and sociability, and arrangements were made to forgive the required dollar for those who could not afford it.[66] A former public school teacher of "great decision of character and pleasant and winning manners" was hired to be on hand at the rooms every day from 2:00 P.M. to 10:00 P.M.

A board of directors of twenty-five women contained "no more than three from any one church." They moved quickly to establish a bureau of employment, a bureau of information concerning board and lodging, and a choral group. They hired a gymnastics teacher and appointed committees to look into industrial conditions.

Money came in from church societies and from the "ladies" as well as from the "girls" themselves. The ladies were urged to interest their servants in becoming members and to volunteer their own services in the rooms.

A class of young teenagers was established to train them to be "serviceable at home . . . moulding them into all that is pure and excellent in character." Since some of these young ones had even smaller children to care for, day care was arranged. Meantime a Lookout Committee mapped the city as a preliminary to going in search of new members. The ladies were concerned that entertainment should also be instructive. Classes in gymnastics, dressmaking, and painting all did well, but a class in German had to be canceled in the absence of applicants. Soon the Lookout Committee reported thirty calls during which it had found "many delightful, thoroughly self-respecting girls." The report spoke highly of the advantages of personal contact.

In the Junior Class, meantime, the young girls were being taught to set a table. One member wondered whether mothers who had to worry about getting food at all might think this an unnecessary frill, but then the same woman waxed poetic about the potential good effects upon the youngsters who, having learned the correct way to set a table, would go on to see the virtues of "the orderly room, the neatly prepared bed, the cleanly bath, the . . . well-mended attire; and so [these] simple lessons shall prepare the way for the inauguration of a revolution in some untidy and careless homes whose end at length shall be godliness."

And so the minutes go on, revealing much more than the secretary could have dreamed, as she divided the world into "ladies" and "working girls," expatiated on the godliness of cleanliness, and reported that "the good seed sown by the association was springing up and flowering into self-respecting womanhood."

By the spring of 1893 the Education Committee spoke hopefully of "the ever-widening scope of our work as indicated by the various classes of girls engaged in it; rich and poor, black and white, protestant and romanist, coming together in helpful contact, envy, jealousy and foolish pride giving way to mutual sympathy, respect and a desire to share all good things with those less favored."

In 1900, in a circular seeking money for a building, the Cambridge Y recounted its history and added a revealing homily: "... Our work which we aim to carry on is preventive more than reformatory. Idleness is never tolerated, but we seek to teach all who come under our influence to be useful and industrious.... [this organization] is auxiliary to none, but is an independent organization of women working for women.... twenty-three hundred women and girls came to our rooms during one month."

Local Ys developed across the country—each working out its own program of "Christian service." The low-cost boardinghouse became a characteristic enterprise, with employment bureaus running a close second. The interaction between the women who raised the money and the women who were their supposed beneficiaries was increasingly complex. When wages were so low inexpensive housing was a boon, but the "ladies" on various boards showed a strong (and unwelcomed) tendency to supervise the lives of their beneficiaries.[67]

As early as 1871 alliances began to be formed among various local groups, and in time a governing body, called the International Board, was established to offer national oversight and guidance. In 1873 the first campus YWCA had been organized in Illinois, and the International Board—which was in reality a national board—agreed to promote campus work. In fact the student groups were often in conflict with the community-based associations; the students, who were mainly in the Middle West, tended to be evangelical and conservative, while the middle-aged women in the East tended to be liberal in their religious views, and moderate supporters of women's rights by conviction. The campus associations combined to set up their own governing body which they called the American Board of the YWCA. For about twenty years the two groups remained separate, and often in conflict, while the student movement grew rapidly and became an important force on many campuses.

A major shift occurred in 1906 when, thanks to the diplomacy and persistence of a woman named Grace Dodge, a dedicated organizer of working-girls' societies, the community-based Y and the student Y resolved their differences enough to agree to establish a single governing board.

What happened next has yet to be analyzed and explained. The student Y, originally the conservative wing of the movement, began to undergo what in time would be a remarkable change. Having begun as a strictly evangelical group concerned primarily with saving souls, bit by bit the young women who joined the association on college campuses moved toward a more radical version of the social gospel than that which guided the community-based associations. By the 1920s the campus Y would be a haven for student radicals, especially those who thought of themselves as Christian socialists. A parallel development took place in the Methodist student movement during the same years. Perhaps the children of the

Methodist missionary women and of the community-based YWCA women elaborated, as children will, the commitments of their mothers.[68]

In the years after 1906 the community-based Y also went through a considerable period of development. It had to wrestle over and over with continuing issues of class and the ever more pressing one of race. Despite considerable conflict, the Y went considerably beyond the other women's Christian movements in both areas.

As early as 1907 the newly organized national board began in a very gingerly way to talk about the problems of black women who were organizing separate YWCA units both in towns and on campuses. Some white southern members were very reluctant to agree that these units should be represented in national conventions. Meanwhile a paid organizer, a black woman, was working with existing and prospective "colored YWCA" groups. By 1911 in Richmond two young white women asked a black woman to convene a group of her friends who wanted to form a Y. According to the record they experienced "fewer difficulties than most places." In Texas, by contrast the "spirit among older white women not wishing to extend the work to colored women" was a problem.

At a general national conference in 1914 there was, the record suggests, a "frank discussion of the colored work with secretaries in the different fields. . . . there is a general awakening in the country over for our colored girls." The record continues: "Just as the immigrant and industrial girls are special girls, so the colored girl is fast coming in for her share of development. We must be prepared to meet her needs. . . . " With all this good will, there was still plenty of tension.

None of this was easy, whether the subject was black women or factory women. Ken Fones-Wolf has described in detail a confrontation in Philadelphia between young women wanting to help factory workers organize unions, and older women who very much resisted the idea.[69] In the end, Fones-Wolf found, the young women won. What is even more interesting is that in the same city's Young Men's Christian Association, where a similar tug-of-war had developed, the manufacturers who sat on the board and supplied the money successfully squelched the pro-union sentiment. The key to the difference, he concludes, "is that male reformers were not involved in building cross-class alliances on gender-related issues" and therefore were more easily split off from their working-class allies.[70]

The YWCA provided an ongoing microcosm for women's efforts to put the social gospel into action. In the 1990s, it claimed to be the largest women's membership organization in the world, with two and a half million members in the United States alone. A dozen books are waiting to be written on the many facets of this far-reaching organization.[71]

All three of these burgeoning "Christian" voluntary associations linked back to the earliest benevolent societies and foreshadowed a more complex future in which the issue of cross-class and cross-race interaction would loom ever larger in women's organizations. All three managed to combine women of conservative and traditional mindset with those who were helping to shape the social gospel. All three developed quite differently from their male counterparts. While the Christian associations were growing, a range of secular associations was taking shape with which they would increasingly interact.

CONSTITUTION
and
SUBSCRIBERS NAMES
OF THE
FRAGMENT SOCIETY,
INSTITUTED BY
FEMALES of BOSTON
October 1812.

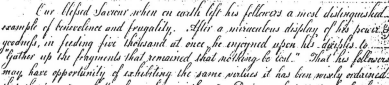

Our blessed Saviour when on earth left his followers a most distinguished example of benevolence and frugality. After a miraculous display of his power & goodness, in feeding five thousand at once, he enjoined upon his disciples to "gather up the fragments that remained that nothing be lost." That his followers may have opportunity of exhibiting the same virtues it has been wisely ordained that the poor "we shall always have with us." Desirous of imitating so bright a pattern, and anxious to alleviate the distresses of the indigent, we have formed ourselves into an Association, to be known by the name of "The Fragment Society." They who love God will love all the human family, and feel a desire as far as their ability extends to promote their comfort & happiness. As members of that family, and conscious of our dependance on the rich bounty of Providence, we wish to cast our mite on the altar of Benevolence. Though our means may be small, yet, by a divine blessing on our humble efforts, we may be able to do something towards relieving the wants, and promoting the comfort of the suffering poor. The design of this Society shall be to assist in clothing the destitute, more especially distitute children, and to loan bedding and infants garments to such mothers as are not able to procure things necessary for their comfort during the month of their confinement. The Society solicit annual subscriptions, and will be

The first page of the Boston Fragment Society Constitution records the premises on which the group was founded in 1812, as well as the origin of its name. (Schlesinger Library, Radcliffe College, Fragment Society Papers. Reproduced with permission.)

Boston June 14th 1843

At a Meeting of the Board of Managers, held at Mrs Francis's.
Present,

Mrs Francis, Pres.
Mrs Clapp, Vice Pres.
Miss B. L. Lane, Treas.

Mrs Shine — Miss Moore
Miss Winthrop — Miss Folsom
Miss Codman — Miss Perry

The Providential Committees report read & accepted. —

Voted. to put it on file.
the Chens:— report read & accepted
Voted— to put it on file.

the following persons having been mentioned and their wants being very pressing, it was

Voted to relieve them by giving them the following Articles

Jos. Boston	Mrs Lauderton	Mrs Childs	1 petticoat
2 shirts, 2 flannels	1 shirt	1 jacket	1 gown
2 yards 6 Napkins	Mrs Clms	1 yd trowsers	1 pr pantaloons
Mrs Perry	2 aprons	Mrs Fitzgerald	1 shirt, 2 aprons

Mrs Bird .... 3 jackets ....
1 gown, 2 shirts ....   3 pr trousers ....
2 flannels ....
Hopkins .... Mrs Bagley ....
Mr Brummet ....   1 pr shoes ....
1 jacket .... Mr Hammond ....
1 pr trousers .... 3 gowns, 2 shirts ......
                                    3 pr shoes, 1 bonnet ..
                                    Or 2 gowns ....

                                    Mrs Hammond .... Mrs Paine ....
                                    1 pr shirts, 3 gowns || 1 pr sheets, 3 gowns ..
                                    1 pr pillow cases .... 1 no. pillow cases ....
                                    2 petticoats, 2 shirts || 2 petticoats, 2 shirts ||
                                    1 robe, 4 flannels .... 1 robe 2 flannels ......
                                    6 Hopkins, 3 caps ..... 6 Hopkins, 3 shirts ...

1 napkin .... 1 Mrs Hunt ....
Mrs Gardner || 1 shirt ....
1 pr shoes .... Mr Godfrey ....
Mr Thomson .... 1 gown ....
1 shirt, 1 jacket ....
1 pr trousers .... Chenith, Hopkins .....
              1 petticoat, 3 pr shoes ...
              3 jackets 3 pr trousers
                       Mr Booth ....
                       1 sheet ....

Voted the Pres. &c be auth orized to close 30 dollars from the Treas.

The twenty third Annual meeting of the Directors of the Fragment Society was held at the house of Mrs D.S. Parker Feb. 12, 1835.

The meeting was opened by prayer by the Rev. Mr Charles Barnard. The follow-ing report was read and accepted.

The season has again returned for the Managers of the Fragment Society to present something by way of report, of their proceedings during the past year, which are as follows:

Received of Subscribers — — $269, 00
Bank Dividend — — 42,
Interest received in the Saving Bank 37,12
Donation 1, 25

Rec'd from the D.S. Parker — 1000, 00
executor of the will of Miss Sarah Jackson, being $1349, 37

Insurance Co. -   — $1899.00
Savings Bank -   — 360
[C]ommon Bank -   — 700
                          $2060

When we contrast this statement with that for 1813, we ask ourselves what is the cause of this falling off of subscribers; there are expended $1,800, amounting $1,800, surely the poor we have still among us, they do not decrease.

The Saviour has told us, the poor we should always have with us, and inasmuch as we would, we should clothe them good. True there are societies of a similar kind, which have grown out of this; and they do much towards feeding the hungry & clothing the naked; but as parents do not like to be laid aside from all usefulness because their children are grown up around them, and taking an active part in the concerns of

By 1835 the Boston Fragment Society was investing money in the Massachusetts Hospital Life Insurance Company and two banks. Page from annual report of the Directors of the Boston Fragment Society, 1835. (Schlesinger Library, Radcliffe College, Fragment Society Papers, Box 2. Reproduced with permission.)

In 1916 the Boston Fragment Society marked the centennial of its formal incorporation with a celebration to which many guests wore the costume of 1816. (Schlesinger
Library Photo Collection, Radcliffe College. Reproduced with permission.)

Friend of Virtue.

" Blessed are the undefiled in the way, that walk in the law of the Lord."—Ps. cxix 1.

| Vol. IX. | Boston, January 1, 1846. | No. 1. |

LEGISLATION ON LICENTIOUSNESS.

The following remarks, so well adapted to promote the cause of Moral Reform, appeared in the New York Observer. The friends of the cause every where, we think, may read them with profit. We hope the perusal may induce those engaged in circulating petitions, to double their diligence.

Ed.

Again, upon the approach of another session of our State Legislatures, we ask the attention of the lovers of virtue to the importance of further legislation to restrain the progress of licentiousness. The vice is flagrant, deadly to individual and social happiness, offensive to God and all decent men, acknowledged on all hands to be a proper subject of legislation, yet hitherto it has passed scot-free, or only so lightly hedged about with law as to have the appearance of being protected, not punished. How to get at it with the arm of law has indeed been a problem. It is a secret vice, yet not so secret as murder. Is murder so private that law cannot reach it?

Not only is it less secret than murder, it is also more destructive to the peace of society! The SIN involved may not exceed that of blood guiltiness, but the misery caused by the assassin, is not to be compared for magnitude and extent with that which is the fruit of licentiousness ; yet the former is justly punished with death, and the latter is not touched.

The PREVAILING argument against rigid legislative enactments to restrain the vice is, that it is impossible to prevent it. That is, society is so corrupt, there is no use in making laws to punish its vices. If it should ever become fashionable to steal or kill, it would be proper, on this principle, to repeal all laws forbidding theft and murder. The same class of moralists who wish licentiousness to go unpunished, would doubtless wish all other crimes, in which they indulge, to enjoy the same impunity. Shall they be gratified?

We do not deny that some virtuous men may think it inexpedient to attempt the suppression of licentiousness by penal enactments, but beyond a cavil the secret of much opposition to wholesome laws arises from a secret love of sin. We make this remark, apparently severe and uncharitable, in full persuasion of its truth, and with special reference to candidates for legislative office. We would have no man of doubtful virtue elected to make our laws. Both of the great political parties have, in their turn, denounced us as opposed to their candidates, when we have raised a feeble but honest voice to put down bad men whom party policy has set up for office. But

First page of *Friend of Virtue,* the periodical of the Female Moral Reform Society, 1846. (Sophia Smith Collection, Smith College. Reproduced with permission.)

11th meeting. May 13th 1885 —
9 members present. at Mrs. John
Hopkinson's. —

Mrs. Arthur Gilman read from
Dr. G. Z. Gray's book, "Husband & Wife."
That Man & Wife are "one flesh",
means one of three things — Either
he becomes hers, & she is the head,
or Each become different, & unite
to form a new flesh, or she
becomes his. — The third is
correct, as shown by Ancient
Customs, by the teaching of the
Old & New Testaments, by the
teaching of the Church's Ceremo-
nial, & by present Customs. —
The Common Sense of the World,
as shown in its legislation

The secretary of the Mothers' Club of Cambridge, Massachusetts, refers to a discussion of the nature of matrimony, 13 May 1885. (Schlesinger Library, Radcliffe College, Mothers' Club of Cambridge, Box 2. Reproduced with permission.)

REPORT OF COMMITTEE
— ON —
WORK FOR GIRLS IN CAMBRIDGE.

Read at meeting held in First Baptist Church, Thursday evening, June 11, 1891.

The W. C. T. U., of Cambridgeport, have for a long time felt the need of some organized work for girls in our section of the city.

A committee appointed to consider this matter have learned that there are about nineteen hundred young women employed in the various large manufactories of our city. If we allow but one hundred more for the number employed in stores and other small establishments, we still have two thousand girls engaged in daily labor, whose evenings are practically their own.

What do we offer these two thousand young women? No public park worthy of mention exists in the city of Cambridge. No gymnasium or opportunity of outdoor or indoor recreation is open to girls, such as are furnished to young men by the Y. M. C. A.

Girls as well as boys must have exercise, variety and amusement, and too many of our girls are left to find these in the miscellaneous companionship of the street. We have no need to dilate on the evils resulting from this condition of things, for these are more patent to all eyes than are the extenuating causes.

Hence it has seemed to the members of the W. C. T. U. that the most important missionary work to be done for girls in our community is not strictly religious, but social. That the girls need first of all a place where they may enjoy safe and wholesome recreation; 2nd — such intercourse as will insensibly elevate their social and moral standards; 3d — intellectual stimulus; 4th — industrial education; 5th — practical instruction, calculated to fit them for the duties devolving upon them as women.

In order to furnish these advantages, the committee of the W. C. T. U. recommend that an organization be formed to be called the Young Women's Christian Association of Cambridge; that this society be under the control of a board of managers composed of ladies representing the various churches of our city; that there be connected with it an auxiliary corps composed of gentlemen, whose eminent usefulness to this organization will be as manifest as is that of the Ladies' Auxiliary to the Y. M. C. A., and that from this corps an advisory board be chosen; that suitable and attractive rooms be obtained and fitted up as reading room, social room, and place for industrial and literary classes; that a competent lady be secured as General Superintendent, whose duty shall be to preside over the rooms and to have oversight of the various branches of work there carried on; that for the summer months a class in calisthenics or light gymnastics be established, outing expeditions be arranged, and the social features of the work be chiefly prominent; that in the fall, sewing and cooking classes be opened, and such literary or business classes as may seem to meet the greatest demand not already supplied by the evening schools of Cambridge; that lectures on hygiene and various

practical subjects be given from time to time; that the girls be encouraged to form among themselves groups and bands for mutual aid in work or study; that weekly prayer meetings be held at the rooms, and that the religious element be an organic part and permeating influence of the work, but not the one to be chiefly prominent.

Feeling that through the meetings of the various churches and of the Salvation Army, our girls receive much more religious instruction than they apply, the committee think it less important to establish another religious centre, than to bring the influences of religion to bear upon them in their application to the work and play of every day life.

Much discussion has been held in the committee relative to a name for the desired association. While entire unanimity exists among its members as to the purpose to be attained, the committee are almost evenly divided on the question whether the Christian character of the enterprise should be embodied in its name. The majority feel that they would not be true to their own purpose, nor to the Lord they serve, if they refuse to place His name upon their ensign. The minority consider success in the work more important than the name under which the work is done, and fear that some careless girls may hold themselves aloof from an organization in which they would seem to rank as subjects for missionary effort. This minority hold that in rejecting the word "Christian" in their recommendation of a name for the society, they are not denying but rather imitating their great Exemplar. He spent most of His public life ministering to the physical wants of the needy ones about Him, and seeking to establish His kingdom in their hearts, before He ever allowed Himself to be publicly proclaimed as "the Christ, the Son of the Living God."

All are agreed, however, under whatever name we come come together, to do with our might what our hands find to do.

We invite the Christian women of Cambridge to join with us in going to our young sisters, less wise and less favored than ourselves, carrying to them the essence of home and good cheer, and refined and Christian intercourse, that we may thus reward those who are now doing well, encourage the ones who need help to do better, and reclaim those that are out of the way. "Being all things to all men we would by all means save some."

Respectfully submitted,

By order of committee,

G. F. LEONARD, *Secretary.*

MRS. F. N. BARDWELL	MRS. W. S. BRAGG
MRS. R. L. SNOW	MRS. B. J. HOYT
MRS. SUMNER ALBEE	MRS. N. H. HOLBROOK
MRS. L. G. CASE	MRS. M. W. CURRIER
MRS. E. J. R. YOUNG	MISS JENNIE HINCHCLIFFE
MRS. JENNIE JONES	MISS MARTHA HARPER
	MISS GEORGIA F. LEONARD.

The Woman's Christian Temperance Union led in the founding of the Young Women's Christian Association of Cambridge, as reported in June 1891. (Schlesinger Library, Radcliffe College, YWCA Papers. Reproduced with permission.)

Members of the Brooklyn Colored Conference of the YWCA, 1915. (Young Women's Christian Association of the USA, National Board Archives. Reproduced with permission.)

Delegates from Kentucky attended the Women's Rights Conference in St. Louis, 1916. (University of Kentucky Photo Archives. Reproduced with permission.)

Officials of the National Association of Colored Women's Clubs met in Texas in 1937. Formed in 1896, the association was dedicated to securing and enforcing civil and political rights, and to promoting interracial understanding. (Western Reserve Historical Society. Reproduced with Permission.)

5

Self-Improvement, Community Improvement

We have to remember that the valuable intellectual development is
self-development.... That is the reason ... uneducated clever women,
who have seen much of the world, are in middle life so much the most
cultured part of the community....

—A. N. Whitehead,
Aims of Education and Other Essays, 1929

"Members," wrote the secretary of the Aesthetic Club of Little Rock,
Arkansas, "have journeyed together through all ages and climes.... they
have gleaned from the fields of literature and art, and have felt the electric
thrill of the mighty movement of our own times."[1] Writing in 1890 she was
summing up an experience common to thousands of women in the
preceding twenty-five years. As the religious associations burgeoned, other
women (and some of the same ones) were enthusiastically establishing a
vast array of secular societies designed for their own education. The war
was barely over when ladies' literary societies—a form of organization
hitherto principally developed by black women—began appearing in various parts of the country. In time these "clubs," as they began to call
themselves, became formidable educational enterprises reaching beyond
the women themselves. Many clubs moved from self-education to community improvement and eventually to national political action. Despite the
existence of masses of data, scholars have only recently begun to pay
serious attention to this phenomenon which appeared in every part of the
country, transformed the lives of thousands of individual women, provided
a support system for virtually every woman of professional or political
or even literary ambition, and, like the religious associations, provided
a safe setting in which women could begin to question the dominant
ideology with its emphasis on competition and profit as the highest values.
The ideas and activities of "organized womanhood," as they liked to call
themselves, were a vital part of the social and political history of the
nineteenth century.

The historian who spends much time with club records is in danger of being carried away by the women's own infectious enthusiasm for their work, to the possible detriment of balanced analysis.[2] The task of separating rhetoric from reality, of understanding who joined clubs and who became leaders, of tracing connections between what the women said they were doing and what they were really doing, of analyzing the true nature of the "female values" that characterized club work, and even of finding a way to measure the significance of the part women's clubs played in the rapidly changing society is formidable.[3] Still, it is necessary to try.

The white women who flocked into literary societies in the late nineteenth century gave no sign of knowing anything about the precedent set by the tiny antebellum community of free black women in eastern cities. These most educationally deprived of all women had long before turned to mutual aid in this arena as they had for other things. The Female Literary Association of Philadelphia, for example, established in 1831, viewed itself as working for self-improvement and thus for the improvement of the whole black race. In the preamble to its constitution the women declared that it was their duty, "as daughters of a despised race," to develop their intelligence and talents in order to break down prejudice. These women not only pioneered in self-help literary associations, but also worked diligently to create and support schools for black people. The records of their societies have rarely survived, and but for the reports of their activities which William Lloyd Garrison published in *The Liberator* they might have vanished altogether from the historical record.[4]

Though literary societies principally for the purpose of self-improvement had not been common among white women before the Civil War, occasionally some small group had cast a long shadow ahead: Hannah Mather's "woman's lodge" in the eighteenth century, a "reading circle" (often of young, single women) here and there in the early nineteenth, an Edgeworthalean Society in Bloomington, Indiana, in 1841, were all signs of the search for mental discipline and a broadened education.[5]

In 1847 Antoinette Brown wrote her friend Lucy Stone about a society of fifty young women in Rochester, Michigan, whose members wrote compositions and engaged in disputation. Brown thought the result had been "rapid improvement in the use of the tongue," and she hoped a few of the members would "go out in the world pioneers of the great reform which is about to revolutionize society," by which presumably she meant woman's rights.[6] A Ladies Library Society devoted to discussing books appeared in Kalamazoo, Michigan, in 1852 and a Minerva Society in New Harmony, Indiana, in 1859. Two members of this last would go on to be national leaders in the postwar club movement. In the South, Sarah Morgan, living in Louisiana, spoke in her diary of a "reading club."[7]

Doubtless there were other forerunners the records of which have entirely vanished.

In the seventies and eighties this kind of association, so long foreshadowed, suddenly took off, witness to some women's urgent desire for formal education. Although schools for women with ambitious curricula had multiplied after Emma Willard opened her seminary in Troy, New York, in 1821, with the avowed purpose of providing a better education than any hitherto available, the demand for formal learning far outran available opportunities. Education was high on the agenda of every group that sought to codify women's goals. In 1848 the Seneca Falls Declaration put the matter baldly: "He [man] has denied her [woman] the facilities for obtaining a thorough education, all colleges being closed against her." It was only a slight overstatement. In private and in public some women expressed a deep yearning for a chance to learn, and while they shared the widespread American view that education contributed to moral development, intellectual curiosity was also a driving force. Learned ladies might be scorned by most men but untold thousands of women, as their diaries, letters, and actions make clear, cherished a secret desire to become just that.[8] Some women also had a point to make: at least since the time of Mary Astell in the sixteenth century, feminists had argued that the difference between male and female intellectual accomplishment was not a function of biology but of differential educational opportunity.

During the Civil War some state universities, deprived of male students, opened their doors to women, and in 1865 full-fledged women's colleges began to appear, but in the 1870s a large number of aspiring women, already married and with children, had no hope of enrolling in Vassar or Smith or the newly coeducational state universities.[9] Literary clubs for "self-culture" proliferated as if some very contagious virus was loose in the female population.

The antebellum literary societies had been purely local and so invisible beyond their own circles that when women in New York and Boston almost simultaneously set out to organize women's clubs in 1868 none of them had heard of any predecessors. Each group thought itself to be original— and for years they politely disputed priority—never recognizing that at the very least both should have bowed to the claims of black women's societies, some of which had existed for forty years, or to those of a group of women in Quincy, Illinois, who had organized a club for "educational purposes" two years before, and devoted twenty-nine weekly meetings to reading and discussing William Lecky's *History of the Rise and Influence of the Spirit of Rationalism in Europe.*

The first two big-city clubs reflected the interests, personalities, locations, and strong urge for improvement of their founders. Members of the New

England Woman's Club (NEWC)—135 came to the first meeting—were of a type principally produced, at least in large numbers, in Boston: confident, intellectual, reform minded, and didactic. Many were single and a number were veterans of Soldiers' Aid. They proposed to "organize the social force of the women of New England, now working in small circles and solitary ways—and to economize time and strength so valuable as theirs, by making this centre of thought and action a centre also of comfort and convenience."[10]

The "centre" meant rooms in the city where women of the leading families, who were gradually moving to the suburbs, could restore the sense of community of an earlier day when they had been able to walk to each others' houses, or to the satisfactions of collective effort they had felt in wartime. Rooms were promptly secured, and the club was underway.

Humility was not their long suit. Once provided with a constitution and a place to meet, the Boston women moved swiftly in a number of directions. A School of Horticulture, someone thought, would widen career opportunities for women, so they set out to organize one. They established a room where working women could come in the evening for rest and refreshment ("with no thought of patronizing them"). They proposed to confront "the vexed problems and difficulties which beset woman's daily life under its best and worst conditions."[11] To this end a committee studied the situation of needlewomen in Boston and discovered nearly twenty-one thousand women working in the needle trades, ranging from highly skilled dressmakers who earned fairly good wages to low-skilled factory workers whose poverty and working conditions appalled them. The clubwomen's first reaction was not to ask how the conditions of work might be changed, but how the needlewomen could be trained for better-paying jobs. They hoped to found an employment bureau "for the higher kinds of labor," and in 1869 examined in detail a German woman's proposal for "forming unions among women to increase their earning capacity, extend their fields of labor; to promote health and education...." An investigation into the conditions of factory workers gave rise to what would become a perennial question in virtually every middle-class women's association: why were poorly paid, exploited women workers so averse to going into domestic service? The perennial proposed solution was a training program to elevate domestic service to a respected occupation, even to a "profession," so that young women would choose it over factory labor and thus also, not coincidentally, provide their patrons with well-trained household help. High-minded rhetoric on this subject always threatened to slide into self-serving discussions of "the servant problem." Clubwomen tended to overestimate the cultural advantages young domestic servants might gain from association with mistresses like themselves, and to *underestimate* dramatically the burdens, psychological as well as physical, that they and most of their friends expected domestic servants to carry.[12] Over the years the women who have argued most forcefully for making domestic work into a "profession" that could attract able practitioners have never shown any inclination to join such a profession themselves. While it pondered the vexed question of domestic service, the New England Woman's Club proceeded to establish committees on public nurseries, public kitchens, and labor schools.

Meantime, lectures on art, music, literature, history, and public affairs took up many meetings as the club drew on the resources of the Boston community to hear about, it sometimes seemed, everything under the sun. In the first year alone meetings were devoted to freedmen's schools, the benefits of association, the status of German women, the Spanish government, dress reform, Charles Dickens, cooperative kitchens, Washington Irving, and the positive philosophy. The mix of "culture" and "reform" must occasionally have been bewildering.

Early in 1870 Lucy Stone came to lecture on suffrage and stirred up so much enthusiasm that, though Boston had not granted women municipal suffrage, the club decided to make up a woman's ticket for town offices. "With the utmost difficulty" two women were found who were willing to be nominated for the School Committee. Fifty or sixty members of the club marched to the polls and cast their votes, in a separate box. A crowd of men and boys gathered in the street and the hall was packed with men eager to see this strange sight. The women and their male supporters were outvoted by the "so-called Democrats—that is the foreign population," but they vowed to do better the next time around. After a good deal of hard work the club did manage to bring about a change in the law so that women were eligible to vote for the School Committee and to serve on it. The first to be elected were, of course, members of the NEWC.

From one perspective this early history exemplified the superficial flitting from topic to topic that critics of women's clubs were wont to dwell on. Lectures followed one another in such quick succession that it was hard to see how any fundamental learning could have taken place, and stirring calls to action often led only to the signing of a petition or the establishment of a committee.

This was, however, only part of the picture. Competent teachers providing classes in literature, botany, physiology, and languages allowed for the systematic study that might have been found in a good college class. Action often followed study: after the members examined the issue of dress reform, which they viewed as a problem in physiology and health, the club set up a store to make and sell sensible clothing. Both this endeavor and the School of Horticulture suffered from the women's lack of business experience, but they learned as they went along. They were more successful in establishing a Latin school for girls comparable to the elite Boys' Latin, which had prepared so many Boston men for leadership.

When a small, tightly organized Committee on Work chaired by Abby May undertook a project—as in the case of the School Committee campaign—things happened. In many of its endeavors, in its failings as well as in its accomplishments, the NEWC foreshadowed the experience of the clubs that came in its wake. Many loyal members felt it to be a vital and effective organization, and the record reveals their inexhaustible capacity for enthusiasm and social experiment.

Inevitably, not all members were enthusiastic. Harriet Hanson Robinson, a self-made woman who had worked in the Lowell mills and knew something of the realities of poverty and working-class life, had been brought into the club by Julia Ward Howe. In her journal Robinson recorded many exciting meetings, but some members were, she thought, snobbish and autocratic. She found Edna Dow Cheney long winded and boring, and recorded her view that no one much liked Abby May, even though she had been elected president. Robinson took particular umbrage at the insensitivity of many of the women to the feelings of women who had not shared their educational and social opportunities. Critical as she was of the failings of the NEWC, Robinson did not doubt the value of association: unhappy in Boston, she and her daughter organized a club in Malden made up of women who shared her general outlook "to secure to all women better moral, mental, physical and social conditions, with a more thorough understanding of the questions of the day and confidence to utter their own thoughts."[13] Meantime, the New England club continued to provide leadership in Boston and to offer a ready platform to women with literary, artistic, or political ambitions. It helped to create a sense of sisterhood among reformers, and in time spun off a number of important institutions.

In 1872, for example, the NEWC founded the Women's Education Association, for the single purpose of promoting the formal education of women. The WEA pressed Harvard to open examinations to women, persuaded MIT to permit women to enroll for instruction in chemistry, organized a summer program in marine biology which in time developed into the world-famous Woods Hole Oceanographic Institution, provided a graduate fellowship for a woman to study abroad, and established a nurses' training school.[14]

Sorosis, New York's first woman's club, derived its name from a Greek word meaning "aggregation" and differed in a number of ways from its Boston rival. Jane Cunningham Croly, a forty-year-old journalist and mother of four, called some friends together to propose the formation of a woman's club for those like herself who "wished for a more intimate companionship with women . . . whose deeper natures had been roused to activity, who had been seized by the divine spirit of inquiry and aspiration, who were interested in the thought and progress of the age and in what other women were thinking and doing."[15]

Sorosis was founded on "womanhood alone"—no men. Many of the first members were, like Croly, career women who felt the need to find support among their peers. They were educated and ambitious and insisted that they were not concerned with benevolence or reform, but only with their own development. It was quite appropriate that they elected Emma Willard— now eighty-one and the archetypal self-made career woman—an honorary member and set up a scholarship fund in her name.[16]

Despite the *Boston Transcript*'s view that "homes will be ruined, children neglected, woman is straying from her sphere," the records of the New England group do not emphasize opposition, and a coterie of Boston male intellectuals seems to have been among its strongest supporters.[17] It was otherwise with Sorosis whose members complained of skepticism, sneers, and sarcasm, "from gentlemen, of course." Alice Cary, the first president, observed that "these sneers and sarcasms are, after all, but so many acknowledgements of our power, and should and will stimulate us to braver assertion, to more persistent effort. . . . "[18] At the end of its first year the executive committee proudly reported that there had been nineteen meetings "rendered conspicuously profitable by conversational disquisition and literary exercises of a high order," and that the club had grown to include eighty-three members.

Sorosis activities were described as intellectual, social, and educational, and members included artists, authors, editors, poets, historians, teachers, physicians, and businesswomen. Though persistently denying any charitable object, the club in its early days could not completely escape the expectation that women's societies would engage in welfare work, and found itself contributing to the Children's Aid Society, the Working Woman's Protective Union, and the Hampton Institute.

The name spread when a member of the New York group moved to a new town or when some visitor took the idea home. There was a Sorosis in Chicago—and one in Elberton, Georgia. Others could be found from North Carolina to California and even on college campuses.

Croly, from the beginning, had more than a local vision. In 1869, picking up on an idea that Emma Willard had proposed in the 1850s, she convened a "women's parliament" to "legislate" on matters of concern to women. It is not clear whether she was naïve or simply using the term metaphorically, but in any case the three-day gathering did nothing more than listen to speeches on such things as kindergartens and hygiene in schools and public institutions, cooperative households and public laundries, and the need to combat corruption in public life. The delegates exchanged information about what they were doing, which was perhaps the principal point.

Another such meeting in 1873 led to the establishment of a permanent organization: the Association for the Advancement of Women which, for the next twenty-five years, convened annually in various cities to discuss women's issues and spread the gospel of "organized womanhood."[19]

These AAW meetings were one of many forces accelerating the formation of women's clubs. By the early 1870s new clubs were appearing across the country, in no particular pattern, in cities and towns and occasionally in rural villages. The idea leapfrogged beyond the Mississippi, so that the first clubs emerged in California at about the same time as in some New England states, and somewhat earlier than in Nebraska. North Dakota had a club or two before New Jersey did. In the South religious associations continued to be the dominant form of organization until women there began to realize that "club" did not necessarily imply suffrage or radical feminism, whereupon black and white women there began to organize literary societies. In 1884 Sallie Southall Cotten, who, a decade later, would become North Carolina's "Mother of Clubs," joined a reading circle formed during a summer session for teachers at the University of North Carolina. "I consider [it] as a *mild form of compulsory education* and that is why I joined it," she wrote. "So I would feel *obliged* to read books which otherwise I would neglect." She reported benefit from her first book on the subject of politics.[20]

Though each club had its own particular set of personalities, leaders, and environmental influences, they shared a strong family resemblance. "Intellectual improvement and mental cultivation" were typical goals. The Chicago Woman's Club, destined to become one of the most influential in the country, set out upon a "united effort towards a higher civilization of humanity." The stated aim of the Woman's Club in Aurora, Illinois, was even loftier: "practical consideration of the important questions that grow out of relations of the individual to society."[21] Occasionally a club grew up around a particular purpose—the founding of a public library or a playground, for example—or set out from the beginning to work for civic improvement, but by and large the earliest goals were grandiose and the early programs a *pot-pourri* of subjects. Shakespeare, the Brownings, and George Eliot led the list of literary topics; history of many different kinds engaged nearly every club. In Atlanta, black women—most of them associated with the black colleges—set up a Chautauqua circle, drawing study materials from the national adult education program based in Chautauqua, New York. In 1885 white Atlanta women organized the Nineteenth Century History Class and embarked on several years' study using a syllabus prepared by Herbert Baxter Adams, a Johns Hopkins historian who agreed to monitor their progress. The history class moved on to a three-year project in political history, and by the late nineties had gained enough courage to undertake a study of the antislavery controversy. Elsewhere, along with Roman Law, Greek Sculpture, and Renaissance Art came programs such as Married Women's Property Laws, The Poor in Large Cities, Recent Trends in Scientific Thought, and Education for Industry. John Stuart Mill's *The Subjection of Women* was a favorite, and the Chicago Woman's Club undertook to read Karl Marx as well. Travel lectures were a staple. With only benevolent and reform societies as models, the women who led these ambitious efforts at self-education had to find their way as best they could. As early as the seventies some Texas clubs enrolled en masse in Anna Tichnor's Society to Encourage Studies at Home which provided instruction and books from Boston. The Decatur, Illinois, Art Club raised money to send three of its members to study in Europe, confident that they would bring home, and share, knowledge about art not easily acquired in the American Middle West.[22] Black women in Kansas alternated study of Shakespeare with attention to fine handiwork.[23]

Underlying what to an outsider must have appeared to be (and sometimes was) considerable confusion of purpose were deeply felt aspirations, a strong and profoundly emotional desire to engage in systematic study. Even the confident women of the New England Woman's Club recognized their need for intellectual discipline, and women in humbler groups forthrightly described deficiencies in their education and tendencies toward superficiality which they were valiantly seeking to overcome. Many clubs eschewed outside speakers, or invited them only occasionally, insisting that members should prepare and read their own papers, no matter how badly, in order to learn how such things were done. Often they recognized that the chief value of these exercises was to the paper-giver, rather than to her audience. One North Carolina woman, whose club was built on members doing their own work, wrote: "I was taking my book club papers as seriously as if they had been college term papers, was studying for them, rewriting, revising. You see I was not doing this for show. I was taking exercise for making muscle, and was trying my strength out upon the minds of my fellow women."[24] While they took umbrage when men joked about them, clubwomen often poked fun at themselves. In 1892 a longtime member of the Quincy Friends in Council looked back to her first essay, taken bodily from a book called *Physiology of the Mind*. She recalled that an older member had praised it by saying she could scarcely believe it had been written by a woman—and, the author of the paper noted ruefully, "the dear lady may well have indulged her doubts!" Later she had been assigned to write a report on Venetian painting. "Think of it friends! A person who knew nothing of art principles, who had never seen a painting, nor perhaps even an engraving, of any work of the Venetian school, with such a theme. . . . Never before had I spent so much labor in the preparation of anything nor, I presume, shall I ever do so again. Everything that I heard or saw seemed to bear a relation to Venetian art, and into my paper it went. . . . "

Still, she concluded, doing her own research was an advance over cribbing from an authority, and added, "I am not deriding those old days of second-hand work. They were a necessary step in the evolution of our club life; they gave us the habit of expressing ourselves on paper; they taught us not to fear the sound of our own voices; they made us acquainted with each other's minds and thoughts. . . . " By 1883, she said, "we had fairly entered upon the period of original thinking. . . . "[25]

In a similar spirit of self-analysis Texas women recorded the great improvement of their federation meetings, due, they thought, to assiduous study of parliamentary procedure and continuous practice in public speaking.[26] Some clubs established the office of Critic: a member assigned to offer detailed comment and criticism, without undue regard for the feelings of the composers of papers. A California club reported regular debates, saying, "The most timid of the club's members have developed a surprising readiness in addressing an audience with clearness and conviction." A North Carolinian spoke of "whett[ing] our minds against one another," and a Connecticut club said of itself: "Its object is improvement solely, there being no time for social enjoyment except at the close of the year."[27] The founder of the Chicago Woman's Club thought seven years of study and practice in writing and speaking a necessary preliminary for "untrained women without business habits or parliamentary experience" to learn how to manage large endeavors.[28] During this period of preparation the club read and discussed David A. Wells, *Recent Economic Changes;* Karl Marx, *Das Kapital;* Henry George, *Progress and Poverty;* and Sidney and Beatrice Webb, *The History of Trade Unionism.* "The women were intelligent and capable," said the report from a club called the Ossoili Circle in Knoxville, Tennessee, "and a field [for action] was all that was necessary to develop latent talent."[29]

Over and over clubwomen spoke of their enterprise as a way of building bridges among women who tended to stick closely to people who shared their own religious, political, or family connections. The club, they believed, fostered tolerance and the exchange of ideas. In 1892 May Wright Sewall, a scholar, teacher, founder of schools, and founder of the National Council of Women, who was also a leader in the club movement and the suffrage movement, mused along these lines:

> The greatest personal and social benefit of the club results from the fact that it removes its members from the exclusive influence of what some women delight to call "our own kind," and brings them at regular intervals,

into the liberalizing atmosphere of a company constituted of many kinds and representing all the creeds and parties found in a community and many different social ranks as well. It was in the woman's club that wives and daughters of business men and of professional men, that business women, teachers, professional women, writers, artists, and that distinct class which, including members of all the others, is separated from all in the public mind, by the phrase "society women," first met on a common plane—on a plane outside of that upon which any one of them habitually stood.

She went on to say that it was in the club that society women discovered the value of "women who pursue serious pursuits" and vice versa. She thought that clubs were the most important influence nurturing religious tolerance, adding that the time had come to bring "the Hebrew and the Romanist . . . into our club membership."[30] It is not clear just how widely her concept of "many different social ranks" extended, or whether she envisioned clubs that would combine working-class or immigrant women with those of the middle class. Still, in light of the rivalry and intolerance that existed between various Protestant denominations as well as the intolerance of Protestants toward Catholics and Jews, there was plenty of work to be done along these lines within the amorphous "middle class."

While women all over the country were busily engaged in trying to make up for their lack of formal education, a small group of women college graduates created an organization for mutual support to carry on the education college had begun. Late in 1881 seventeen women representing eight colleges and universities took the first steps leading to the formation of the Association of Collegiate Alumnae, whose announced purpose was "practical educational work." Before long there were branches in other towns, and the original mandate proved to be a broad one; for while these young women graduates set out to improve their Greek and Latin they also embarked on a scholarly study of domestic service in the United States, a "scientific" study of the condition of Boston schools, and other projects aimed at community improvement. At the same time they raised money to provide recent graduates with fellowships for foreign study.[31]

The self-improving club whose principal purpose is to educate and inform its members has—like the benevolent society—survived into our day, a recognizable descendant of its earliest progenitor. But many of the original literary clubs went through a dramatic transition from an exclusive focus on "culture" or self-education to a concern with community needs. The transition came about in different ways in different places. The minutes of a small, local club in Massachusetts provide an illuminating and sometimes amusing close-up view of one group as it strove for self-discipline and evolved from self-absorption to community concern, and as it became steadily more political while issuing constant disclaimers that it was doing so.

The Mothers' Club of Cambridge came into being in 1878 when a group of "earnest young mothers" decided to join forces to consider the problems of raising children.[32] The group began with eight women and grew to forty, a number which would remain the norm for the rest of its life. The young mothers, mostly wives of academic and professional men, were bright, well educated, often witty, and easily distracted. They measured themselves by high standards, and were exceedingly concerned about raising honest, truthful children and maintaining well-ordered households. They also worried about their own intellectual development and wondered constantly how they could find more time for "mental effort." They repeatedly resolved to be more systematic.

In the early days members dutifully set themselves weighty subjects upon which they took turns writing essays, but it was hard to keep the discussions focused. The early minutes resemble a stream of consciousness. On 23 November 1881, after a meeting in which the discussion had strayed to fashion, the merits of flannel underwear, the dangers of tight lacing, and Cambridge social life, the secretary recorded three suggestions:

1. That they should consider discussing the essay of the day, on which some member had undoubtedly worked hard.
2. That perhaps a meeting on mental concentration would be in order.
3. That they consider "whether such a meeting as this, although ... very lively and social, does not justly expose us to the reproach of being a do-nothing society.

(One's mind jumps to those early benevolent societies with their constitutional prohibitions of gossip.)

At the next meeting these minutes were objected to as being too personal, but were finally accepted, after which the members discussed home life, dancing, boys and smoking, obedience, truth telling, simplicity in entertaining ... and several other subjects. Later meetings dealt with Christmas gifts (Did children get too many? Should they be forced to give some of their presents to poor children?) and the desirability of giving only plain, serviceable garments to servants so as not to foster a love of dress (one skeptic inquired whether it was any of the mistress's concern if her servants wanted finery). A lecture on the evils of sweets led to the revelation that in most kitchens gingerbread and cookies were the usual snack for children, and that "very little use was made of graham bread."[33] Another meeting focused on self-control—a quality they agreed was highly desirable for mothers and most likely to be acquired by prayer. What should children read? How could they be taught manners? (The subject of table manners came in for a good deal of attention and gave rise to the intriguing suggestion that the way to go about it was one implement at a time: first the knife, then the fork, and so on.) Should boys be taught to sew and dust? Proponents and opponents were equally vehement. Was college a good thing for boys? Someone spoke up in favor of college for girls.

In January 1884 after a paper on "Hurry," which recommended early breakfasts and trust in God, there was an animated discussion of the virtues of early rising. Most of the mothers thought it essential to a well-organized day, but Helen Brooks declared the habit unhealthy and bad for the eyes. If her friends could have known that she would eventually live to be ninety-two perhaps her advice would have carried more weight. Most of the members saw themselves as leading harried lives due to their own much-deplored lack of system and the nature of a mother's responsibilities. One member read aloud an article by Dr. Elizabeth Blackwell on home management which suggested, among other things, cooperative kitchens and neighborhood laundries, as well as lower standards of housekeeping to allow more time for reading and intellectual improvement. A "fast and furious discussion" ensued.

Someone read a sermon on the subject of not letting one's life be eaten up by small duties. The women responded with considerable skepticism, suggesting that the author was undoubtedly a bachelor, and that it was a "man's sermon for men." Stella Gilman, who admitted a mischievous desire to stir things up, read from a book that described the woman's role in marriage as one of complete subjection to her husband. The secretary felt "forced to record" that one member laughed the whole time and that there was a constant "undercurrent of murmuring." At the end the club adopted by acclamation a resolution saying that the members did not think that wives should be "entirely gobbled up by husbands."

By 1886 the club had decided to have an occasional outside speaker, agreeing that they would discuss the substance of the lecture at the following meeting so they could speak their minds without danger of hurting the visitor's feelings. These discussions exhibited verve, insight, and strong opinions.

Sometime in the early nineties the minutes began to reflect a subtle change in direction. Increasingly programs included papers with titles such as "The Need of a District Nurse in Cambridge," "The Tenement House," or "An Eight-Hour Law." Speakers tended to be people who were actually working in various reform movements, and for the first time club members joined in signing a petition to the local government.

What was happening? For one thing the mothers, and their children, were now fourteen years older, and interests were shifting from immediate familial concerns to those of the community. For another, the popular and serious press were devoting a great deal of space to proposals for social reform, and then as now, the citizens of Cambridge were doubtless in the vanguard of such discussions. The club undertook, rather cautiously, to support the work of one member who had established a mothers' club in a local settlement house. Though members persisted in identifying the enterprise as "Mrs. Currier's poor mothers," some of them became deeply involved in the work and the club as a group began to take some responsibility for keeping the settlement going.

Intellectual improvement did not cease to engage them, but there was also talk about the possible usefulness of electing some of their members to the School Committee, and one member proposed quite simply: "We should try to make some combined movement for public improvement," suggesting that the municipal government would be a good place to begin. After some discussion the members agreed to spend the following year trying to learn about local government. They proceeded methodically, inviting experts of various kinds to inform them, and doing considerable research themselves. One member investigated the Municipal Court and the county jail. Others examined the Board of Health, the schools, the hospitals, and district nurses, as well as the overseers of the poor. More and more, local reformers were invited to speak.

The sixteenth of April 1896 marked an important turning point. The essay for that day described an experiment being tried by clubs in a number of places: vacation schools for children who had nothing much to do when school was out. Their interest engaged, perhaps by the statement that Cambridge was getting a bad reputation for petty crime committed by just such idle children, the mothers set up a committee to look into the matter. Two women, Helen Brooks and Helen Almy—wives, respectively, of the president of the Consumers' League and a municipal judge—became the prime movers in what would develop into a major community project, a case study in what was coming to be called "municipal housekeeping." Brooks and Almy, with the help of a few other members, organized public meetings, negotiated with the city for the use of a school building, found teachers, raised money, circulated petitions, and recruited sixty-eight boys to take part in the first summer's experiment. Dedicated teachers tried to meet the children on their own ground and to use the techniques of Froebel, Pestalozzi, and John Dewey to engage their interest. The program was an overwhelming success: only one or two children dropped out, and a large number for whom space could not be found begged to be allowed to join. With this evidence in hand Brooks and Almy persuaded the School Committee to allocate more space, and to admit girls. The second summer more than two hundred children took part. When some older boys who felt left out began to disrupt the playgrounds, the women found a Pied Piper in the form of a gifted Harvard student who managed to engage the big boys' attention and take their minds off bullying the younger children.[34]

By 1900 the community had come to view the vacation school as so essential that the committee was able to induce the local government to take it over. Now that they were seasoned old hands as organizers and lobbyists, the women persuaded the city to create a number of additional playgrounds. In an odd twist the club as a whole refused to take credit for these accomplishments, insisting that they had been the work of "a committee of ladies from the Mothers' Club." Nevertheless the projects proceeded in what would come to be a standard pattern: the club began a program, and as soon as the community was ready to support it, turned it over to the local government and went on to tackle other needs. Buoyed by these experiences, the club paid increasing attention to local and national social problems, and from time to time organized lobbying campaigns such as one directed at abating the "smoke nuisance." Members continued to work at the settlement house and in the playground program. They continued to watch over the vacation schools and to encourage the city to expand them. They supported candidates for the School Committee—and were shocked when one of the women they had helped to elect came to tell them about the "graft and political intrigue" of her colleagues on the committee. Political maneuvering apparently had not discouraged her, however; she wanted to run again and hoped for their support.

By 1916 enterprising daughters of club members often came to talk about their careers, whether in social reform or in such things as landscape gardening. One gave a stereopticon lecture on her climb of the Matterhorn; the club members, approaching a sedentary stage of life, were glad they could experience such things at second hand. When the World War began, the Mothers' Club followed developments in Europe largely through letters from *daughters* who were serving overseas. Sons were rarely mentioned.[35]

As the women grew older the number of projects diminished, but interest in public issues was unabated. After the passage of the Nineteenth Amendment, Cornelia James Cannon, a leading activist, urged them all to join the League of Women Voters. There is no record of how many followed her advice.

As late as the 1930s an astonishing proportion of the original members were still on the rolls. Instead of taking in younger women, this club had encouraged succeeding generations to set up their own mothers' groups, thus keeping the membership and ties of the original intact. As they moved into their sixties and seventies the women continued with miscellaneous self-education and public concern. Then came Pearl Harbor. After some discussion, the members agreed it would be wise to suspend activity until the war was over. Thus after sixty years in which they had been a marvelous microcosm of women's club life, and of the life cycle of a woman's club which did not seek to become a permanent institution, the Mothers' Club of Cambridge adjourned *sine die*.

The Mothers' Club was always local, and had in fact resisted attempts to bring it into association even with other local groups. It was also unusual in its lack of interest in self-perpetuation. But the *process* by which the members moved from self-development to community development was typical of many groups that seemed to share some inner dynamic leading them to feel at some point that they had done enough for themselves and now owed something to the larger community. And, like many others, the Mothers' Club refused to admit it was in politics long after the reality of its political influence was visible for all to see.

Pressure for clubs to take on community problems came from external as well as internal forces. Jane Croly took the lead again, this time by initiating the formation of a General Federation of Women's Clubs. The Association for the Advancement of Women had served its day; it began and remained an elite group. The idea of a more broadly based organization had begun to percolate as early as 1882 when the Indianapolis Woman's Club had suggested a cooperative program that would provide for systematic exchange of constitutions, ideas, and information. Nothing had immediately come of this suggestion, but as the time to celebrate the twentieth anniversary of Sorosis approached, a committee sent letters all over the country seeking to interest clubwomen in the possibility of a federation.[36] Ninety-seven clubs were invited to send representatives to a gathering in New York. Sixty-one delegates from seventeen states, including three from California and one each from Louisiana and Tennessee, responded and agreed to launch a General Federation of Women's Clubs. A year later the federation held the first of the biennial conventions which would become a major source of communication among women from all parts of the country who met to exchange ideas. For delegates from local clubs and state federations the biennial provided a combination of serious work, inspiration, and escape from the confines of daily life. Over and over women left these meetings with renewed energy and new ideas.

While the newspapers dwelt upon the dresses, jewels, flowers, and food that ornamented the conventions, the women themselves generally had far more substantive concerns. On one Sunday morning when the biennial was meeting in Denver, delegates filled twelve pulpits in the city churches, and Jane Addams gave a lecture for children in the afternoon.

A series of sophisticated presidents used the conventions to encourage an ever-increasing concern with social and economic problems, first in communities and later in the country as a whole. A Louisiana woman attending her first biennial in 1900 wrote home that she was very much impressed with the organization and efficiency of the national leaders and went on to say that she observed "a fast growing spirit of altruism among club members," that instead of the pursuit of self-centered literary culture women were taking an interest in the town library and the public schools. "The key woman," she said, "strives for the solution of questions of wage-earning women, of the underage working children, of the Consumers League, of sanitation and of the political equality movement."[37] The conventions also provided an arena for political ambition, as women who aspired to national visibility competed for federation office.

If the biennial was a showcase for the accomplishments of women's clubs, it also displayed some of their weaknesses. Southern delegates were, for the most part, adamantly opposed to including representatives of black women's clubs, or individual black women—such as Josephine St. Pierre Ruffin or Fannie Barrier Williams—who had been admitted to previously all-white clubs. A particularly bitter fight was precipitated in 1900 when the executive committee of the federation voted to admit the Woman's Era Club of Boston, a black women's group organized by Ruffin, and was repudiated by the convention which then, as a kind of half loaf, offered to seat Ruffin herself as a representative of the Massachusetts State Federation of which she was a member. She stood on principle and refused.

By that year there were black women's clubs in many local communities, as well as a National Association of Colored Women's Clubs. Though these clubs were interested in self-education and particularly in art and music, they were also profoundly committed to changing the image of black women in the white mind. Part of the impetus for the formation of the National Association in 1896 had been a particularly obnoxious characterization of black women written by an American male journalist to an English friend, who had asked questions about Ida B. Wells's antilynching lectures in England. It rarely occurred to white women, as they began to link their own clubs in city and regional federations, that it would have made sense to include the black clubs as well. In Kansas an otherwise unidentified black club member wrote bitterly that her friends would not intrude themselves where they were not wanted, but added: "In localities where women are estimated by their intelligence, refinement and ability to do good club work, it may be a common sight to see a colored woman a member of a white woman's club, but it is not at all likely that we will see such a sight as that in Kansas soon."[38] Nor was it likely in many places. North, south, east, and west, racism was pervasive, and black women club leaders carried a heavy burden of rejection and limited resources.[39]

While all this was going on, another form of organization sought to unite the large federations of women both in the United States and in other countries. In 1888 an international council of women had met to celebrate the fortieth anniversary of the Seneca Falls Convention, and during that meeting a committee chaired by Frances Willard was appointed to develop "the simplest form of organization" to bring together "workers committed to the overthrow of all forms of ignorance and injustice, and to the application of the Golden Rule to Society, custom and law."[40] Willard's committee drew up simple, one-page constitutions for both a National and an International Council of Women. The national group was to meet every three years, the international one every five years with representatives "irrespective of race or creed." Frances Willard was first president of the national council. Millicent Garrett Fawcett, a leader of the English suffrage movement, was the first international president; other officers included two Americans, a Dane, and a French woman.

The year 1893 in some ways marked a turning point in the club movement. It was the year of the World's Columbian Exposition, otherwise called the Chicago World's Fair, which celebrated (a year late) the four hundredth anniversary of the European discovery of America. Much the most far-ranging exposition yet undertaken in the United States, the fair was destined to affect many areas of the nation's life, from city planning to public health. Henry Adams thought it the greatest opportunity for education he had yet encountered. For American women the fair provided an extraordinary opportunity to see themselves brought together in panoramic display. If Adams had turned his keen eye on women at the fair he might well have seen the future there as he did when he examined the mechanical exhibits.

Thanks in part to the power of their developing network of organizations, women had forced their way into the preliminary planning for the exposition. Unwilling to meet Susan B. Anthony's demand for equal representation of women on the commission it was establishing to run the fair, Congress had compromised by providing for a separate (but not quite equal) Board of Lady Managers to be made up of two women from each state, appointed by the male commissioners. The result was a mixed array of women, some of whom were chosen for their relationship to powerful men, others for their own accomplishments, mostly in voluntary associations. When Bertha Honoré Palmer, wife of a Chicago merchant prince, was asked to head the Board of Lady Managers, the commissioners assured her that she would not need to work very hard. Window dressing was surely what they had in mind. Palmer, an unusually talented and well-educated woman, had attained social position through her marriage to a wealthy man nearly twice her age, but she had also shown a strong independent bent which took her at an early age into the Chicago Woman's Club and the WCTU. She had no intention of being a token. It would not be the last time that men in power would choose a woman for her presumed pliability only to find out their mistake when it was too late.

With the combined weight of many women's organizations at her back Palmer proceeded to wrest from the United States Congress more than it ever intended to give and from the exposition commissioners concessions they had not dreamed of. None of this came easy, and in the process Palmer ranged the world looking for international support, and traveled the country encouraging the formation of local and state "Columbian societies" in which women raised money and prepared their exhibits. Some of the money went to build an impressive Woman's Building, designed by Sophia Hayden, a young woman architect, and planned to show the world every aspect of women's work, paid and unpaid.

Among the early projects of the Lady Managers was a Dormitory Association which sold shares and built low-cost dormitories to permit women of limited means to come to the fair. Shares of stock could be used to pay for housing; and, at forty or fifty cents a day, thousands of impecunious women were able to visit the exposition, to learn, if they could, what it had to teach.

The complex organization of the fair included the Congress Auxiliary—a body charged with setting up "congresses" on hundreds of subjects; science, religion, anthropology, technology, and many other fields were to have their own convocations of scholars and practitioners. One of Palmer's achievements was the commitment from the men in charge to include women in each one of these congresses; in the end, a fourth of all the congress speakers were women.

There was also the question of juries to judge various exhibits. Palmer liked to say that when she insisted on equal opportunity for women to be jurors, one commissioner, in his ignorance, suggested that women should form the whole jury in "areas where they had made significant contributions." She said she modestly asked for only 50 percent representation, since, had his generous offer been accepted, none but women would have been jurors.

The first auxiliary congress to convene was the Congress of Representative Women, a week-long affair that brought women from many countries together with American leaders. It attracted enormous attention; crowded audiences filled the various auditoria to hear what women had to say.[41] Meanwhile, in the Woman's Building, conferences, meetings, and conventions went on all summer as national women's organizations convened the faithful, and a vast array of papers were read.[42]

None of this was as easy as it sounds in the telling. Palmer and the Lady Managers had to fight constantly for a fair share of federal appropriations. The commissioners were never as willing in practice as they were in conversation to share power with the women and only constant vigilance held them to their commitments. All of Palmer's diplomatic skills were required to protect women's share in the proceedings.

Nor were her own constituents always united and supportive. In addition to rivalries and jealousies on the Board of Lady Managers, made up as it was of many ambitious women, from time to time disaffected individuals took issue in public with Palmer's leadership. While privately she was willing to recognize that when women were fully engaged in public work they would inevitably differ as men did, she felt that for the moment their precarious position demanded an outward show of unity. She viewed attacks on her leadership as weakening the whole woman's cause. Most of the time she kept her temper and tried to bring her critics along.

In two important areas Palmer and the Lady Managers revealed the depth of certain nineteenth-century assumptions about class and race. First, though Palmer herself felt that the needs of working women should be a primary focus of the women's part in the fair, and though her opening speech was a stirring call for social justice for wage-earning women, she and many of her colleagues assumed that they knew what should be done for working women. It seems not to have occurred to them to ask representatives of wage-earning women to speak for themselves.

A similar unexamined assumption shaped their reaction to the vehement demands of black women that they be included in the planning and execution of affairs related to women at the fair. The first such demand came from a group of black women in the District of Columbia; the most famous came from Ida Wells-Barnett, who published a stirring pamphlet on the exclusion of black people, men as well as women, from the exposition. The one black Lady Manager (from Buffalo, New York) was not on record on the issue. Mary Logan, a white Lady Manager from the Middle West, had found little support when she tried to secure representation for black women, and in the end the managers temporized by appointing a white woman to represent black interests.[43] A handful of very well known black women addressed meetings, but black women's associations were ignored. In both cases Palmer and her colleagues revealed their profound belief that educated prosperous white women like themselves not only would but should set the agenda for the burgeoning woman's movement.

The thousands of women who took part in the fair from small towns and the countryside as well as from cities were affected by the experience in many different ways.[44] At one end of the spectrum were women like Ellen Martin Henrotin, a Chicago society woman and club member who was catapulted into national leadership when Bertha Palmer gave her responsibility for women's participation in the Congress Auxiliary. The skill and acumen she demonstrated in that position led to her election the following year as president of the General Federation of Women's Clubs, from which position she exerted a powerful influence not only on the federation itself, where she pushed hard for the study of what she called social economics, but on the woman's movement as a whole. Henrotin was an organizer, and during her presidency the number of clubs doubled and twenty new state federations were formed.[45]

At the other end of the spectrum were the thousands of women who were exposed for the first time to the accomplishments and the organizations so tellingly displayed not only in the Woman's Building but—thanks to the persistence of Henrotin and the Lady Managers—in many other exhibits as well, and who listened to women speaking in any one of the two hundred auxiliary cultural, artistic, and scientific congresses they happened to attend.

Everywhere she looked such a visitor would have found evidence of the pervasive network of women's organizations. The Connecticut Lady Managers, to take only one example, having surveyed their state, reported in impressive detail not only on the conditions of women working in industry in Connecticut but also on the 724 voluntary associations whose work they described.[46] Reports from other states were similarly impressive. It is not surprising to find that one outcome of the fair was a rash of new organizations—ranging from the North Carolina Federation of Women's Clubs to the National Council of Jewish Women and the National Home Economics Association.[47]

The part women played in the various congresses was a tribute to the effectiveness of self-culture and a forecast of what might come next. Of the middle-aged women who spoke in the Woman's Building, a handful had professional training, but more often they had been educated at a seminary or by private tutor. Among the younger speakers—some still in their twenties—were graduates and faculty members of Smith, Vassar, and Barnard. The proportion of silly or irrelevant speeches was small: many were well organized, thoughtful, and substantive.

The lectures fell into three broad categories, each representing one aspect of a complex associational life. One type carried forward the tradition of self-culture: "Life and Times of Isabella of Castile," "Moorish Women as I Found Them," "Katrina in *The Taming of the Shrew*," "Zuni Rituals," for example. A second category focused on the history of women or their present needs and status: "Women in Journalism," "Economic Independence for Women," "Women as Political Economists," "Industrial Women." A third group of talks dealt with social reform: "Woman, the Inciter to Reform," "The Industrial Revolution of the Past Century"—which advocated the single tax—"Effective Voting," "Education of the Deaf," "Is Labor Dignified?" and so on. Notable in this third group were hard-hitting descriptions by Anna Julia Cooper and Fannie Barrier Williams of the problems faced by African Americans.

Two noteworthy speeches called upon clubwomen to take a close look at themselves. Anna Garlin Spencer, a forty-two-year-old Unitarian minister from Providence, Rhode Island, spoke on "Advantages and Dangers of Organization." After a comprehensive and insightful summary of the history of American women's organizations, Spencer went on to raise a warning. She thought that separate organizations, necessary as they had been in the beginning, might now be limiting women's further development. Indeed, she argued, it had come to be easier for women than for men to achieve what she called "intellectual and moral development," with the result that a gulf was developing between clubwomen and "all but professional and learned men," a gulf which she believed hurt both. The implication was that women who had time for self-education were outdistancing husbands, and that working in associations that included men might help to bridge the gap.

Spencer's second warning was even more pointed: having come this far—and she gave women's associations full credit for their accomplishments—she argued that the time had come for women to take more responsibility for knowing what they were talking about and understanding the full implications of things they might propose to do. Spencer said, "Mind, I do not say that the ignorant woman must grow wise before she belongs to a club seeking wisdom. On the contrary . . . she may gain far more, and sooner learn to give as she gains, than in any separate study. But this I do say, the ignorant woman must know her ignorance and long to grow wise before she can gain anything but a foolish, make-believe knowledge from the brightest club."[48] She went on to paint a chilling picture of danger ahead. She pointed out that women's organizations had become so respected that "small natured, pretentious, vain and selfish women," were joining simply to share in the prestige and not at all because they were committed to the larger goals of the group; she quoted a newspaper advising a woman who had asked how she could acquire social standing in a new community: "join two or three popular charitable associations."[49] She said that it had become fashionable for a woman to belong to literary clubs, adding that "many a woman thinks she is 'cultivated' because she hears swiftly forgotten papers by the bushel. . . . "

These warnings came not from uninformed outsiders, but from a leader who had taken part in a number of associations, who understood their history well and who would continue to be active in years to come. Spencer was not proposing that women abandon their organizations but that they recognize the hazards of rapid growth and of becoming fashionable. The response of the audience is not recorded, but Spencer's talk made it clear that the convention that women would never criticize each other in public was coming to an end.

On a day set aside to do honor to the city where the fair was taking place,

Sarah Hackett Stevenson, a medical doctor, gave a speech entitled "Chicago Women." The occasion might seem to have called for conventional praise, but Stevenson evidently saw it as an opportunity to voice some serious concerns. Coming upon her lecture in the midst of the more orthodox ones is rather like walking into an ice cold shower. She intended to talk, she told the audience, not just about the small, and by inference very privileged, group of clubwomen but about all Chicago women—the 150,000 domestic servants, the 5,000 factory workers, the 3,000 teachers, and the uncounted numbers of what she labeled "plain home women." She wondered just how much clubwomen really knew about the domestic workers, mostly immigrant girls, who were "taking care of our homes at the greatest possible expenditure of resources, at the greatest possible extravagance." As a medical doctor she expressed horror at the poorly prepared food and unsanitary conditions in many well-to-do houses which she attributed to the failure of employers to make an effort to understand the need for education of their servants. She worried, too, about the isolation of servants and factory workers, who had no models for achievement: "If you were to know them intimately and analyze their aspirations you would find their standard of getting on in the world is a purely material one, just like ours. . . . Have we as individuals or our boasted and influential clubs, anything to give these women of domestic and factory life?" She went on to ask what the clubwomen really knew about the public schools: "Do we not feel that our school work is finished since we have helped to place two women on our school board,—and left them to their fate?"[50]

Even more than Spencer, Stevenson spoke from the inside. She had been superintendent of the WCTU Department of Hygiene, member of the elite Fortnightly, president of the Chicago Woman's Club, leader in the Illinois Social Science Association (which was largely a women's organization), and had had dealings with many others.[51] She emphasized the need for education and reflection on the part of "plain home women" who, because there were so many of them, had the greatest opportunity for influence of all, and who should feel profoundly responsible for using that influence wisely.[52]

There is no way to know who heard what or to measure the subtle effects of the fair experience on such a diverse group of women as those who came to lead, to follow, or simply to look and listen. Local records show, however, that the fair was followed by a wave of energy and organization, which many women said reflected the emphasis on the power of "organized womanhood" they had seen and heard in the Woman's Building.[53]

A North Carolina woman, whose presence at the Exposition came about only because a Lady Manager fell ill, provides a case study of its transforming power. Sallie Southall Cotten, who appeared earlier in this chapter when she joined a reading circle to force herself to read improving books, was forty-seven years old with no experience in public life when—thanks to her husband's political friendship with the Governor—she was appointed an alternate Lady Manager. After a summer in Chicago Cotten came home to launch a career that would last the rest of her life. She organized first individual clubs and then a North Carolina federation; she preached the gospel of "organized womanhood" from one end of the state to the other—and elsewhere. She encouraged women to take themselves seriously, and took her own work seriously as well. She became perhaps the most admired woman in North Carolina and toward the end of her life she was hailed in Boston as the "Julia Ward Howe of the South." The reaction of this southern lady to being compared to the author of the *Battle Hymn of the Republic* was not recorded.[54]

It seems likely that there were many Sallie Cottens, and many other women who shared some part of her vision and energy as a result of their encounters with other women in Chicago. An overall evaluation of the effects of the experience would require us to see the world from many different angles, from one side of the country to another, from—almost—one woman to another. There can be no doubt that the exposition was a major milestone in the history of American women's associations, one which made it possible to see what lay behind the statement, used often in the 1890s, that the nineteenth century had been "the woman's century."[55]

Amid all this activity it was inevitable that sentiment for woman suffrage would spread. But Susan B. Anthony expressed some concern. "I have been curious to learn," she told the Congress of Representative Women, "that all roads lead to Rome."

> That is to say, it doesn't matter whether an organization is called the King's Daughters, the partisan or nonpartisan Woman's Christian Temperance Union; whether it is called a Portia club, a sorosis, or a federation of clubs, a missionary society to reclaim the heathen of the Fiji Islands or an educational association; whether it is of the Jewish, of the Catholic, of the Protestant, of the Liberal, or the other sort of religion; somehow or other, everybody and every association that has spoken or reported has closed with a statement that what they are waiting for is the ballot. . . .[56]

She went on to say that while many of the other organizations had very large membership, there were no more than seven thousand dues-paying suffragists, and that if all the professed suffragists would join the National American Woman Suffrage Association, the United States Congress might prove more respectful of women's demands.

Of course Anthony knew as well as anyone that the woman's rights movement—as it would continue to be called—had made considerable progress as part of the vast expansion of women's associational life since the end of the Civil War. In the late 1860s, indeed, the movement had seemed to be in a promising mode. When the Iowa legislature passed a suffrage amendment and an informal club of Iowa lawmakers not only devoted four meetings to the subject but also invited a suffrage activist to present her case, women on the spot had been optimistic.[57] When the committee on suffrage of the 1868 constitutional convention in Texas brought in a majority report in favor of woman suffrage or when nine thousand Kansas male voters—one-third of the electorate—actually cast a ballot in favor of enfranchising women, suffragists grew more hopeful.[58] In one state after another new suffrage organizations, made up largely of young, often well-to-do, women, had begun to appear and in some places, again principally in the Middle West, male opposition seemed to be evaporating. For the moment it appeared that vigorous agitation and haphazard local organization would be enough: the walls would soon tumble down.[59]

Meantime, however, politics were becoming more complex in the East. At the first postwar Woman's Rights Convention meeting in New York, antislavery men who before the war had seemed committed to woman's rights, and especially to woman suffrage, now argued that the first consideration must be to seek enfranchisement of freedmen, not only as a matter of justice but to ensure Republican control of the South before the Confederate states were readmitted to the Union. Pushing for so unpopular a cause as woman suffrage, they argued, would create an unnecessary hindrance to the rapid achievement of black suffrage. They suggested that the women put aside their own interests and work for the rights of black men.

The issue was divisive. Some women, typified by Elizabeth Cady Stanton, thought that if black suffrage was to come through a federal amendment woman suffrage must come too. She was outraged at the thought that illiterate men might vote when educated women could not. Others, typified by Lucy Stone, were more willing to consider the freedmen's needs as greater than their own, to hold back while black men sought their rights. Thus began a series of disagreements, disappointments, and conflicts that would divide the prewar leaders, and prevent women in places like Iowa and Ohio from taking full advantage of the promising fluidity of the immediate postwar period.

One outcome of this division was the formation of two so-called national associations. First, Stanton and Susan B. Anthony created the National Woman Suffrage Association, with the intention of allowing women to speak for women, though in the end they relied on some men for help. Initially the organization's chief purpose was to tie woman suffrage to any constitutional amendment granting the vote to freedmen. Despite its ambitious name, there were years when the National Woman Suffrage Association consisted principally of the unremitting labor of Susan B. Anthony; the brilliant oratory of Elizabeth Cady Stanton; their short-lived newspaper, *The Revolution;* a small coterie of devoted grassroots activists; and a mailing list of several thousand friends and acquaintances.[60] They did manage to stage a convention of women's rights advocates each year in Washington, D.C., and to convert a few members of Congress. Though both had many admirers, Stanton and Anthony were also often criticized for radical views and unseemly behavior. While it lasted *The Revolution* drew on Stanton's talents as a publicist and offered its readers a rich diet of reform ideas. Subscriptions were rising rapidly when the paper ran out of money, and Anthony, upon whom the practical side of the National always rested, could find no angel willing to take a chance on so risky a venture. She closed it down and set out to pay off a ten thousand dollar debt with the income from lectures. From that point on the National had no easy channel of communication with women in the rest of the country.[61]

A temporary alliance with Victoria Woodhull, whose presentation of the argument that the Fourteenth Amendment did in fact enfranchise women had intrigued a congressional committee in 1871, embroiled them in a far-reaching controversy when Woodhull first advocated free love in her paper, *Woodhull and Claflin's Weekly,* and then revealed the existence of an extramarital relationship between the wife of one ardent suffragist and the president of a rival suffrage group. Lucy Stone, in particular, was sure her erstwhile friends and colleagues were doing the cause great harm. In Iowa, according to Louise Noun, the "free-love storm" frightened away timid supporters and left the whole movement in something of a shambles. In this context the Iowa legislature felt free to renege on its earlier commitment to a state suffrage amendment.

Lucy Stone and her husband, Henry Blackwell, had responded to the Stanton-Anthony initiative by forming their own "more representative" society, the American Woman Suffrage Association, which, they said, would permit power to remain in local communities. They implied, with some justice, that the National Association was run by Stanton and Anthony from the top and that it had made little effort to set up a system for representation of local groups, though women from eighteen states had been present at the founding. In contrast the AWSA had adopted a carefully drawn constitution, demanded proper credentials of the women who attended its conventions, and offered membership to any woman willing to pay a dollar dues. It also had a male president and equal numbers of men and women in policy-making positions.[62] The American established a close and fruitful relationship with the New England Woman's Club, and shared headquarters in Boston with the New England and the Massachusetts Woman

Suffrage associations. Stone and Blackwell were involved in all three, and within the state of Massachusetts they demonstrated impressive organizational and financial skills. Lucy Stone was able to secure donations and—as benevolent societies had so long done—encouraged older suffragists to write the society into their wills.

They also initiated *The Woman's Journal.* Established as a joint stock company, it would become the best and longest lasting woman's rights newspaper ever published. In addition to the *Journal,* Stone inaugurated a series of suffrage tracts, modeled on the ubiquitous religious tracts, and urged suffragists to make the rounds of "every house in town or village" with tract in hand, as so many of them had done in antislavery petition campaigns.[63] Both groups depended upon reason and oratorical splendor, and lengthy petitions to legislative bodies, to persuade men to give women the right to vote. The conventional wisdom has it that the National wanted to go by way of a federal amendment and the American concentrated on state legislatures. In fact either would have welcomed any degree of enfranchisement.

Though the National (Stanton and Anthony) and the American (Stone and Blackwell) were increasingly at odds and members of each said many harsh things about the other, this bitterness chiefly affected people in close proximity to the leaders. Local suffrage groups often seemed quite unaware of the rivalry between the two national organizations and welcomed representatives of either with impartial hospitality. Various women made abortive efforts to heal the split, but fundamental differences in outlook and deep feelings of personal grievance at the top prevented any unification.[64]

For the next twenty years a handful of eloquent women crisscrossed the country, enduring cold, heat, sooty trains, shared beds in frontier cabins, flies, bedbugs, and mosquitoes, and occasional hostile audiences, as they preached suffrage. Hundreds of young women and girls, including some who would become powerful leaders in the next generation of suffragists, would later testify that their interest in the cause had been aroused in one of these meetings. The suffragists often crossed the trail of Frances Willard, who was speaking diligently in the cause of temperance and the "Home Protection Ballot" and organizing local units of the Woman's Christian Temperance Union wherever she went. However much some of the leaders of each movement wished it were otherwise, temperance and suffrage were intertwined from the beginning. Susan B. Anthony and numbers of others of the first generation had begun careers of activism in the prewar temperance movement. Amelia Bloomer's *The Lily,* for example, began as a temperance journal, and later incorporated woman's rights and dress reform. There were many vigorous suffragists in the post-1874 WCTU, and in the

South that organization provided the only safe haven for women who believed in suffrage. Some leaders moved back and forth between the two movements, identifying themselves with one or the other depending on which seemed most likely to gain a hearing in a given time and place. It is difficult to untangle the lines of influence, which clearly ran both ways. Willard and Anthony remained on good terms most of the time.

The substance of suffrage lectures, which were generally to mixed audiences of men and women, varied with the predilections of the lecturer and her judgment as to what would persuade her hearers. Anthony, in particular, sought to awaken people, especially women, to what was to her an obvious fact: that with the ballot women would have a better chance of economic independence. Others stressed natural law, property rights, woman's moral superiority—or all three.

In a number of places groups of women experimented with the tactic of going to the polls and voting as if they had every right to do so.[65] In 1872, along with fifty friends, relatives, and sister activists, Anthony registered and voted, and was arrested for her pains. She had hoped to bring about a verdict that could be appealed to the Supreme Court to test the proposition, first elaborated by Francis Minor in St. Louis, that the Fourteenth and Fifteenth amendments had already enfranchised women. Although she refused to pay the hundred dollar fine that was the result of a directed verdict, to her great disappointment the state refused to press the case, thereby depriving her of the opportunity to appeal. All she gained was one more occasion for speaking all over New York state on the issue of women's rights.

In the eighties the two NWSA leaders, Anthony and Stanton, with the help of Matilda Joslyn Gage, gathered all the records and reminiscences they could lay hands on, wrote long introductory essays reaching back to antiquity for the roots of women's oppression, and published the first three volumes of *The History of Woman Suffrage,* which they then distributed to libraries all over the country. This enterprise was a major propaganda effort as well as a major historical one.[66]

In the absence of effective record keeping in either national suffrage organization, there was no way to know how many women nominally belonged. It is even more difficult to determine the number of suffragists whose principal activity was in other organizations. Beyond the enfranchisement of women in two thinly settled western territories, Wyoming and Utah, the most visible practical achievement of the movement in the twenty-five years after the Civil War had been the adoption of school suffrage, or municipal suffrage, in many states. In some places—as in Boston—this had been the achievement of a woman's club. Similarly, when the Indiana legislature passed both a suffrage and a prohibition amendment in 1881, the most effective lobbyist was a suffragist who spoke in the name of the WCTU.[67] In Ohio, Louisa Southworth, chairman of NWSA's committee on national enrollment, collected forty thousand names by 1888 and made regular trips to testify before the Ohio legislature. Since she was also chairman of the Franchise Committee of the Ohio WCTU she could wear the hat that seemed most useful at any given moment.[68] In Illinois, Elizabeth Boynton Harbert, who at twenty-seven had organized a suffrage association in Iowa, was one of the founders of the Illinois Social Science Association, which, though its principal purpose was said to be to bring a scientific outlook into reform, also planned to promote woman suffrage. Clearly some of the most dedicated suffragists did not think suffrage organizations were always the best way to reach the goal.

As early as 1868, thanks to a personal friendship with Senator A. A. Sargent of California (said to have been a spokesman for the transcontinental railroads), Stanton and Anthony had secured the introduction of the amendment that would ultimately become the nineteenth. Senator Sargent also precipitated a lively congressional debate on the subject when he tried to attach a woman suffrage amendment to a bill to set up the territory of Pembina (later North Dakota). In the course of the debate, congressmen voiced nearly every argument, pro and con, that would be heard over and over in the ensuing fifty years.

This had been the state of things in 1890 when a younger generation of women, led by Alice Stone Blackwell, brought about at last the unification of the organizations. Stubbornness on both sides about giving up a treasured name made necessary the unwieldy label of National American Woman Suffrage Association, with the equally ungainly acronym NAWSA. It was for this group that Susan B. Anthony spoke at the World's Columbian Exposition in Chicago.

The propensity of women to set up associations appeared just as powerfully among those opposed to suffrage as among its supporters. In 1895 ten socially prominent Boston women invited a carefully selected list of people like themselves to form a Standing Committee with the intention of forming an association to resist the demand for woman suffrage being placed before the Massachusetts legislature. A hundred women responded to the invitation and agreed to establish the Massachusetts Association Opposed to the Further Extension of Suffrage to Women. In background these women were not remarkably different from the suffragists, except that they were a little richer, and a little more linked to the mercantile and manufacturing elite. They were nearly all active in other associations, and some held political appointments. Their methods were indistinguishable from those of the suffragists: parlor meetings, pamphlets, speakers, and testimony before legislative committees.

There is some evidence that the idea for an organization of women to oppose suffrage came from a state senator, who did not have the nerve to stand against the idea himself, but thought a group of women organized to prevent their own enfranchisement would provide a way for male legislators to legitimate opposition.

From Massachusetts the antisuffrage movement spread. As suffrage advocates were increasingly better organized, so was the opposition. The failure of every state suffrage referendum between 1896 and 1910 was partly due to the effectiveness of the antis, as they were called. They had, of course, the advantage of defending the status quo.

Understanding the history of women's associations would be easier if the women had moved in lockstep through stages of development: from religious societies to self-improvement clubs, to civic improvement, to suffrage and so on. But no such tidy order emerges from the record. Groups with different purposes emerged at the same time, and what is more confusing, their boundaries were anything but fixed. Self-improvement soon spilled over into civic reform, with traditional charity thrown in for good measure. Music and art clubs looked out of their windows and were soon planting trees or creating orchestras. Almost everybody spoke in religious language to some extent, and however much they argued and divided internally, clubwomen presented themselves to the outside world as models of harmony and talent.

The individuals who surface from the mass of members are as difficult to categorize as are their organizations. Farmers' wives joining village clubs in Kansas were a far cry from the elegant spouses of wealthy businessmen who led the Chicago Woman's Club from one triumph to another, and both were quite different from the journalists and writers who predominated in New York's Sorosis, or the women workers in a thousand "working-girls' societies." Black clubwomen were most often members of the growing black middle class, and were sharply different from their sisters in the black working class, but they also differed in important ways from white middle-class clubwomen. Ethnic communities had their own clubs and their own variations on the type. There was a great deal of sisterhood, and a great deal of conflict, most of it carefully hidden from public view.

Critics found the clubs superficial, yet member after member testified to their transforming influence upon themselves. Both were right in some circumstances. What one can say with assurance is that the urge to self-improvement took both women and their associations a long way from where they started. The next step in the untidy evolution of women's associations would be the spreading practice of what they came to call municipal housekeeping.

6

Inventing "Progressivism":
Municipal Housekeeping

Unquestionably the great majority of voters in this country are dissatisfied with existing political and social conditions. . . .

—Benjamin DeWitt
The Progressive Movement, 1915

The adventurous member of the Cambridge Mothers' Club who proposed to her friends that they "make some combined movement for public improvement" echoed a keynote that was already reverberating through the far-flung network of women's organizations, gathering force as it went. The call for such improvement was everywhere.

The idea that women as the center of home life were responsible for the moral tone of a community did not vanish, but increasingly it was said that such responsibility did not end with the four walls of a home, but extended to the neighborhood, the town, the city. In 1910 Jane Addams summed up what had become the conventional wisdom: "If a woman would keep on with her old business of caring for her house and rearing her children she will have to have some conscience in regard to public affairs lying quite outside of her immediate household. The individual conscience and devotion are no longer effective. . . . "[1]

Addams would have defined "public affairs" very broadly; the president of the black woman's club in Tuskeegee, Alabama, was more concrete: "Good women try always to do good housekeeping. Building inspectors, sanitary inspectors and food inspectors owe their positions to politics. Who then is so well informed as to how these inspectors perform their duties as the women who live in inspected districts and inspected houses, and who buy food from inspected markets?"[2]

After the Civil War urban problems multiplied. The largest cities experienced extraordinarily rapid growth. New immigrants from the European and American countryside were crowding into broken-down housing, searching for employment, struggling to cope with unfamiliar police and local courts, creating problems for themselves and for the community.

Habitual ways of handling such things as transportation, garbage disposal, housing, petty crime, or emergency relief were no longer adequate. An array of spontaneous civic organizations, reform mayors, and muckraking journalists focused attention on what Lincoln Steffens labeled "the shame of the cities." Women's organizations were among the first to recognize and begin to deal with many practical issues.

The term "municipal housekeeping" conferred an air of respectability upon what might otherwise have been considered unseemly public or political activity, but behind that innocuous label lay a considerable measure of "discontent with existing political and social conditions"—on the part of people who were not yet voters—first expressed in systematic efforts to improve village, town, or city life.[3]

The way women approached local problems varied depending on the setting: big cities called forth behavior different from what might appear in a small town, but the range of tasks they undertook was much the same in either setting.

Chicago represented one end of the spectrum. It contained as remarkable a group of women leaders as has been seen in this country before or since. While the political history of the city for the two decades after the Columbian Exposition could be (and has been) written in terms of mounting and seemingly intractable urban problems and of corruption linking aldermen with colorful names such as "Hinkey Dink" Kenna and "Bathhouse" John Coughlin to businessmen making impressive fortunes from city contracts, it could equally well be written as a case study in the growing influence of organized women.[4]

One center of this influence was the Chicago Woman's Club, the prototype "department club" which had allowed itself seven years of study to prepare for what would become a vigorous program of municipal reform.[5] The club played a key part in a large and increasingly influential network of women. In 1889 it had supported the founding of Hull House. The circle that grew up there around Jane Addams, Florence Kelley, Julia Lathrop, and Alice Hamilton linked itself on the one hand to every national progressive individual or organization, male or female, and on the other to the literally dozens of women's organizations in the city, beginning with its own Hull House Woman's Club but including the WCTU, the YWCA, the Women's Trade Union League, the Association of Collegiate Alumnae, the elite Fortnightly, and the radical Illinois Women's Alliance. The work of preparing for the Columbian Exposition had brought together most of the white Chicago women's associations and both Bertha Palmer and Ellen Henrotin had relied heavily on their skill and experience. The fact that more than four hundred members of the Chicago Woman's Club took part in various congresses at the fair was a measure of their involvement.

In 1894 just as the post-fair economic depression was creating a new challenge, the club sponsored a symposium entitled "What Has the World's Fair Done for Us," and by April it had organized a very large meeting on the relation of women to modern industrial conditions. Not content with talk, the club set up a system of relief for women thrown out of work by the depression.

The club extended its reach through a number of institutions of its own creation: the Women's and Children's Protective Agency, which provided free legal counsel; the School Children's Aid Society; the Model Workshop and Lodging Association; the Municipal Order League; and the Political Equality League. From these sprung kindergartens, low-cost housing projects, women's trade unions, visiting nurse associations, and a major ongoing effort to improve the public school system.[6]

So large and diverse a collection of women required strong leadership to contain the inevitable conflicts, disagreement on priorities, and competition for leadership—but the net result was impressive. At one time or another every project in the municipal housekeeping repertoire appeared in Chicago led by one or many women's associations.[7] Sarah Hackett Stevenson's astringent observations in 1893 remind us that their achievements were matched by impressive failures, but despite her tough analysis of these failures Stevenson herself continued to find women's organizations the best means to reform goals, and her own career was testimony to the breadth and depth of the work of organized women in the city.[8]

In Philadelphia, to take another big-city example, the New Century Club, which had been engaged in what it called "practical philanthropy" and self-education since 1877, in 1893 spun off a Woman's Health Protective Association which immediately attracted two hundred members.[9] The new organization set about studying the way municipal departments were organized to deal with public health. Committees were established on contagious diseases, water supply, street cleaning, garbage and ashes, trolleys and the sweating system. The Water Supply Committee began to study methods of filtration suitable to Philadelphia's water source and—among other things—put together "a committee of ladies" from several organizations to visit Louisville, Kentucky, which was said to have an exemplary filtration system. After careful study the committee concluded that the alum which Louisville was using was too dangerous in the amounts that would be needed for their own city. Back home the women sought expert advice from a Boston engineer and with his help came up with a plan for a system suitable to Philadelphia which they presented to the mayor. Effective publicity aroused public sentiment to support a bond issue. In due course, thanks in large part to the committee's work, Philadelphians could at last drink clean water.

The Woman's Health Protective Association's Committee on Contagious Diseases, with help from the County Medical Society, built a hospital and persuaded the board of health to begin medical inspection of schoolchildren. Other committees functioned in what they labeled "the same thorough and systematic way," until "public officials, at first doubtful and reluctant, now welcomed the cooperative influence of the Woman's Health Protective Association, while the membership had grown to upward of four hundred." A branch in the lower part of Philadelphia joined in the work of cleaning up schoolhouses and building playgrounds. The women envisioned a branch in each ward of the city.[10] Reflecting the spirit of the times, the Philadelphia WHPA, after a good deal of internal disagreement about the best use of members' energy, agreed to join in a national organization of Health Protective Associations; forty clubs and societies sent representatives to its first national convention.

While women in cities struggled to find ways of dealing with spreading slums, air and water pollution, overcrowded public schools, and political corruption, inhabitants of many smaller places, particularly those that had been recently settled, began to look around in dismay at rickety buildings, dusty main streets, piles of garbage attracting flies and rats, stinking gutters, sewage pouring into rivers and harbors, water not fit to drink, milk that caused babies to sicken and die. Some thought with nostalgia of tree-shaded New England villages, of neat public schools and libraries, of pleasant churches and other amenities they remembered in longer-settled eastern places. Many middle western and western communities, intent first on economic survival, had failed to create most of the conditions that people associated with "civilization." Poverty and a widely scattered population had much the same result in the South. Harbors and waterways had been turned to industrial use in many places with no apparent thought of what was being lost. In one rough western or southern town after another, women, in particular, wondered if they were destined to live in frontier style forever.

El Paso, Texas, was one of many small frontier communities where women organized themselves to create a decent environment in which to raise children. The beginning was typical: a Child Culture Study Circle organized in 1891 was soon followed by a club to study literature and current events. Then came the Woman's Club which began at once to tackle what one not-very-admiring historian of the town called a "wild, uncouth, uncivilized and un-Christian" place. True to form, the club combined study and action, interspersing an analysis of the uses of kindergartens with lectures on Roman history, and building a library while it also studied principles of sanitation. Playgrounds and compulsory school attendance were next on the agenda. Then, with spades and hoes in hand, the women went forth to improve the appearance of the town, an experience that led them to begin studying forest conservation. In order to draw in the men, they initiated a Civic Improvement League, which commandeered twenty wagons for a massive town cleanup. By 1911 the club was proposing to establish a home for delinquent boys and in 1914 the *El Paso Herald* announced that it was doing more for "civic betterment" than any other organization in town.[11]

While the El Paso pattern was typical of what happened in many small towns all over the country, another Texas city provided a case study of women brought together by disaster. In 1900 a great hurricane swept Galveston with 100-mile-an-hour winds and tidal waves which wiped out a large part of the city. Six thousand people died, and the situation became so desperate that corpses were burned in huge funeral pyres. Some survivors thought Galveston was finished for good.

In March of 1901 a group of experienced members of church and benevolent societies joined forces to establish a Women's Health Protective Association which went to work on two immediate problems—transferring bodies which had been buried in makeshift graves to a formal cemetery, and planting grass and shrubs after tons of fill, pumped in to raise the level of the island, had killed what vegetation had survived the tidal wave. By the time the immediate crisis had begun to diminish, the WHPA was well established, and moved on to deal with problems of public health and sanitation so starkly revealed during the disaster. In the wake of the hurricane Galveston had devised a commission form of government, which was soon being hailed as one of the significant inventions of the municipal reform movement. The WHPA went to work to persuade the commission to adopt city ordinances covering a wide range of health and sanitation issues ranging from milk inspection to tuberculosis clinics. By this time the association had four hundred members and had become an essential part of the reviving community.[12]

Some variation on these stories could be written for a thousand towns.[13] Even rural villages that might seem too small to support a woman's association devised their own version of municipal housekeeping. One project, independently invented in a dozen places, suggested how many small-town women had recently left the hard life of farm wife. In a number of places clubwomen observed that on Saturday afternoon all the country people came to town, and while the men bought supplies, visited the saloon, or arranged to sell corn, wheat, or cotton (and enjoyed opportunities for sociability), women and children sat patiently or impatiently in wagons, or stood around on street corners, cold in winter, sweltering in summer. Mothers with babies presented a particularly long-suffering image. Clubs in Texas, Iowa, Kansas, and Minnesota, and doubtless elsewhere, set about securing a room or a small house which could be converted into a social center for the country families. The response was instantaneous (in one town sixty families came the first day the social center was open) and in some places country women were persuaded to join a town club. In others the project widened to become a community center for the town. Organizers spoke explicitly of bridging the gap between themselves and rural women whose experience had so recently been their own.

A Texas woman, reminiscing years later, caught the flavor of informality which characterized these small-town developments:

> I grasped at the Shakespere [*sic*] Club (and Mrs. Dibrell who also was blessed (or cursed) with an urge to do what she could in return for the gift of life) as a drowning man at a straw. We—rather she—the rest of us helped—formed a Village Improvement Society (a few objected to the term "village"). I was chairman of the committee that persuaded property owners to plant all of those trees . . . and then persuaded the city fathers to have them watered. Then we raised enough money to build two large club rooms with folding doors. One we met in and used as a library the other we furnished free with maid service to the bedraggled, tired country women for their babies when they shopped on Saturdays. . . . [14]

In 1906 Mary I. Wood, director of public information for the General Federation of Women's Clubs, summed up more formally not only what women were doing but the ideology with which they justified their activity:

> Very early the club women became unwilling to discuss Dante and Browning over the teacups in some lady's drawing room . . . while unsightly heaps of rubbish flanked the paths over which they had passed in their journey thither. They began to realize that the one calling in which they were, as a body, proficient, that of housekeeping and homemaking, had its outdoor as well as its indoor application. . . . It was this knowledge, the extension of the homemaking instinct of women and the broadening out of the mother instinct . . . that led them out into paths of civic usefulness. [15]

One searches Wood's book or any other standard source in vain for evidence that enthusiastic white clubwomen were aware that black women were equally eager to follow "the mother instinct . . . into paths of civic usefulness." Though black women established Shakespeare and Browning clubs, Chautauqua circles and music clubs, they seldom had the luxury of confining themselves to "self-culture." The needs of the black community were so pressing that community improvement nearly always became their major focus. After 1890 secular clubs joined the missionary societies in trying to force the white world to face up to the injustice of violence, lynching, disfranchisement, and Jim Crow laws, as well as of the popular stereotypes of themselves. [16] Their Sisyphian task was epitomized in the poignant motto of the National Association of Colored Women's Clubs: "Lifting as we climb." The association stated its purposes vigorously:

> To secure and enforce civil and political rights for ourselves and our group.
>
> To obtain for our colored women the opportunity of reaching the highest standard in all fields of human endeavor.
>
> To promote interracial understanding so that justice and goodwill may prevail among all people.[17]

Black clubwomen were alternately sympathetic to and repelled by the lives of "our poor benighted sisters of the plantation," but reason told them that improvement in the educational level and living standards of *all* black people was necessary to secure their own position in the world. Mary Church Terrell spelled this out in 1901:

> In no way could we live up to such a sentiment ["lifting as we climb"] than by coming into closer touch with the masses of our women. . . . Even though we wish to shun them, and hold ourselves entirely aloof from them, we cannot escape the consequences of their acts. So, that, if the call of duty were disregarded altogether, policy and self-preservation would demand that we go down among the lowly, the illiterate, and even the vicious to whom we are bound by the ties of race and sex, and put forth every possible effort to uplift and claim them.[18]

Even more vehemently than white women, black women emphasized the home as the vital center of reform, and taught gentility as a counter to racial stereotypes, particularly those that labeled all black women as immoral. From Boston to Tuskegee, Alabama, urged on by national leaders like Josephine St. Pierre Ruffin, Hallie Quinn Brown, Fannie Barrier Williams, Mary Church Terrell, and Victoria Earle Matthews, they developed neighborhood community centers and set about dealing with the problems on their doorsteps.

The Atlanta Neighborhood Union, established by Lugenia Hope, wife of the president of Morehouse College, and a group of faculty wives, was one of the most impressive. Born in St. Louis, Hope had worked for a benevolent society in Chicago and spent some time at Hull House. Along the way she had developed a salutary confidence in her own ability and a vision of the potential power of women working together. The union, organized in neighborhood units, tackled most of the pressing problems of black city life: education, day care, health, family life, housing, and recreation. Part of Hope's genius was her ability to involve people in meeting their own needs. She encouraged neighborhood women to take their problems to the city council and the state legislature.[19] The union helped to create kindergartens and day nurseries, provided aid for families in trouble, founded missions for girls coming to the cities in search of work, and, occasionally, cooperated warily with white women. As part of a survey of the segregated black schools in 1912 and 1913 it not only documented the deplorable conditions that made a mockery of the "separate but equal" doctrine but also forced both white women activists and the mayor to look at unpleasant realities.

In the North and Middle West an extraordinary group of leaders, many of them originally from the South, established associations to provide help for young black women, fresh from farms and plantations, coming to the city for a better life but knowing almost nothing of what awaited them. Victoria Earle Matthews's White Rose Mission in Brooklyn, for example, tried to help these young immigrants find housing and friends. In Cleveland, Jane Edna Hunter founded the Phillis Wheatley House for much the same purpose.[20] Segregated units of the YWCA took up part of the task.

Despite the enormous obstacles, some changes were brought about.[21] In time black women's clubs undertook much of the grassroots organizing for the National Association for the Advancement of Colored People and the National Urban League.[22]

By 1914 the NACW claimed fifty thousand members in twenty-eight federations and over a thousand clubs. Everywhere the work was similar: homes for the aged, for working women, and for unwed mothers; hospitals in towns where white hospitals refused admission to black patients; neighborhood clinics; employment services; kindergartens where there had been none for children of either race, along with training programs for kindergarten teachers; libraries; settlement houses; and so on and on. Individual clubs went to great lengths to raise money for small scholarships to help young people go to college. Theirs was a special kind of municipal housekeeping, carried out with limited resources, which meant that the women themselves did a great deal of hands-on labor in their projects. They learned more from white women than white women were willing to learn from them. This story is only beginning to be reconstructed, and as far as I have been able to determine, black women's wide-ranging contributions to civic improvement have never been mentioned in any of the standard works on the age of reform, whether contemporary or those written by historians.[23] Even white historians who have recognized and implicitly castigated the racism of white progressives seem unaware that black women across the country were creating their own brand of "progressivism."[24]

When Radcliffe College established an oral history program focused on the careers of black women leaders, in one case after another it became clear that their careers had been built through voluntary associations. Christia Adair, for example, born in 1893 in Texas, began in the AME church and a mothers' club developed in cooperation with white women to remove a gambling den from her community.[25] She went on to organize a club and to become a volunteer secretary for the NAACP. The NACW, in which she was also active, was not, in her view, for the women who were doing well, but for "the woman who needs us." Frankie Adams, born in 1902 in Danville, Kentucky, began her career in the YWCA, with a focus on improving wages of industrial women. Still another, Norma Boyd, born in 1888 in Washington, worked through Alpha Kappa Alpha, a black women's sorority, to open jobs to black women. Ella McCabe, also born in 1888, found her *metier* first in the WCTU and later in an improvement club of her own organizing in which among other things she promoted the study of black history. There is scarcely a woman in this collection of interviews who had not worked in close association with other women.

Among both white and black women's organizations there was a steady concern for education of all kinds. Since women often joined together in the first instance for self-education, it was not surprising that they went on to build thousands of public libraries. As one part of this effort to bring books to people they invented the travelling library (ancestor of today's bookmobile).[26] For many years carefully packed boxes of books crisscrossed the rural parts of many states, all under the supervision of the federations of women's clubs.

The work of creating institutions of higher education for women or opening existing institutions to them is a story in itself.[27] Women's educational societies, for example, created Pembroke and Goucher, step by step brought Radcliffe into being, pushed many state universities into admitting women students, and had a great deal to do with persuading state legislatures to support higher education for women. Clubs regularly raised money to provide scholarships for young women, and the Association of Collegiate Alumnae provided support for post-graduate study abroad. Colleges for black women, created initially by missionary societies, could count on continuing support from secular clubs. The symbiosis is clear when one realizes that the great black women school builders—women like Lucy Laney, Nannie Burroughs, and Mary McLeod Bethune—were also leaders in women's clubs.

While women's efforts on behalf of the education of their own sex were basic to its rapid expansion, their work for public education affected children everywhere. At the third biennial of the General Federation of Women's Clubs a resolution was adopted recommending to all the member clubs "a study of the science of education and of educational conditions existing in their home cities, to the end that the united influence of women's clubs may be exerted for the betterment of the state system of education, from the kindergarten to the university."[28] No single activity of women's clubs was more ubiquitous. Propelled by the belief that "what you would have appear in the life of the people you must put into the schools," and a long tradition of seeing the right training of children as the best hope for improving society, associations everywhere, white and black, assumed an ongoing responsibility for local schools. In small towns and large cities they built playgrounds, inaugurated school lunch and school garden programs, introduced art and music as well as domestic science and manual training into classrooms, experimented with kindergartens, initiated school-based adult education programs, arranged for medical inspection of children, and found ways of using school buildings for community centers. Taking seriously the injunction to study "educational science" they read and discussed Froebel and John Dewey; in Georgia the federation of women's clubs published the *Southern Educational Journal.* Many club members had been teachers and had firm ideas about what schools should be doing. They visited schools, studied school laws, and cooperated with local, state, and national education associations.[29] The Woman's Association for the Betterment of Public School Houses in North Carolina took on the formidable task of creating better school buildings (for white children) in a rural state where resources for public education were very scarce.[30] Parent-Teacher Associations grew out of an organization called the Congress of Mothers, and despite the name, were principally women's associations. Black schools, poorly funded by local and state governments, were especially dependent on the voluntary work of women's associations.

In large cities involvement with public education and the effort to put women in positions of responsibility could become extremely complicated, as in Chicago when Ella Flagg Young (with the support of the women's clubs) became the first woman superintendent of schools and then found herself in combat with the politically appointed school board, which refused to re-elect her, despite her record of having solved a good many of the school system's most pressing problems. In this crisis the Chicago Woman's Club and a group of other women's organizations called a mass meeting, which demanded—and got—Young's reinstatement.[31]

By the end of the first decade of the twentieth century the drive to improve community life had gained a good deal of momentum, and in 1912 the National Municipal League discovered women. It commissioned Mary Ritter Beard, then in her thirties and part of a circle of young radicals, to make a study of women's work in civic reform. Clinton Rogers Woodruff, of the Municipal League, introducing Beard's book, fully adopted the women's own explanation for their work: "Women by natural instinct as well as by long training have become the housekeepers of the world, so it is only natural that they should in time become effective municipal housekeepers as well. This book demonstrates how successfully they may fulfill this role."[32] The book described literally thousands of municipal reforms and community improvements carried out by women's clubs. Beard's chapter headings suggest how wide ranging these activities had become: education, public health, the social evil [a euphemism for prostitution and venereal disease], recreation, the assimilation of races, housing, social service, corrections, public safety, and government administration. Filled with revealing information, the book is disconcertingly light on documentation. Though she may be overwhelmed by the evidence of women's multifarious civic achievements, the scholar in search of data must continually wonder about reliability.[33] Yet if some of the accomplishments detailed in the Beard book are overstated, the record is still extraordinary.

Beard used women's work in public health to illustrate the process which had become almost standard. First, she said, it was necessary to build a strong organization made up of members who were prepared to study thoroughly the details of engineering, taxation, and budget making. Since women could not vote, they needed also to understand the techniques of indirect influence in order to promote the election of officials who shared their concerns. There was no rest for the weary, for even with the "right" men in office only constant vigilance could make sure campaign pledges were carried out. The women also had to understand the ways in which contractors and businessmen sought political influence for their own gain, in order to guard against being undermined from that quarter. And, to top it all, they had to "overcome the reluctance of public officials to take women seriously" on the one hand while they persuaded apathetic citizens of the importance of what they were doing on the other.[34] This was a tall order indeed, and it could not be expected that every club was able to juggle all these complex and difficult tasks.

Many must have done so, however, since public health was one of the major areas in which women's clubs brought about significant, measurable change. Cleaning up the milk supply was a favorite enterprise. As towns and cities grew, most of their inhabitants could no longer get milk directly from the cow but had to depend on commercial dairies. En route to the consumer there were multiple opportunities for contamination. Since milk was a primary food for children such contamination posed a major hazard to infant and child health. The disturbingly high rate of infant mortality in the United States (it was tenth among the nations of the world) had come to be a progressive rallying cry. One approach, which many clubs followed, was to set up pure milk stations to sell clean milk at cost. Needless to say such activity was viewed as unfair competition by commercial vendors, who were thereby pressured to clean up their own supplies.[35]

When efforts to deal with the problem directly proved inadequate the women campaigned to force local government to regulate the production and distribution of milk. In 1913 the Civic Committee of the Woman's Club of Orange, New Jersey—to take one example—offered the services of its own secretary to the health department to encourage the city to make a study of the local milk supply. The department agreed to appoint the club secretary as temporary special milk inspector, and allowed her to use its laboratory to test six hundred samples from many commercial sources. Predictably, a considerable number of the samples were contaminated, and the club published her findings both to warn consumers of the hazards they faced and to build public support for an ordinance requiring municipal inspection of milk, which the club had drafted and which was in fact adopted.

Variations of this project took place in hundreds of communities, with consequences that sometimes went beyond the milk supply. Dr. Josephine Baker, a public health pioneer in New York, pointed out that while clean cow's milk was certainly better than contaminated milk, the real problem was to make sure mothers could nurse their infants, which was difficult when women were forced to work at heavy, demanding jobs while they were feeding babies. Mary Beard summed up the point: "The question of poverty, that skeleton in every social closet, looms up here with an insistency that nothing will banish. No kind of philanthropy will solve the requirements of infant welfare when poverty or labor conditions are the root of the problem. Babies' milk thus becomes essentially a social-economic problem."[36]

The pattern exhibited by the Mothers' Club of Cambridge vacation school project was repeated over and over: womens' clubs identified problems or needs, initiated projects to meet them, and then, when their efforts were successful, persuaded local governments to take responsibility, while the club went on to the next challenge. This was a favorite tactic of library associations; it was followed in many places where clubs initiated well-baby clinics, school lunches, kindergartens, and literacy programs which became so successful that citizens of the town insisted that the government sustain them.

The implications of this kind of success were not much thought about in the beginning. When a project clearly benefitted the community, it was logical that the community should pay for it. In time however it became clear that in giving up control women's groups sometimes had to watch the work they had initiated become mired in politics, or allowed to drop by civil servants who lacked commitment. When they handed over the actual conduct of programs, women's associations found themselves propelled into a watch-dog function in an effort to keep government agencies on what they considered to be the right track.

By the time Mary Beard undertook her study it had come to be taken for granted in many communities that when problems were recognized, women's associations would undertake to deal with them, yet very little evidence remains of the concrete ways they went about their self-imposed tasks day-to-day: how they raised money, who was pressed into service when manual labor was required, how other kinds of assistance were recruited and paid for, and the way one project led to another. The sources for reconstructing their accomplishments are numerous but it is difficult to discover how the process looked from the inside. Minutes, newspaper clippings, correspondence, an occasional memoir, and records of institutions women created help, but they leave many questions unanswered. There are, however, a few things that can be said with certainty.

First, as in the Cambridge Mothers' Club, civic projects rarely engaged all the members of a particular association. Every club had its quota of members whose motivations were personal and self-centered, and whose understanding of community issues was minimal—the kinds of women pictured by Sarah Hackett Stevenson and Anna Garlin Spencer in their warnings delivered at the Columbian Exposition.

In 1904 the *Atlantic Monthly* published a revealing article by a woman who had, apparently, made her living on the club lecture circuit. While she admired some manifestations of club work, and spoke highly of certain big-city clubs (Chicago, Denver, and Cambridge), she described in disturbing detail the gap between the ambitious goals described by national officers and the feeble response of some local groups. She pointed to the futility of listening to lectures, which so many clubs were wont to do, lectures which stirred up members on one major issue after another in what she described as "an infinite process of stimulation and exhaustion" but from which no action followed. She was cautiously optimistic about the phenomenon of municipal housekeeping but she offered a devastating description of women who had no clear idea of the meaning of the terms they used (she spoke especially of the phrase "social economics") and who flitted through one subject after another without grasping any of them.[37] The ambivalence of this observer's reaction reflected one part of the reality. While for some the club was a genuine tool for social change, or was in fact "the middle-aged woman's university," for others it was a place to see and be seen, to acquire a patina of information and "culture," and to meet the right people.

A single large "department club," the common form by the first decade of the century, might encompass both the best and the worst of club possibilities. Since each department organized its own work one might be blessed with intelligent, energetic leadership, while another remained peacefully at anchor, listening to lectures and accomplishing very little. When a public library was built, a new subject introduced into the public schools, a water supply cleaned up, there had always been a few women willing to work long and hard, who had both the ability to rally others to join them and the administrative and political skills to carry out complex programs. And it was just such women whose enthusiasm for clubs ran highest, and for whom the experience was profoundly important.

Doubtless many clubs embarked on projects which were never finished, or set goals which were never achieved, but the evidence of failure has rarely been preserved. Reading the enthusiastic reports of successful ventures, it is not hard to imagine other cases where a group, in a flush of enthusiasm after hearing a speech or reading a book, decided to initiate some community improvement which it was unable to bring off for lack of knowledge, commitment, resources, or sustained leadership.

The conventions of nineteenth- and early-twentieth-century discourse generally forbade women to speak ill of each other in public, so the published records tend to be one long paean of praise for achievement. Even Mary Beard, who in later work would demonstrate a sharp critical mind, seems to have accepted at face value most of what she read or was told about women's work in the municipalities, with only an occasional glance at the inevitable conflicts and human orneriness to which women were not immune.

Since leadership was a key factor in the growth, development, and effectiveness of women's clubs it would be enlightening if we could find out in what ways the women who emerged as leaders differed from the rank and file. While some attention has been paid to the class origins and educational background of club leaders in particular localities, most of what can be said about personalities, motivation, and methods must be highly impressionistic.[38] Their own published statements and those of their contemporaries reflect the prevailing socialization: since women were expected to be good mothers, and to be compassionate and moral, these qualities were emphasized. Even the terms in which women praised each other for administrative ability or oratorical skill were highly stylized. Club presidents, for example, were women of "fine culture and great insight," of "tact, high character and freedom from aggressive methods"; "gracious," "cultivated," "brilliant," "earnest," "devoted" were the common adjectives. In the South, particularly, but in most other places as well it was always emphasized that no neglect of home was involved in carrying even the most weighty administrative responsibilities.

In spite of the difficulty of seeing through these conventional terms of praise, it is clear that the women who emerged as leaders, especially those who rose rapidly from local to state to national visibility, though a diverse group, shared certain characteristics.[39] They had in common a better than average education, whether acquired at a formal institution or by their own efforts.

Some effective leaders organized one association and gave their lives to it. Alice Birney (1858–1907), for example, conceived the idea of the National Congress of Mothers to promote scientific child study. The organization she initiated in 1897 had instant appeal, and state congresses rapidly followed. Eventually her association developed into the National Congress of Parents and Teachers. At the other extreme were women who joined every organization in sight, though inevitably they could only do serious work in one or two.

Ambition was an essential quality for any woman who took on the pain and strain and unremitting labor of sustained leadership. Just as every presidential contender, invited to state his reasons for running, announces that he has a deep and abiding desire to serve the country, so women in positions of leadership were apt to explain themselves in terms of a desire to serve. Clearly many had a profound, sometimes obsessive, urge to bring about certain changes in the larger society, but equally clearly most of them enjoyed public speaking, enjoyed the use of their inborn or acquired skills, and used these skills to gain power and visibility. They were not, on the whole, given to modesty.

Despite the gradual opening of the professions to women, opportunities for the exercise of ability and ambition, especially for married women, were still comparatively few. Able, ambitious women gravitated to voluntary associations where they could create impressive careers.

While most club leaders were mothers of several children, they were more likely to have small families or to be childless than was the average American woman. Being widowed or divorced often set a woman on the road to achievement, though others married two or even three times. One striking group was made up of very wealthy women—Bertha Honoré Palmer and Ellen Henrotin in Chicago were good examples—who divided their time between traditional social life and hard work in one or several voluntary associations and who appeared to delight in the independent identity their leadership provided. Other wealthy women, of whom Margaret Dreier Robins of the Women's Trade Union League is a good example, simply eschewed high society and spent all their time and most of their money on voluntary activities.[40]

By the turn of the century women with college degrees made up an ever-larger proportion of club membership, a change which was reflected in the educational achievements of the leadership group as well. In view of the stereotype fostered by cartoonists and detractors, it is worth noting that many women began to work in voluntary associations at an early age, and some national leaders were barely in their forties.[41]

Almost any woman with professional or career ambitions beyond the clubs themselves kept one foot in the voluntary world. Women doctors and lawyers, and indeed professionals of all kinds, took a continuing part in one or several associations and brought to the shaping of a distinctively female professional style the background, training, and values acquired there. Sarah Hackett Stevenson, who has already appeared in these pages, was altogether typical. She was a highly regarded doctor, with a wide-ranging career in medicine. Yet somehow she found time to be not just a member but a leader in several associations. She was president of the Chicago Woman's Club, an active member of the Fortnightly and of the Twentieth Century Club, and helped create the Illinois Social Science Association. California's pioneer lawyer Clara Foltz was an ardent creator of women's clubs. Florence Kelley, though immersed in her professional responsibility as executive secretary of the Consumers' League, found time to chair committees for the General Federation of Women's Clubs, as did Julia Lathrop, the first head of the Children's Bureau.

Lathrop was in some ways an archetype of the volunteer turned professional. Drawn to Hull House by Jane Addams, she worked as both volunteer and political appointee in a wide range of social welfare posts in Illinois. When the women's organizations finally succeeded in persuading the president and Congress to create a Children's Bureau in the Department of Labor, they also supported Lathrop to be its first head. She brought to government service a distinctively female way of looking at the world. Not only did the bureau under her guidance push for many structural changes in the way the government took responsibility for children, it also functioned in a highly personal way. Thousands of women wrote to the agency as if it were a personal friend, and responses were often in the same vein. Lathrop incorporated women she knew through her voluntary-association connections into its work. A woman writing from Chicago in what appeared to be desperate need might find herself being visited by a club member whom Lathrop had asked to investigate the case. Looking back in 1939 Josephine Roche, who had been part of Lathrop's network, asserted that the women who supported the Children's Bureau were "determined that human welfare, human conservation, be made the first concern of, the first charge on government."[42] Indeed the Children's Bureau was a marvelous combination of the long benevolent-reform tradition and the new faith in social science, as college graduates came to work for it; these young women set out to reduce the high infant mortality rate using some of the methods they had learned in college and some with which their mothers would have felt quite at home.[43]

As one state after another adopted woman suffrage and women began to run for public office, clubwomen brought their experience to bear on political campaigns, with remarkable success when one considers that men in political parties were unlikely to provide much support for women candidates. A classic example was the election of Florence Ellinwood Allen, of Ohio, to the state Supreme Court. Another was the election of Nellie Nugent Somerville to the Mississippi legislature.[44]

To turn the lens another way, virtually any woman of achievement in any field (with some, but not universal, exceptions in art and literature) maintained strong connections with the voluntary associations in which most had gotten their start. As time went by, many women moved back and forth from voluntary to paid responsibilities, as when North Carolina women, for example, first lobbied for and achieved a law establishing welfare departments in every county, and gradually women who had worked for the reform were appointed county welfare directors.[45] In many states as suffrage opened doors for women in government, male politicians turned to clubs and associations in search of qualified appointees.

Sometimes women who began working as individual crusaders turned to women's clubs when they realized the need for broader support. Albion Fellows Bacon was a talented and well-to-do middle-class woman who was suddenly introduced to the housing conditions of poor people in her town, Evansville, Indiana, when her children caught scarlet fever from a working-class child and it occurred to her to investigate the source. After what almost amounted to an apocalyptic vision, she made herself into a one-woman housing reformer, but in time she found it necessary to mobilize the women's clubs of Indiana in order to achieve the legislation she so much wanted to see adopted.[46] Madeline McDowell Breckinridge of Lexington, Kentucky, who became the leading progressive in that state, started working on her own but soon realized the value of organizing other women to support the plans she was so good at making. As a very young woman she caught the spirit of the settlement movement and envisioned a settlement in the Kentucky mountains—which she was able to create with the help of a women's church society. For the rest of her short life she conceived reform projects and then organized women to help carry them out. These projects included a community center in Irishtown, a poor section of Lexington, an antituberculosis campaign, the Kentucky Equal Suffrage movement, and—just before her death—the campaign to promote United States membership in the League of Nations. The *Louisville Courier-Journal,* writing in her praise in 1913, noted that she had accomplished so much it would be easier "to tell what she has not done than to give the data of her various and far-reaching philanthropies. . . . to get at Mrs. Breckinridge you must get at the organizations she has created. . . . "[47]

"Municipal housekeeping" made communities all over the country healthier and more livable. Perhaps a partial reason for its curious absence from standard histories of the age of reform is that historians are drawn to situations of conflict. The battle between reformers and bosses was a great drama. One has only to read Lincoln Steffens's *Shame of the Cities* side by side with Beard's *Women's Work in the Municipalities* to see why the first would attract more readers than the second. The women's work, while it often transformed the health and appearance of whole towns, was on the whole not controversial and only occasionally posed a threat to existing political structures.

A second part of the answer may lie in the ever-present problem of the way assumptions shape perceptions. Men who had had no first-hand exposure to the work of women's clubs tended to think of them as frivolous; hence when clubwomen behaved in decidedly unfrivolous ways, the fact did not register. Some men, of course, did notice. The Palo Alto, California, *Times* was one of many newspapers that paid attention. In 1904 it noted: "There has never been in the town another organization so earnest and energetic as the Woman's Club nor one that has accomplished anywhere near such good results for the town."[48] Across the continent a North Carolina newspaper editor observed: "The improvement of health, the betterment of morals, the modernization of education and the humanizing of penology are perhaps the most vital matters of government in which North Carolina women have interested themselves. Any one who can deny either that all these things need improvement or that the activity of the Federated clubs has improved them betrays a startling ignorance of the facts in this state."[49] Meanwhile, among certain groups of organized women, the concept of "civic improvement" was being radically broadened to include work for what was called social justice.

7

Inventing "Progressivism": Social Justice

By universal consent, this social crisis is the overshadowing problem of our generation. In the world of thought all the young and serious minds are absorbed in the solution of social problems.

—Walter Rauschenbusch,
Christianity and the Social Crisis, 1910

In 1906 Zona Gale, a young novelist, newspaperwoman, and poet with an interest in public affairs, wrote about a process she had observed in Wisconsin women's clubs:

The initial steps usually include "clean up" days, the buying of trash baskets, prizes for back-yard improvement.... Next comes constructive work in beautifying.... This leads naturally to work for sanitation ... [to] medical inspection of school children, the tuberculin testing of cattle ... then ... the element constructive as well as preventive: playgrounds ... investigation of the treatment of juvenile offenders, ... of child labor, of factory and shop conditions in general—hours, sanitation, wages and so on, gradually *to the whole underlying industrial situation and to the economic conditions which have begotten it* (italics mine).[1]

She went on to speak of "the great new current of social consciousness which is pouring round the world."

For many women municipal housekeeping had been concrete, tangible and satisfying. The consequences were generally good for everybody. Harmful bacteria in milk and water were no respecter of persons; playgrounds and libraries were at least as useful to the middle class as to anybody else. Children from every kind of family might be found in public schools. Gale's observation, linked to Mary Beard's comment some years later about "the skeleton in every social closet," which was that "no kind of philanthropy will solve the requirements of infant welfare when poverty or labor conditions are the root of the problem," suggests that a new stage in women's activism, more radical than anything since antislavery, was leading to a reexamination of the fundamental structures of urban-industrial society.

For some middle-class women the need to cross class lines, to form alliances with working-class women, was increasingly apparent.

Reaching this point had taken a long time. For decades women's associations had recognized "poverty and labor conditions" as problems. Benevolent women and moral reformers, as they discovered how difficult it was for widows to support themselves and their children, as they observed the abysmal pay of sewing women, or as they tried to contend with the economic lure of prostitution, had begun to realize that however much the United States might be a land of opportunity, it was not necessarily one for self-supporting women. As more and more women were drawn into the industrial work force, successive economic depressions underlined the problem. References to the difficulties of working women ran through the records of many antebellum associations, and from time to time wage-earning women themselves organized to make forceful statements about their exploitation. But for the most part these insights had led only to compassion, charity, and—on the part of the working women themselves—sporadic efforts to organize or to strike.

As industrial capitalism developed, so did women's awareness of some of its consequences. One of the first projects of the New England Woman's Club, for example, had been a study of the situation of sewing women in Boston. The club's experiment with a "Friendly Association" for working women led to the creation of the Women's Educational and Industrial Union, an organization focused on the problems of wage earners. The WEIU soon had more members than its parent organization and was copied elsewhere. In 1883 after Harriet Townsend, a member of the Association for the Advancement of Women, invited Abby Morton Diaz of the Boston Union to talk, "sixty of Buffalo's most courageous women" agreed to set up their own WEIU. Townsend's hope was that the organization would be "a Union of all classes and conditions of women."[2] Women in a number of other towns modeled cross-class associations on the Boston Union.[3]

There had been other tentative efforts to reach across class boundaries. In 1869 Lucy Stone joined some women from the shoemakers union, the Daughters of St. Crispin, to urge a ten-hour law upon a committee of the Massachusetts legislature.[4] Susan B. Anthony had also tried to link suffrage with the labor movement, but male unionists found her emphasis on women's rights unacceptable and many wage-earning women doubted that suffrage would help their situation.

In many ways the eighties and nineties were seminal decades for the developing concept of social justice. The widespread influence of Henry George's *Progress and Poverty,* Bellamy's *Looking Backward,* and H. D. Lloyd's

Wealth vs. Commonwealth indicated that many people in the Anglo-American world were trying to understand the changes that assailed them on every side. Questions raised by some among the rising generation of intellectuals added to the ferment. A group of young academic social scientists, some of them educated in Europe, came into adulthood "acutely sensitive to the social and political unrest around them, and introduced their concerns to a generation of students in some of the leading universities."[5] Some of these men were close friends and allies of the women who were leading organizations. Much of the ideology of social justice was shaped in the settlement houses, in discussions that included European as well as American reform thinkers. The ideas developed in these gatherings were rapidly transmitted through the tight network of women's organizations, and began to be reflected in their talk and more concretely in the things they were choosing to work on.[6]

Mary Livermore, Abby Morton Diaz, and Lucy Stone were only the best known of those who joined Nationalist Clubs inspired by Bellamy's book, and several—Livermore among them—began to call themselves Christian Socialists. Caroline Severance was one of this group. A founding mother of both the NEWC and the Los Angeles Woman's Club, she wrote and talked endlessly to businessmen hoping to persuade them of the virtues of profit sharing.[7]

In 1888 more than twenty Chicago women's organizations ranging from the Woman's Club to the Trades and Labor Assembly combined to form the Illinois Women's Alliance to work for improving the situation of sweatshop workers. In the same years Frances Willard, as president of the WCTU, worked closely with the Knights of Labor, dreamed of a united farmer-labor-woman's political party, and in time also came to call herself a socialist.

After 1891 the spirit of the developing social justice movement was more and more visible at Hull House. In that year Florence Kelley arrived to take up residence and almost immediately found a job investigating sweatshops for the federal Department of Labor. She had barely unpacked her bags when the Chicago Woman's Club invited her to explain the sweating system to its members. She urged them to set up a committee on the subject and engaged their interest in her proposal for a stiff factory inspection law.[8]

After beginning to build a base of support in the women's organizations, Kelley and her coworkers dragged a reluctant committee of the Illinois legislature through some of the worst slums where women and very young children were slaving in the garment trade, sometimes in rooms where family members lay ill with smallpox. Persuaded by what they had seen, the committee recommended and the legislature adopted—with strong support from the Illinois Women's Alliance—a comprehensive factory inspection law which among other things established a mandatory eight-hour day for women and children. Years later Kelley mused on the fact that the bill had become law without significant opposition. She speculated that most Illinoisans outside of Chicago still thought of themselves as rural people and had not yet recognized the existence of manufacturing as a major part of their economy. As for the manufacturers themselves, she suggested, experience had misled them: they simply did not believe any such law would be enforced. They discovered their mistake when Governor John Peter Altgeld appointed Kelley factory inspector. She proceeded to vigorous enforcement with the result that opposition quickly solidified and the pathbreaking law was declared unconstitutional.[9] The whole process, however, served to educate the women involved who would continue for decades to work for the regulation of child labor and for legislation setting minimum wages and maximum hours for women workers.

The mood of Chicago women activists in the year the Factory Inspection law passed was suggested by Bertha Honoré Palmer's speech at the opening of the Columbian Exposition's Woman's Building. She told her audience that the key issue for the future was that of working women. After an ironical bow in the direction of the male view that "every woman who is presiding over a happy home is fulfilling her highest function," Palmer pointed out that only a minority of women were in a position to live up to this description, and castigated the "idealists" who did not understand how many women were forced to earn their own bread. She accused men of fearing competition from women in the work force. "Freedom and justice for all," she asserted, "are infinitely more to be desired than pedestals for a few."[10]

Palmer's friend and protégé Ellen Henrotin went further. As president of the General Federation of Women's Clubs she undertook to encourage clubwomen to study what she called "social economics." In 1899 the United States Department of Labor published a forty-page bulletin introduced by Henrotin and based on twelve hundred replies to a questionnaire the department had sent to women's clubs. In the midst of her detailed summary of the specific activities clubs had reported, Henrotin observed that "club members seem to have become convinced that the science of economics is at the bottom of nearly all their problems."[11]

Under Henrotin's leadership the General Federation of Women's Clubs established a Commission on Industrial Problems Affecting Women and Children and invited John Mitchell of the United Mine Workers to address a biennial convention. Four years later the Chicago Woman's Club sponsored a large conference on women in modern industrialism in which each department of the club was asked to focus on the "the status of woman as an economic and financial factor and the consequent change in her family and social relations."

The changes in focus which Zona Gale had observed and which Henrotin had tried to encourage can be seen in a more detailed look at the records of women's clubs in Wisconsin. There, 70 clubs had formed a state federation in 1896; by 1910, 172 clubs with 7,350 women were at work. The federation had begun in the usual way with standing committees on such things as education, libraries, and art, but by 1899 three papers at the state convention dealt with "the industrial question as it relates to women and children," and a lecture from Kelley inspired the group to establish a standing committee on the Consumers' League. This committee in turn encouraged clubwomen all over the state to make surveys of the conditions in local factories and to report violations of the factory act.[12]

Clubs, missionary societies, the WCTU, the YWCA, as they discovered the realities of wage-earning women's lives, undertook to organize working women's associations of various kinds hoping, as the New England Woman's Club had once said, not to condescend. In Philadelphia in 1882 the conservative New Century Club had allowed Florence Kelley, just out of Cornell, to use its name and its building to establish the New Century Guild, an evening school for working women. Younger members of the club provided instruction to the overflow crowds of young workers who showed up chiefly anxious, as Kelley remembered it years later, to learn arithmetic and French. For several decades the guild continued to provide adult education for working women.

In New York, Grace Dodge, heiress to railroad millions, made the creation of working women's organization her life work.[13] The report in Croly's volume on "Working Girls' Clubs" reveals some assumptions but also suggests just how pervasive was the activity that fell under this heading. Commenting on a convention of such societies held in 1890 an anonymous reporter wrote: "This convention was a revelation to a public that had only known working girls through the whining and crying of sentimental sympathizers who had nothing in common with working girls themselves. The keynote which the convention struck was Education and Cooperation. The papers and discussions by the girls were marked by thoughtful intelligence, as interesting as to many unexpected.... The convention accomplished a great work.... it established the working girl in a new light in the eyes of the public."[14]

When they were initiated by middle-class women many of these societies focused initially on providing for the "girls" things they could not afford themselves, on what might be called amenities and manners, and on low-cost housing. The more astute organizers soon realized that what wage-earning women needed were saleable skills and the power to demand better wages and hours. The Women's Trade Union League was one result of this understanding. Organized in 1903 under the wing of the American Federation of Labor, the league brought together women active in the trade union movement and a group of "allies" from the middle-class voluntary associations. The WTUL set out to organize industries built on female labor, especially the clothing industry. Local branches were established in New York, Chicago, and Boston, and later in a number of other cities. The New York branch had considerable initial success, especially in the garment trades where it played a key role in the great garment strike of 1909. Rich and poor women stood together on picket lines and went to jail together. There were similar stirring strike experiences in Chicago, and the emotional aftermath of the Triangle Shirtwaist Fire in New York 1911 gave an added impetus to the high hopes that by working together in unions and appealing to public opinion, women could bring about a great improvement in wages, hours, and working conditions. The organization pressed Congress to set in motion an investigation of the condition of women and child laborers in the United States. The findings of that study, published as a Senate document, *Report on the Condition of Women and Child Wage Earners in the United States,* provided the basis for a decade of legislative effort. While the WTUL was active in the North and Middle West, in the South, in Richmond, Atlanta, and New Orleans, women's clubs worked with the Knights of Labor, local assemblies of which continued long after the national organization had diminished in significance.

Many organizations became more radical during the great depression of 1893. Hull House, for example, lost some of its financial support when residents began taking part in strikes or when Jane Addams tried to explain to Mr. Pullman why benevolent paternalism was not a satisfactory answer to working people's needs. In the wake of the depression the Woman's Christian Temperance Union deplored the concentration of economic power in the hands of a few capitalists and advocated a "change of ownership," pointing out that the general benefit of mankind "cannot be expected as long as these great wealth-producing interests are in the hands of individuals or private corporations. The only other ownership, is, of course, the national government."[15]

There was no single philosopher of social justice, but Jane Addams was probably the one most influential among women. In 1902 she published *Democracy and Social Ethics.* It was soon required reading in many women's organizations. Addams argued that eighteenth-century democracy with its concern for the right of an individual (male individuals at any rate) to choose those who governed was an inadequate concept for the complex urban-industrial world. If democracy was to mean anything in this new world, she said, it must take on a social dimension. It was not enough to assume responsibility for individuals who might need opportunity or material aid; the time had come when a person dedicated to the democratic ideal had to assume responsibility for the structure of the society, for the well-being of people one did not know and probably did not at all understand. Furthermore this responsibility included respecting and learning from such people.[16] Addams's voice was widely heard: she spoke around the country to women's clubs and on college campuses and developed many of her ideas in articles for popular journals. Her *Newer Ideals of Peace, New Conscience and an Ancient Evil,* and *Twenty Years at Hull House* were read and discussed in women's clubs and missionary societies, as well as in the women's colleges.[17]

Ellen Henrotin's emphasis on "social economics" and her statement that women were more and more seeing social problems as problems in economics reflected a change in the basis for action. Municipal housekeeping had often been built on careful fact-finding; now, as college graduates moved into positions of responsibility in women's organizations and in the professions, there was an increasing emphasis on research and statistical analysis as the necessary preliminary to action. Like their academic contemporaries, women advocates of social justice were turning more and more to what they defined as "social science" for guidance.[18] The careful basic research conducted by Pauline and Josephine Goldmark in preparation for Louis Brandeis's landmark brief in the case of *Muller v. Oregon* was a good example. *Muller* established the right of the state to regulate hours of women's work.[19] Along with Sophonisba Breckinridge, Grace and Edith Abbott, Josephine Roche, Helen Sumner, and others like them, the Goldmarks represented a transition generation of reformers who saw themselves as social scientists, but who were still very much a part of the traditional voluntary association network.

The Russell Sage Foundation, founded by Olivia Sage, set the tone for the future when it funded the massive Pittsburgh Survey, a comprehensive study focused on a city which epitomized the urban-industrial society.[20]Much of the basic work of the survey was conducted by women. Following a similar impulse, the Boston Women's Educational and Industrial Union began to support careful studies of the fields in which women generally worked. These included such work as Susan Kingsbury's compilation of labor laws and Louise Bosworth's *The Living Wage of Women Workers.*[21]

The women who took part in the growing social justice movement were almost invariably strong suffragists. As legislation came to the center of attention, indirect influence was frustratingly slow. The rising generation of suffrage women included more and more college graduates, many of them scornful, as younger generations are wont to be, of the slow progress of their elders. In 1890 the young women had helped bring about the unification of the two national suffrage organizations and by the turn of the century they were initiating a new kind of campaign tactic, as they moved out of parlors to street corners and public places, speaking to anyone who would stop to listen.[22] One of their number, Carrie Chapman Catt, became head of the NAWSA Organization Committee. Catt, at age twenty-seven, had led the canvassing for a municipal suffrage petition in Mason City, Iowa, which only ten women in the whole town failed to sign. In Colorado and Idaho, in 1893 and 1896, she had helped organize campaigns that brought suffrage to both those states.

Some suffragists were beginning to make a serious effort to enlist wage-earning women in the cause. Harriot Stanton Blatch, home from England, organized an Equality League of Self-Supporting Women in New York. She invited working women of all sorts to join, and in short order nineteen thousand had done so.[23]

Earlier efforts to convince shoe binders and textile workers that suffrage was in their interest had met with considerable skepticism among women whose highest priority was wages and steady work. Perhaps Blatch found it easier to get a hearing in the context of an increasing commitment among middle-class women to protective legislation for women workers. Despite a number of successful strikes, and a good deal of useful experience for women who later became leaders in the labor movement, organizing women workers was difficult. The nature of women's employment, the tendency of many young women to think of their wage-earning years as simply a prelude to marriage (though many, had they realized it, were destined to be wage earners all their lives), the lack of understanding and support on the part of the men who ran the American Federation of Labor, the complexity of trying to operate a cross-class association—all required endless patience, more as it turned out than the middle-class women in the Women's Trade Union League had been able to muster. Gradually the WTUL turned from organizing women to helping the Consumers' League mobilize women's associations to lobby for protective legislation.[24]

The Consumers' League was another center of social justice thought. Though it had a male president, most of the work was done by women members. The league had begun in New York City with the idea of bringing the power of consumers to bear on manufacturers in an effort to improve working conditions. One of its earliest projects had been to publicly recognize department stores that treated their employees well and to identify (as places to be avoided) those that did not. The next step was the creation of a "white label" to certify that clothing had been made in clean surroundings by workers who received fair pay. The idea took hold, some manufacturers changed their ways to meet the standards required for the label, and local leagues were organized in a number of cities. By 1899 there were enough local groups to form a national federation. Florence Kelley as executive secretary expanded the range of activity. She traveled the country urging women's clubs to investigate working conditions in their own localities, to set up consumers' leagues if none existed, and to support legislation limiting child labor and establishing minimum wage and maximum hour laws.[25] Alongside these activities a small network of Socialist women's clubs, some in cities but some also in Middle Western country towns, contributed to the discussion of working-class issues.[26]

The growing concern about infant mortality and child labor led women's organizations to join in a major national legislative effort. The Children's Bureau in the Department of Labor, examined in Chapter 6 as an example of women's way of becoming professional, had come into existence almost entirely as a result of the leadership and grass-roots support from women's associations.[27] The initial proposal to set up a federal bureau which would gather data bearing on "the health, the efficiency, the character, the happiness and the training of children" had come from Florence Kelley and her friend Lillian Wald of the Henry Street Settlement in New York. The high level of infant mortality and the absence of accurate data on such things as "the birth rate, preventable blindness, congenital and preventable disease, infant mortality, . . . juvenile delinquency, dangerous occupations, . . . crimes against children," made it easy to persuade women that the federal government, which was in the habit of making substantial appropriations to study such things as hog cholera or the spread of the boll weevil, should evince at least a measure of concern for the children of the nation. The future of children, Florence Kelley believed, "depended on . . . the slowly growing power of women as citizens."[28]

A bill establishing a federal bureau to address such concerns was first introduced in Congress in 1906. Strong opposition expressed in the most sarcastic terms came particularly from southern senators representing textile states where child labor was widespread, and despite support from the National Child Labor Committee, the Consumers' League, many churches, and virtually every woman's organization in the country, the bill failed. In 1910 Theodore Roosevelt urged its passage, and finally in 1912, after much debate in Congress and vigorous lobbying on the part of women's organizations, the bill establishing the Children's Bureau was finally passed. The women rallied, as we have seen, to support the appointment of Julia Lathrop, a veteran of Hull House and the Chicago social justice movement, as its chief. This very modern agency, which diligently gathered statistics and made scientific surveys, also reflected its descent from the long history of women's voluntary welfare work as it deployed volunteers, from medical doctors to clubwomen, to carry out part of its responsibilities.[29]

Support for the Children's Bureau demonstrated a pattern that was more and more common among reformers as the twentieth century got underway. Men and women worked together in national organizations such as the Consumers' League, the National Child Labor Committee, or the National Association for the Advancement of Colored People, while the grass-roots support for major legislative changes such as the state minimum wage laws, workman's compensation, the Pure Food and Drug Act of 1906, child labor laws, antilynching laws, and the like was largely generated by the women's associations which had a firm base in communities.[30]

The term "social justice" must have had an ironical sound to leaders of the black women's organizations—what else had they been striving for all along? As their struggle continued, they too were developing more coopera- tive relationships with men, through the National Association for the Advancement of Colored People (which included both men and women and was dominated by white people) and the Urban League. Slowly and against great odds, these organizations were bringing some changes which could be traced through the pages of W. E. B. Du Bois's journal, *The Crisis,* or in the work of women like Ida Wells-Barnett whose antilynching cam- paign hit at the heart of injustice to black people. In the first decades of the twentieth century, local and state black women's clubs were gaining confi- dence and political sophistication, though they were still chiefly visible to their own communities.[31] The most important forces making for change were only visible in hindsight: the rising level of education, the overseas experience of black soldiers in World War I, the great exodus of black people from the South, Marcus Garvey's Back to Africa movement, and the beginnings of the cultural phenomenon of the Harlem Renaissance.[32]

The home missionary societies, black as well as white, whose part in developing the social gospel we have already examined, increasingly empha- sized economic and industrial issues. In 1918 the National Council of Women for Home Missions added to its list of books *The Path of Labor: A Symposium.* Chapters covered city industries, mountain and mill people, lumber camps and mines, and—significantly—Negro laborers. Four years earlier the author of this essay, Lily H. Hammond, a longtime leader in southern Methodist home missions, had published *In Black and White: An Interpretation of Southern Life,* in which she argued forcefully for the rights of black people to equal justice in the courts, to decent housing and fair wages, and for the responsibility of white women to take the lead in achieving these goals. "Being a woman goes deeper than being of this race or that, of this or that social station," she wrote, "women should stand together for the womanhood of the world."[33] Here and there other white women heard Hammond's message, and within the limits of their back- ground and socialization tried to follow her lead. In the small college town of Athens, Georgia, to take one example, the white Woman's Club joined with the black Woman's Club to establish a day-care center for black children, and in the process the white women found themselves speaking in a black Baptist church.[34] With such small steps was the first post-Reconstruction redirection of race relations built. The white women who believed in crossing racial barriers constituted a small minority, but one that was destined to grow in significance as the years passed.

A handful of northern white women were also seriously concerned about justice and opportunity for African Americans. Jane Addams and Ellen Henrotin, for example, went to the 1899 biennial of the National Association of Colored Women, and Addams was one of the founders of the NAACP, but for the most part the social justice train ran on two tracks, one white, one black.

The reform ferment built toward a political climax in 1912. Woodrow Wilson, sensing the mood of the country, came out of the Democratic National Convention with a "progressive" platform and went to the country promising a New Freedom. Theodore Roosevelt, thwarted in his bid for the Republican nomination, summoned a mixed crew of reformers, social workers, and veterans of the social justice wars to support a Progressive Party, its platform a summary of the causes women had developed over the preceding forty years.

A close look at the Progressive Party Convention and the subsequent campaign provides good evidence of the extent to which women's organizations of many kinds had constructed the foundations for the social justice movement.

More than a score of women sat as delegates at the convention, and Jane Addams was one of the seconders of Roosevelt's nomination. The newspapers were fond of saying that her support was worth a million votes, and one, at least, reported that the managers of the convention thought her presence more important to the chances of the new party than that of the Republican governors who had enlisted in the Bull Moose camp. When Albert Beveridge in his opening speech laid great stress upon the influence of women in the Progressive movement he was cheered enthusiastically. A Brooklyn newspaper wrote that even the most cynical politicians were conceding the importance of women's support. "The women," the editor went on, "are not deceived as to the motives of the politicians. . . . They believe that the new party needs them just as much as they need the new party. . . . [This fact] has given them a chance that women never had in a national convention before."[35] One sign of the situation came when Roosevelt reversed his earlier position and came out "flat footed," as he put it in a telegram, for woman suffrage.[36] When the issue of seating black delegates from the South split the convention, Addams stood against TR and supported their right to be seated, yet she remained part of the inner circle. Evidently he could not afford to be estranged from the women, disfranchised though many were.[37]

Jane Addams had written the position paper upon which the social and industrial justice section of the platform was based. When the convention ended, women set up their own Progressive Party headquarters in Chicago specifically to work with all kinds of existing women's associations. On 2 October 1912 Mary Foulke Morrisson, suffragist and longtime reformer, wrote a letter to women's organizations all over the country: "Now that a party has arisen pledged to a consistent and thorough going effort to secure social and industrial justice, its appeal to the club women of this country is direct and powerful, for it not only recognizes the importance and need of these things for which they have been striving, but also the necessity of their direct cooperation if these things are to be achieved. . . . "

She went on to list the platform items that she thought were most important to women: equal suffrage, prohibition of child labor, prohibition of night work for women, an eight-hour day for women and young persons, pensions for sickness, provisions for unemployment and old age. She suggested that each of them proceed at once to organize a Women's Progressive Association.[38]

In addition to the planks Morrisson cited, the section of the platform labeled "Social and Industrial Justice" called for legislation to deal with industrial health and safety; minimum wages for working women; prohibition of night work for women; one day's rest in seven for all wage workers; abolition of the convict contract labor system; publicity as to wages, hours, and conditions of labor; an end to illiteracy; and support for labor organization.[39]

Jane Addams campaigned all over the country for the party. At a giant meeting in Carnegie Hall in which Rabbi Stephen Wise spoke for Wilson and William S. Bennet for Taft, the *New York Evening Mail* thought that Addams would be "the figure upon which the interest of the audience will be chiefly centered. . . . She typifies a new and great hope in American affairs."[40] Across the country the editor of the Colorado Springs *Gazette* wrote that "the social and industrial planks of the Progressive platform have a vital bearing and influence on the everyday life of women . . . " and hoped the crowd to hear Addams would be one of the largest ever assembled in El Paso County.[41] Over and over the press observed that the effective work of women in the campaign was giving impetus to the support for woman suffrage.

The Democrats won, but the principal elements of the Progressive platform did not disappear, and in 1916 the Democratic party felt it necessary to incorporate many of its planks. It was at least symbolically significant that Wilson, running on this platform, thought he had lost the election until the vote of California, a woman suffrage state, changed the result in his favor.

After 1914 the commitment of many women's groups to the social justice agenda was complicated by the outbreak of war in Europe. Some of the most powerful leaders turned their energies to the women's peace movement. The political and social programs of many voluntary associations were hampered as some of their best workers turned full time to the Red Cross, to raising money for war bonds, to the practical tasks of saving food and caring for the needs of soldiers. However, a close look shows that "war work" in many places was defined very broadly. In Virginia, for example, the woman's division of the Council of National Defense had a child welfare committee which proceeded to set up pure milk stations, establish well-baby clinics, provide school lunches, put on a baby health exhibit at the state fair, which included black as well as white children, and establish a new boardinghouse for working girls.[42] This elastic definition of war work prevailed in many states.

The suffrage movement, though also complicated by the war, continued to gather momentum. First the Congressional Union, and then the National Woman's Party, headed by two energetic young veterans of the militant English movement, had offered enough challenge to the unwieldly National American Woman Suffrage Association to bring forth new vitality.[43] In 1915 Carrie Chapman Catt was drafted to take over as president. She laid out a plan which included careful organization from the level of the neighborhood to that of the congressional district, and on to Washington where Maud Wood Park and Helen Gardner headed an astute lobbying effort. The combination of this program, the stimulus of the militants, and the war-related conversion of Woodrow Wilson to the cause led to the adoption of the Nineteenth Amendment in 1920.

By the time the war ended, the cross-class social justice movement which women's associations had done so much to create had made some progress toward establishing the principle that federal, state, and local governments had a responsibility for just treatment of wage workers and for the health and welfare of children. Textbooks, which must always make neat beginnings and endings, picture the Progressive movement as ending with the coming of World War I, but reality is not so tidy. In fact the newly enfranchised women carried elements of the movement right into the otherwise reactionary 1920s. Once suffrage was achieved the leading white women's associations combined to form the Women's Joint Congressional Committee. The first major item on its agenda was a bill to establish joint federal-state programs of prenatal care and medical attention for babies, the so-called Sheppard-Towner Act.[44] Building on the lobbying skills developed in the suffrage movement, the combined women's groups (which ranged from the DAR to the Women's Trade Union League) pushed the bill through Congress and similar joint legislative committees in the states worked for the necessary state appropriations. This law was achieved over the adamant opposition of the American Medical Association and other male-dominated groups.

In most states newly enfranchised women were prepared with a legislative agenda that included ratification of a federal child labor amendment, limitations on hours and minimum wage laws for women, public health measures, and support for various welfare institutions. The work was uphill, to say the least, as in Georgia where despite a sustained effort to persuade the legislature to pass a bill limiting hours of work for women, the opposition of mill owners was too strong, and the bill—though approved by a committee—never got to the floor of the legislature.[45] In Virginia, on the other hand, eighteen of the twenty-four bills proposed by the newly formed League of Women Voters passed the first postsuffrage legislature. These included limitations on the hours of work, public health, prison reform, and uniform guardianship and property laws.[46] Similar patterns emerged in other states.[47] In many towns and states veterans of the missionary societies, the club movement, and the suffrage movement ran for office, promising to clean up their towns and work for reforms in the states. A considerable number were elected.

In the troubled area of race, too, the work accomplished in the first two decades of the social justice movement began to have some effect in the 1920s. Nearly every southern state had its commission on interracial cooperation, and while women were at first excluded, they insisted on their qualifications for taking part in this highly controversial cause.[48] In 1930 much of the work of white and black women in this area would come into focus when Jessie Daniel Ames founded the Association of Southern Women for the Prevention of Lynching. Its history brought together many of the streams of activity detailed here: growing as it did out of the women's missionary societies, the suffrage movement, the YWCA, and the organizational efforts of the women's committee of the Inter-Racial Commissions. The association, small and much criticized at first, in time enrolled thousands of white southern church women in a successful effort to use the image of the southern lady as a weapon against lynching.

The structure and network of women's associations that had developed over the preceding hundred and twenty years continued into the decades after suffrage, but with significant changes. New groups were called into being by changed circumstances and they competed for leaders; older associations were affected not only by that fact but by the widening of professional opportunity. Women who once would have found their careers in voluntary work were now able to teach, to preach, to run businesses, and practice law and medicine. Some of the most inspiring leaders were caught up in the peace movement, or were—as they aged—tired and disillusioned by the aftereffects of the great Red Scare.

One lively new group was the League of Women Voters—successor to the suffrage movement but different in fundamental ways. The large amorphous membership claimed by NASWA evaporated when the Nineteenth Amendment was ratified. Those people left to form the new League of Women Voters were the most active local, state, and national suffragists, many of whom were also veterans of the social justice movement. Maud Wood Park, the first national president, brought to the organization political acumen and diplomatic skills of a high order. Julia Lathrop and Jane Addams chaired committees and endowed the organization with their standing in the world of reform. State and local leagues were often similarly led by veteran social justice-suffragists. The national program brought together three central themes: social welfare, the special needs of women and children, and a concern for efficiency and economy in government. It also carried forward the intense interest in the conservation of natural resources so long nurtured by the women's clubs. While it led the Women's Joint Congressional Committee into action in Washington, in the states and local communities the league set out to teach new women voters how to be politically effective. Its citizenship schools were models of cooperation between women's groups and academic political scientists.[49] "Know Your Town" studies proliferated, initiating new women voters into the intricacies of local government.

While the LWV developed in the direction of expertise and sophistication in Washington and detailed research in towns and states, the General Federation of Women's Clubs, which had been of central importance to the municipal housekeeping movement in the three decades after 1890, found itself losing ground both in membership and quality of leadership. Whereas once every kind of club had joined the federation, there was now much more specialization. In local communities some once highly effective clubs fell back upon passive recreation: musicales, lectures and book reports.[50]

During the latter part of the 1920s and in the early days of the Depression the women's movement seemed to have lost its momentum, and social justice along with it. When Franklin Roosevelt took office, however, new life appeared in both. Susan Ware has identified twenty-eight women who held office in the New Deal days, many of whom had cut their teeth in the social justice or suffrage movements or both.[51] Most of these women had been active in at least one, and usually several, women's organizations. The Trade Union League, the Consumers' League, suffrage organizations, and the League of Women Voters led the list but there were many others. Social justice principles shaped legislation such as the Wagner Labor Relations

Act, the Fair Labor Standards Act, and numerous other pieces of New Deal legislation. Ware writes that "women in the network . . . participated in most of the Roosevelt administration's initiatives in the social welfare field in the 1930s." Not since the 1912 campaign had the close association of women's voluntary associations and the social justice movement been so visible.

8

As Organizations They Could
Ask and Gain

The story of organized womanhood does not end in the 1930s. World War II and the affluent society, the "other Americans," the civil rights movement, the revival of feminism, the shifting focus of foreign and domestic policy, drugs and alcohol, neighborhood deterioration, environmental disasters—all presented new or continuing challenges and gave rise to a bewildering proliferation of single-issue associations. Many of these new voluntary organizations included both sexes, but the traditional clubs, the League of Women Voters, the YWCA, the American Association of University Women, and many others held to their single-sex structure and kept resolutely on while in inner cities new forms of all-female self-help groups began to appear.[1] The last half of the twentieth century will provide plenty of food for thought to the scholar interested in voluntary associations.

Any stopping place must be a little arbitrary, and is determined by what the writer knows most about. The weight of this book lies in the years before suffrage, though I have taken a brief look at the two decades that followed in order to indicate how women with the vote both built on the past and went beyond it. Believing as I do that American society changed almost beyond recognition after 1941, I have not ventured beyond the beginning of World War II.

My conclusions are for the most part implicit or explicit in what has gone before, but just as a road map at the beginning may help the reader see what is coming, a summary at the end may reinforce the central argument.

It is safe to assume that none of the women who joined Isabella Graham in the Society for the Care of Poor Widows with Small Children had the faintest notion of reorganizing the way Americans took care of poor people or educated the young. In retrospect, however, they and others like them set in motion certain kinds of behavior, and began to formulate certain kinds of questions that became more pressing as the population grew and women and children, particularly, became more and more vulnerable to the vagaries of the market. By choosing an all-woman mode of organization they set a pattern whose implications reached far into the future.

Women in antislavery, moral reform, and temperance organizations were aware that they wanted to change social behavior in certain ways, but it was only in the late nineteenth century that many women began to think about more general forms of social reorganization.

When the WCTU moved rapidly from the destruction of saloons to the building of institutions for women and children, when the missionary societies, observing the consequences of poverty for the home life they considered essential to the next generation, began to turn from the study of the Bible to the study of their own communities, as wage-earning women experimented with all-woman unions, as one middle-class group after another turned to the needs of "our working sisters," they were all laying the foundation, creating the state of mind, which would characterize much of women's organized effort in the four decades after 1890. When a Denver woman's club in all innocence took as its motto "from each according to his means, to each according to his need," with "earnest intention to establish that rule as the working principle of our social order," it was an effort to formulate for itself the creed Jane Addams summed up: "[when] the identification with the common lot which is the essential idea of Democracy becomes the source and expression of social ethics."[2]

For more than a century the focus had been on women and children; gender and childhood constituted women's point of entry into progressivism. Bertha Palmer's statement in 1893 could stand for what came to be the general view: "We find everywhere . . . overcrowded industrial centers, factories surrounded by dense populations of operatives, keen competition, many individuals forced to use such strenuous effort that vitality is drained in the struggle to maintain life under conditions so uninviting and discouraging that it scarcely seems worth living. It is a grave reproach to modern enlightenment that we seem no nearer the solution of many of these problems than during feudal days."[3] She added, "It is not our province, however, to discuss these weighty questions, except in so far as they affect the compensation paid to wage earners, and more especially that paid to women and children."

Not the unfairness of the wage system in general, but its manifest pressures upon women workers led women's organizations to begin to talk about the need for minimum wage legislation. The image of little children working in mills led women to question the functioning of the industries from which many of them had received great material benefits. It was concern for women, children, and family life which had led church women, decades before the theologians began to formulate what would be called the social gospel, to talk about the social dimension of Christianity.

The idea of making government at some level responsible for social welfare had a long history among women. At least as early as the 1830s some women's organizations had turned to government to solve problems that had proved too much for voluntary effort alone. The whole municipal housekeeping effort had been based on certain assumptions about the government's responsibility for community (as opposed to individual) well-being and had constituted an implied critique of the way communities were functioning. Women certainly did not set out to build what we now call "the welfare state," but in the process of trying to solve one concrete problem after another in the face of the often implacable opposition of businessmen of many kinds and even of professional bodies such as the American Medical Association, they turned to the state and federal governments as the only sources of countervailing power. In the process they persuaded governments to take on many of the responsibilities for human welfare that they had themselves originally assumed, as well as those for which they had developed the rationale. Women were of course not the only architects of the welfare state. Much of the actual legislation had to be, in the nature of things, the work of men. Men were active in almost every aspect of the social justice movement. Certainly, too, other industrial nations have gone down the same road with quite different leadership. But in the American setting the work of women in their associations over nearly a century and a half shaped the ideas, brought about the grass-roots support, and gave our federal-state welfare structure much of its characteristic form.

Though early women's voluntary associations had no conscious end in view except to do God's work in the world, the idea of joining together as women, once established, took them in many directions. The institution of the voluntary association came to have a somewhat different meaning for women than it had for men. The latter, who had access to all the major institutions of the society, found associations a convenient way to get certain things done. Sometimes—as in the Masonic orders, for example—they offered a way to assert masculinity or to define the male sphere, a place to do business or enjoy sociability with no women around. But whatever their real or ostensible purpose, most male associations constituted a small part of their members' lives.[4]

For women—cut off as they were through most of the years considered here from the political party, the bench, the bar, the Congress, the city council, the university, the pulpit—voluntary associations became a place to exercise the public influence otherwise denied them; in a sense they provided an alternative career ladder, one that was open to women when few others were.

By using associations women found a way to shape community life and to influence American concepts of community responsibility and social welfare. Churches, orphan asylums, homes for the aged, juvenile courts, playgrounds, libraries, women's colleges, kindergartens, and well-baby clinics are only a few of the community structures that we now take for granted, but which were first inaugurated by some women's association. If we could somehow imagine American community existence without any of the institutions, programs, and ways of doing things that have been put in place by organized women there would be little need to argue this point. In the process of trying to improve community life women identified a substantial number of emerging social problems, beginning with the problem of poverty and going on to such things as slavery, education, alcohol abuse, prostitution, women's wages, child labor, industrial pollution, occupational health and safety, the depletion of natural resources, juvenile justice—the list could grow very long. In responding to these needs women sometimes worked with men; more often they carried on the separatist tradition.

Consequences for community life went in tandem with consequences for the women themselves. As they worked together they learned how to organize, administer, handle money, speak in public, deal with legislatures, deal with each other. The societies were miniature republics in which to learn about politics. For many women the result was a new self-image, a new self-confidence. Nineteenth-century women spoke often of being brought out of themselves, of learning about a world beyond their previous experience, of trading self-absorption for community responsibility, a change which, once accomplished, they found rewarding. The most active were challenged to think about the world outside their doors as had never been the case before, especially when organizations gave them chances to travel, to see other ways of life. Many southern women lectured around the country for the WCTU, while northern women came south, and Frances Willard liked to claim that her organization had helped heal the wounds of the Civil War. Suffragists, too, were highly mobile. By the end of the century women had abandoned their old habit of apologizing when they expressed opinions on political and social issues. Reading their own words it is possible to sense the exhilaration some women found in discovering their own capacities—whether to sway an audience, organize a fund drive, learn about things hitherto the monopoly of male college graduates, to observe and begin to understand general patterns of human behavior. For some people introspection is the key to developing potential; for many, however, feedback and group interaction is essential to personal growth. Creative women found just this milieu in their associations.

More pragmatically, women found support in their organizations when they wanted to run for office or carry out particular projects. They also found support in time of trouble, especially in the common nineteenth-century situation of losing husband or child or both.

Implicit in the argument of this book is a somewhat old-fashioned view of the Progressive era.[5] The women I have identified as "inventing Progressivism" from the 1880s on into the 1920s were characterized by a combination of moral fervor and dismay at what their communities and the country seemed to be becoming. Women's organizations were early on the scene, identifying issues and devising strategies.

From another angle of vision, this study shows that over time and despite widely different purposes, women's voluntary associations share some common characteristics:

They almost always have several purposes, some explicit, others implicit. The sociological concept of "goal displacement" could be illustrated in one organization after another. Related to this we can discern a marked tendency for goals to converge. The WCTU began with alcohol and moved to social welfare; the moral reformers began with prostitution and moved to welfare; missionary women began with saving souls and moved quickly to bodies as well. Even the Association of Collegiate Alumnae, the most "intellectual" of all the associations, engaged in traditional benevolence, studied the needs of domestic servants (partly for their own benefit, of course), and cooperated with the Women's Trade Union League. Until the post-1920 Red Scare, patriotic societies such as the DAR could be found working for women's higher education and supporting the Sheppard-Towner Act. The historian (and doubtless the reader) must often fight off a sense of *déjà vu* as wheels are constantly reinvented by associations that have no idea that someone has tried it all before—sometimes a long time before.

There is almost always a considerable gap between the policies and plans of national officers and boards and those of local units. This gap seems to vary with the size of the community: local organizations in big cities come closer to what national leaders envision than do those in small towns. National organizations tend to be hierarchical and run from the top. Local groups are likely to operate on consensus.

Leaders, who gather in national and international meetings, testify before Congress and state legislatures, and speak in public at the drop of a hat, live to some extent in a different world from the ordinary members, but they try to keep the channels of communication open. And whatever the reality, national leaders seldom fail to give credit for any success to the grass-roots membership.

In all their organizations women raise money in a variety of mostly labor-intensive ways and spend it with extraordinary care. They rarely count the cost of their own labor, even though it often far outweighs actual money resources in the conduct of the organization's affairs.

Some associations adapt, grow, and constantly evolve. Others become obsolete and fade into obscurity. It is not always clear what makes the difference. The contrast between the WCTU, once the most vibrant of American women's organizations, and the YWCA is a case in point. The first has dwindled to virtual invisibility (though alcohol abuse is if anything a more serious problem now than it was in 1873); the second has grown until it can claim to be the largest women's voluntary association in the world. Yet in the beginning they drew on the same pool of people and ideas.

As long as women had virtually no access to the professions or business the leadership of voluntary associations was of an extremely high caliber. All the ability that in the male half of the population was scattered in dozens of directions was, in the female half, concentrated in religious and secular voluntary associations. This changed as women had more opportunities, both because of the growth of specialized organizations and because doors to professional and business life began to open.

No woman's voluntary association, including those of socialist women, escaped the issue of conflict between public and home responsibilities. Try as they would to take their domestic responsibilities into the public arena and thereby erase the barrier between public and private, women were often on the defensive about the possibility that they were neglecting home duties. They were vulnerable to the often-repeated charge that they were "unwomanly." Women's associations have tended to operate within the prevailing social norms, yet by their very existence—and especially when they have been effective—they have helped to change those norms.

A few other general points emerge from this study. "Organized womanhood" represented an effective communications network; ideas traveled fast. Committees on exchange were one of the early inventions of the General Federation of Women's Clubs, but ideas moved from place to place in many less formal ways as well.

Black women and white women followed parallel but quite separate tracks. Despite many similarities in their interests and methods of work, the two seldom intersected. Until the early twentieth century, the vast majority of the white women in these pages shared the nearly universal assumptions of their time, and only occasionally managed to look upon black or Asian women as anything more than possible recipients of their good works. The few exceptions were almost always members of organizations with a strongly religious orientation. The three white groups from which occasional enlightenment on the race question emerged early were the home missionary societies, the WCTU, and the YWCA. With a few notable exceptions, clubwomen exhibited strong prejudice, and suffragists made concessions to what they took to be southern intransigence in the interest of what they saw as the larger goal. The first white secular organization to show any leadership on the question of race was the League of Women Voters, which in a few southern towns in the 1920s began to examine its own community situations. In that decade the slowly developing racial concerns of the women's home mission societies, the YWCA, the LWV, and the women's divisions of the various interracial commissions in the South made possible the significant breakthrough represented by the Association of Southern Women for the Prevention of Lynching. But even in establishing that remarkable group Jessie Daniel Ames felt, according to her biographer, that "in the context of the Jim Crow South white women could fight more effectively for social justice in the male world of state-sanctioned violence," so it was an all-white organization. By 1940 lynching was on the decline, but it was not until the *Brown* decision in 1954 that the long, slow preparation to deal with race began to bring other concrete results as some southern white women mobilized to promote peaceful integration of the public schools.[6]

The situation of black women was complicated by the environment of racism in which they were forced to operate. As they organized their own associations the question of whether they wanted to join with white women or to avoid them was inevitably shaped by the demeaning experiences to which they were often subjected. Darlene Clark Hine has recently argued that black women over the years have been forced to develop what she calls "a culture of dissimulation." An occasional woman like Ida Wells-Barnett spoke her mind and attacked white people with all her considerable eloquence, but many black women simply avoided the subject, got such help as they could from their white counterparts, and kept their bitterness to themselves.

The growth of bureaucratic forms of organization has been one of the defining characteristics of the twentieth century, and voluntary associations were not immune. As the rest of the society became more highly structured, so did they. From the beginning women wanted to be orderly and systematic; by the late nineteenth century there were women making a good living teaching parliamentary law to leaders of women's groups. By the early twentieth century this penchant for system and order moved into a more bureaucratic phase, as paid staff members were added to the national offices, and new layers of organization appeared.

Most of the associations treated here have been made up of women who, for lack of a more precise term, we call middle class. As such they exhibited whatever middle-class consciousness existed in this country. They were also sometimes incubators of such a consciousness.[7]

A class so varied that it encompassed people as diverse as Bertha Palmer and Abigail Scott Duniway, Ida Wells-Barnett and Mary Church Terrell is not susceptible to very specific definition. Most of the white women who joined any of the societies described in this book were town or urban dwellers of northern European descent, and they were firmly embedded in the culture those terms evoke. They would have liked community life to conform to their own not particularly analytical version of a Christian commonwealth so long as it did not take away their own comforts. It did not occur to most of them that it was presumptuous to tell poorer people what they should want or how they should behave or to try to help them move into the middle class by encouraging self-respect, by offering employment services, by providing child care, and above all by providing education. Indeed a penchant for didacticism ran deep in the nineteenth-century American middle class. But there were significant leaders who did understand presumption, who did work *with* rather than *for* people, and who could entertain analyses of social problems that called for radical restructuring of the society. These women helped to change the climate of opinion with respect to "the poor."

In thinking about what they define as class behavior, modern historians are apt to underestimate the reality of religious motivation. When Nancy Cott writes, "Religion stretched before the convert a lifetime of purposeful struggle. . . . it provided a way to order one's life," she is speaking as a contemporary who tends to see an instrumental choice where nineteenth-century women would have said they were following the dictates of divine truth.[8] In our day evangelical language has been preempted by fundamentalists and television evangelists, and for that reason has acquired a faintly disreputable aura among intellectuals. We must never forget that the effort to "bring people to Christ" or to save them from sin were enormously energizing concepts for women in missionary, moral reform, temperance, and antislavery societies. It is important to remember that the earliest white efforts to cross the racial barrier came from women in religion-based associations. If we impose contemporary values we may miss the point. Carl Schorske understood this when he wrote of late-nineteenth-century Vienna: "Where intellectuals of the next generation would see puritanical repressiveness, Sifter saw *Sittlichkeit und Ernst* (morality and sobriety) like a moralist of the eighteenth century. Where his successors would see petit bourgeois narrowness, he found civic uprightness; where they pallor and weakness, he clarity and purity."[9] To borrow from Schorske's formulation: where we see self-righteousness and condescension, nineteenth-century people saw uprightness and virtue. Victorian language sounds so excessive in a minimalist world, and the convention of never speaking ill of anyone in public is so antithetical to late-modern thinking, that we are in danger of failing to understand just how strong-minded many of these women were.

Few comfortable well-to-do people in any time or place, and of either sex, seriously try to think of a society different from that in which they find themselves. The wonder is not that so many women were unwilling to risk their own position for principle but that a few were and that a considerable number spent their whole lives trying to change things for women not at all like themselves.

Historians, like psychologists, are rarely willing to rest content with what people say about their motives. We tend to ask, What were their real reasons? Nancy Cott has suggested that "religious activities can be seen as a means used by New England women to define self and find community, two functions that worldly occupations more likely provided for men."[10] Mary Ryan, writing of a slightly later period, thinks women's associations were one way the middle class defined itself and shaped its fundamental values.[11] Nancy Hewitt thinks the real purposes were different in each of her three categories of women's groups, with each seeking to shape the community to a vision of social order derived from their particular class and cultural roots.[12]

All of these observations reflect some part of the reality. We can add that women enjoyed the sociability of meeting with neighbors and kinfolk in a setting that eschewed the frivolity that years of socialization had trained them to avoid. Such groups provided a place where hopes and fears could be shared, children and husbands analyzed without fear, and reassurance for religious fears could be found.

One final word. I hope this book is a good beginning, but it is only a beginning. There is an immense amount of exciting data waiting for scholars who will go seeking local records, oral histories, private correspondence, and who will approach the subject from many different perspectives: race, class, ethnic group, region—each had its particular form. The more we learn the more we will understand about the society that has shaped us all.

The Broad Reach of Municipal Housekeeping

A narrative description of the municipal housekeeping movement hardly conveys its breadth. I have compiled the following summary of the manifold pieces of that giant effort from the data in Mary Ritter Beard, *Women's Work in the Municipalities* (New York, 1915).

Education

I. Political activity
  —lobbying to make women eligible to vote and hold office in school elections
    —electing women as school inspectors
    —promoting women as school administrators
    —supporting child labor laws
II. Curricular innovation
  —kindergartens
  —household arts
  —vocational education for girls as well as boys
  —physical education, with special emphasis on girls
  —parent education
  —sex education
  —special education for handicapped children
  —"Americanization" classes for immigrants, adults and children
  —vacation schools
  —school gardens
III. Structural innovations
  —visiting nurses
  —visiting teachers
  —vocational guidance
  —employment bureau
  —development of schools as community centers
  —school libraries

IV. Physical concerns
  —better school buildings
  —sanitation in schools
  —aesthetic development through better design, decoration, furnishing

Public Health

I. Political activity
  —antispitting ordinances
  —medical inspection of schools
  —abolition of poisonous matches
  —support for studies of occupational health hazards
  —housing legislation
  —support for federal Children's Bureau
  —support for birth registration laws
  —regulation of milk supplies
  —pure food and drug legislation
  —regulation of dumps, slaughterhouses, and other perceived health hazards
  —support for required food inspection (as interim measure members of women's clubs served as volunteer food inspectors)
  —regulation of water supply
  —enforcement of garbage disposal ordinances
  —smoke abatement ordinance
  —noise abatement ordinances
II. Institutions
  —hospitals
  —dental clinics
  —free dispensaries
  —well-baby clinics
  —ambulance services
  —tuberculosis sanitoria
  —open-air schools
  —district nurses
  —baby-saving conferences and expositions
  —school lunch programs
  —Society for the Study and Prevention of Infant Mortality
  —public baths
  —public laundries
  —street cleaning programs
  —programs for elimination of flies, mosquitoes, rats

The Social Evil (prostitution and venereal disease)

I. Political activity
  —support for vice commissions
  —support for scientific study of prostitution and v.d.
  —laws to raise the age of consent
  —support for laws to close houses of prostitution
  —monitoring judicial decisions having to do with prostitutes, for the protection of the women
  —threatening recall of judges whom they took to be prejudiced against women

II. Institutions
  —Immigrants Protective League
  —Juvenile Protective League
  —committees for the protection of girls
  —travelers' aid society
  —societies for the suppression of commercialized vice
  —detention homes for delinquent girls
  —committees on sex hygiene of various clubs and federations

Recreation

I. Political activity
  —legislation to regulate dance halls
  —legislation to regulate motion pictures
  —support for public financing of recreation

II. Institutions
  —playgrounds
  —creation of dance halls where no liquor would be served
  —formation of working girls' clubs and societies
  —recreation centers for working women
  —municipal concerts, choral societies, orchestras
  —development of drama and pageant as alternative forms of recreation
  —organization for "safe and sane" Fourth of July
  —development of schools as social centers
  —libraries of games for lending

Assimilation of the Races

I. Study
  —study of foreign cultures

—survey of industrial and educational problems of immigrant communities
—study of conditions of Negroes in cities
—conferences on Americanization
II. Institutions
    —Immigrants Protective League
    —North American Civic League for Immigrants (men as well as women belong)
    —settlement houses
    —Urban League (men as well as women)
    —NAACP (men as well as women)

Housing

I. Political activity
    —tenement house legislation
    —service on regulatory bodies
    —support for state housing legislation
    —support for better wages
II. Study
    —surveys of housing conditions
    —study of alley dwellings in Washington, D.C.
    —study of housing conditions of blacks in Richmond, Va.
III. Institutions
    —Octavia Hill Associations
    —homes for working women
    —building of various types of model homes

Social Service

I. Political activity
    —support for mothers' pensions
II. Institutions
    —National Consumers League (included men, but largely the work of women)
    —Travelers' Aid Society
    —Woman's Department of the National Civic Federation
    —state conferences for social service
    —Associated Charities
    —Jewish Social Service Federation
    —public health exhibits of many kinds
    —schools of social work

Corrections

I. Institutions that women support or in which they take an important part
   —probation
   —police matrons
   —policewomen
   —juvenile courts
   —women judges
   —prison investigations
   —civil service reform
   —prison reform
   —legal aid
   —reformatory institutions

Public Safety

The major work of women in this area has been disseminating information about fire prevention.

Civic Improvement

I. Study
   —city planning
II. Political activity
   —city parks
   —elimination of billboards
   —protection of trees
   —creation of municipal art commissions
   —support for municipal forester
   —preservation of natural areas
   —creation of city planning board
   —creation of metropolitan planning districts
III. Practical work
   —tree planting
   —cleanup programs
   —street lighting
   —creation of art galleries
   —improvement of cemeteries
   —encouragement of garden clubs

Notes

Introduction

1. Rudyard Kipling, "The Butterfly That Stamped," in *Just So Stories* (Garden City, n.d.), 226–27.

2. Eva Perry Moore, "Educational Work of Women's Clubs," *Publications of the Association of Collegiate Alumnae,* Series 3, no. 3 (Feb. 1890): 33–34.

3. "Matronage: Patterns in Women's Organizations, Atlanta, Georgia, 1890–1940" (Ph.D. diss., George Washington University, 1978), 11.

4. The institution of the voluntary association has been available, and used by, people of all political and social persuasions. Many communities run the gamut from the Ku Klux Klan to the Green Party. So, too, with women—in our own time the pro- and anti-abortion groups are equally visible (men, of course, belong to both); women organized to support the ERA and to oppose it. Phyllis Schlafly has her legions as does Eleanor Smeal. Most of the women in this book are to be found on the reform side of the political spectrum. The other side of the spectrum deserves its historian. Donald Mathews and Jane De Hart, *Sex, Gender, and the Politics of ERA: A State and the Nation* (New York, 1990), examine the women's organizations set up specifically to oppose the Equal Rights Amendments.

5. As historians have recently begun to try to define the process by which a middle class separated itself both from the working class and from the tiny self-defined aristocracy, they have begun to see voluntary associations as one of the tools of this self-making, though there is as yet little agreement as to when or just how this process took place. "Middle class" is more difficult to define than "working class," or even "upper class." The difficulty of finding a generally acceptable definition is visible in Stuart Blumin's painstaking attempt to do for the middle class what E. P. Thompson did for the English working class. After wrestling with the problem for nearly three hundred pages, Blumin concludes that: "During the nineteenth century many Americans came to experience class not as part of a national consensus of values but in daily routines and social networks that made their lives visibly similar to those of some people and visibly different from those of others. . . . In nineteenth-century America, 'middle class' represented a specific set of experiences, a specific style of living, and a specific social identity—a social world, in sum, that was distinct from others above and below it in the tangible hierarchy that was society." It is hard to disagree with such a formulation, but it is also difficult to apply

such a general definition. See Blumin's *The Emergence of the Middle Class: Social Experience in the American City, 1760–1900* (Cambridge, 1989).

In an earlier work Mary P. Ryan argued that characteristically middle-class values were developed in women's associations and then taken back into the home. See her *Cradle of the Middle Class: The Family in Oneida County, N.Y., 1790–1865* (Cambridge, 1981). Influenced by Ryan's analysis, John S. Gilkeson gives temperance and antislavery crusades (male and female) part of the credit for the development of a "middle-class consciousness." When he writes that voluntary organizations "mobilized thousands of shopkeepers and artisans [and] crystallized middle-class consciousness," he is surely not speaking of women. Yet his list of middle-class values was comprised of those promoted by many of the women in this book: sobriety, strict Sabbath observance, domesticity, self-improvement, purposive use of spare time. If I read him right he equates middle class with respectability, thus detaching it from any necessary economic status. Working-class women certainly had their own standards for respectability. Did that automatically make them middle class? John S. Gilkeson, *Middle-Class Providence, 1820–1940* (Princeton, 1986), 3–11ff.

Part I

1. Henry Adams, *History of the United States of America during the First Administration of Thomas Jefferson* (New York, 1889), 1:1.

Chapter 1

1. L. H. Butterfield, ed., *Adams Family Correspondence* (Cambridge, 1963), 1:370.

2. Historians have used the term "benevolent society" to designate a variety of types of association. I use it here as the women did themselves—to mean the spontaneous local groups, including missionary and mutual aid societies, which began to appear in the 1790s and a version of which can be found in many communities today. The term has also been used to describe national organizations such as the American Tract Society, the American Bible Society, the American Sunday School Society—the so-called "benevolent empire." These organizations included women but were run by men, and the historians who have written about them have focused on men. See for example, Clifford S. Griffin, *Their Brothers' Keepers: Moral Stewardship in the United States, 1800–1865* (New York, 1960), which ignores women. See also Charles I. Foster, *Errand of Mercy: The Evangelical United Front 1790–1837* (Chapel Hill, 1960).

3. Linda K. Kerber, *Women of the Republic: Intellect and Ideology in Revolutionary America* (Chapel Hill, 1980), xii.

4. Joan Jensen, *Loosening the Bonds: Mid-Atlantic Farm Women, 1750–1850* (New Haven, 1986), discusses this decline in public aid for dependent groups; see chapter 4, "The Social Geography of Dependency."

5. There have been a good many undocumented assumptions about the "leisure" available to middle-class women in the antebellum years. Perhaps a few very wealthy women did have time on their hands, but generally the wives of professional and business men worked hard. See, for example, Susan Hopper Emerson, ed., *Life of Abby Hopper Gibbons Told Chiefly through her Correspondence*, 2 vols. (New

York, 1896, 1897), or Anna Davis Hallowell, ed., *Life and Letters of James and Lucretia Mott* (Boston, 1884), for the extremely demanding daily lives of two women married to intermittantly prosperous Quaker merchants. Or see Harriet Beecher Stowe's hilarious description of writing her books with a baby on her knee and the household swirling about her, in Annie Fields, ed., *Life and Letters of Harriet Beecher Stowe* (Boston, 1897), chapter 5, especially 125–33. Another Beecher sister believed that only a woman in the best of health could survive the labor required of a minister's wife. See the revealing correspondence in Jeanne Boydston, Mary Kelley, and Anne Margolis, *The Limits of Sisterhood: The Beecher Sisters on Women's Rights and Woman's Sphere* (Chapel Hill, 1988), 339–40.

6. Frank Warren Crow, "The Age of Promise: Societies for Social and Economic Improvement in the United States, 1783–1815" (Ph.D. diss., University of Wisconsin, 1952).

7. Janet Wilson James, "Hannah Mather Crocker," in Edward James, Janet James, and Paul S. Boyer, eds., *Notable American Women* (Cambridge, Mass., 1971), 1:406–7. It is at least symbolically significant that Hannah Mather was a great-granddaughter of Cotton Mather, who in his day had promoted the formation of male associations for self-improvement. Hannah had ten children and cared for her aged parents. At sixty-six she published *Observations on the Real Rights of Women* and a book on Freemasonry in which she wished that "some respectable ladies would join in a society . . . [to] promote Science and Literature." It is recorded that she was a Federalist who took a lively interest in public affairs. Edward James kindly supplied these details from Janet James's notes.

8. Mary Beth Norton, *Liberty's Daughters* (Boston, 1980), 179–88, especially 185.

9. Linda K. Kerber, "Daughters of Columbia: Educating Women for the Republic, 1787–1805," in Stanley Elkins and Eric McKitrick, eds., *The Hofstader Aegis: A Memorial* (New York, 1974), 36–59.

10. An excellent discussion of this phenomenon is Richard D. Brown, "The Emergence of Urban Society in Rural Massachusetts, 1760–1820," *Journal of American History* 61, no. 1 (June 1974): 29–51. Brown's explanation for the increase in the number of voluntary associations is "the interaction between the Revolution, the Second Great Awakening and its secular counterpart, the flowering of a romantic view of progress, and commercial development and population growth. Together these events brought much of urban society to country villages, making their old cultural isolation obsolete" (45).

11. It is important to note that even groups attached to a particular church were usually created by women, not by the church hierarchy.

12. Communication among members of widespread kin networks promoted this similarity. See for example, Lucretia Mott, writing to her mother-in-law on 2 Feb. 1820: "A few members of this district have in contemplation to form a society for the relief of the poor. . . . if it is not asking too much, I should like to have a copy of your constitution . . . " Hallowell, ed., *Life and Letters,* 71.

13. Dorothy Sterling, *We Are Your Sisters: Black Women in the Nineteenth Century.* (New York, 1984), 105–18.

14. Mary Bosworth Treudley, " 'The Benevolent Fair': A Study of Charitable Organization among American Women in the First Third of the Nineteenth Century,"

Social Service Review 14 (Sept. 1940): 509–22, has a thoughtful discussion of the problems that work relief has always presented. She used the records of a number of early-nineteenth-century benevolent societies.

15. This distinction between worthy and unworthy poor is one of the strongest themes running through all the records of white benevolent societies. The idea is embedded in the history of charity. Gertrude Himmelfarb, *The Idea of Poverty* (New York, 1984), has an illuminating discussion of the distinction as it developed in England.

16. See *New York Times*, 6 Dec. 1959, 91, for an article about the 153-year history of the Graham School, successor to the Widows Society orphanage.

17. Joanna Bethune, ed., *The Power of Faith Exemplified in the Life and Writings of the Late Mrs. Isabella Graham* (New York, 1843).

18. See especially Ryan, *Cradle of the Middle Class*, chapter 3, and Christine Stansell, *City of Women: Sex and Class in New York, 1789–1860* (New York, 1986), chapter 2 and passim.

19. See Robert Dalzell, Jr., *Enterprising Elite: The Boston Associates and the World They Made* (Cambridge, Mass., 1987), chapter 5, for an illuminating discussion of this issue. Also M. J. Heale, "The New York Society for the Prevention of Pauperism, 1817–1823," *New-York Historical Society Quarterly* 55, no. 2 (Apr. 1971): 153–76.

20. As the colonial historians make ever more fine-grained studies of seventeenth-century village life it is clear that most villagers watched over each other's behavior without shame. It is not clear when it became uncommon for the "better sort" to be thus observed. The poorer people continued to be subject to such oversight; indeed they still are.

21. Records of the Cambridge Female Humane Society, Arthur and Elizabeth Schlesinger Library of the History of Women in America, Radcliffe College, Cambridge, Mass.

22. Constitution in Sophia Smith Collection, Smith College, Northampton, Mass.

23. Constitution of the Bristol R.I. Female Charitable Society, Sophia Smith Collection, Smith College, Northampton, Mass.

24. Jack Larkin, "An Extended Link in the Great Chain of Benevolence: The Shrewsbury Charitable Society," essay written for the Community in Change Project, Old Sturbridge Village, Mass., Oct. 1979. It is regrettable that this splendid essay, a model of its kind, has never been published.

25. The prohibition of gossip was common and perhaps with good reason. Only a month after Lucretia Mott had asked advice of her mother-in-law about the procedure for establishing a charitable society, James Mott was writing his parents that she was very much discouraged because "most of the conversation at the several meetings . . . has not been very interesting, or instructive; being too much of what is called gossip . . . " Hallowell, ed., *Life and Letters*, 72–73.

26. Minutes of the Chesterfield Benevolent Society in Hopkinton, New Hampshire, Schlesinger Library, Radcliffe College, Cambridge, Mass.

27. Records of these societies are in the Lynn Historical Society, Lynn, Mass.

28. Mary F. Kihlstrom, "The Morristown Female Charitable Society," *Journal of Presbyterian History* 50 (Fall 1980): 255–72.

29. Carol Lasser, "A 'Pleasingly Oppressive Burden': The Transformation of

Domestic Service and Female Charity in Salem, 1800–1840," *Essex Institute Historical Collections* 116, no. 3 (Apr. 1980): 156–75.

30. Dorothy Sterling, *We Are Your Sisters.*

31. Anne M. Boylan, "Women and Politics in the Era Before Seneca Falls," *Journal of the Early Republic* 10 (Fall 1990): 365–85, shows how early white benevolent societies were able to get some money from city governments on the grounds that they were bearing part of the welfare burden of the community.

32. Savannah in 1800, with a population of 6,000 about equally divided between white and black, had only 204 white female children under age ten, yet apparently enough of them were orphans to call forth this pioneering effort.

The records of southern women's benevolent societies are indistinguishable from those in other parts of the country, and it is clear that societies existed even in small communities. Evidently these groups were a response to something more than simply industrialization or "modernization." There is no case to be made for southern exceptionalism from the voluntary association evidence.

33. Augustus Longstreet Hull, *Annals of Athens* (Athens, Ga., 1906).

34. Suzanne Lebsock, *The Free Women of Petersburg: Status and Culture in a Southern Town, 1784–1860* (New York, 1984), 197.

35. Barbara Bellows, " 'My Children, Gentlemen, Are My Own': Poor Women, the Urban Elite, and the Bonds of Obligation in Antebellum Charleston," in Walter J. Fraser, Jr., et al., eds., *The Web of Southern Social Relations: Women, Family, and Education* (Athens, Ga. 1985), 51–71. See also Jane H. Pease and William H. Pease, *Ladies, Women and Wenches: Choice and Constraint in Charleston and Boston* (Chapel Hill, 1990), chapter 6.

36. "Beginnings of Common School System in the South," *U.S. Bureau of Education Report, 1896–97* (Washington, 1898), chapter 29, 1394–97.

37. Anita S. Goodstein, *Nashville, 1780–1860: From Frontier to City* (Gainesville, Fla., 1989), 59–61.

38. All of the preceding quotations about the society are from the Revised Constitution and By-Laws of the Raleigh Female Benevolent Society with Reports of the Society from Its Commencement (Raleigh, N.C., 1823).

39. Keith Melder, "Ladies Bountiful: Organized Women's Benevolence in Early Nineteenth Century America," *New York History* 65 (1967): 240; Mrs. W. A. Ingham, *Women of Cleveland* (Cleveland, 1893), 139; and Kathleen D. McCarthy, *Noblesse Oblige* (Chicago, 1985).

40. Alice Tarbell Crathern, *In Detroit Courage Was the Fashion: The Contributions of Women to the Development of Detroit from 1701 to 1951* (Detroit, 1953), 20–26.

41. Darlene Clark Hine, "Black Women in the Middle West: The Michigan Experience" (1988 Burton Lecture presented at the 114th Meeting and State History Conference of the Historical Society of Michigan).

42. Anne Firor Scott, "Mormon Women, Other Women," *Journal of Mormon History* (1987): 2–49.

43. Rowena Beans, *"Inasmuch . . . " The One-Hundred-Year History of the San Francisco Ladies' Protection and Relief Society* (San Francisco, 1953). All quotations in this and the next paragraph are from this study, pp. 28, 29.

44. This is in contrast to some self-righteous benevolent societies which refused to care for children whose mothers were prostitutes.

45. *The Steeple* 26, no. 9, published weekly except Christmas by the First United Methodist Church, Athens, Georgia. Close to home I find the following note in the *Newsletter* of the Inter-Faith Council for Social Service in Chapel Hill, N.C., Mar. 1988, vol. 8, no.1 [looking back fifteen years]: "The initial impulse for calling this organization into being was to meet some very pressing needs . . . the moving spirits were the Chapel Hill church women. . . ."

46. Edwin W. Rice, *The Sunday School Movement and the American Sunday School Union* (Philadelphia, 1917), 57.

47. Heale, "The New York Society for the Prevention of Pauperism."

48. Lebsock, *Free Women,* chapter 7. The whole of this chapter is relevant to my discussion here. See also Hallowell, ed., *Life and Letters,* 136, for evidence that the last national women's antislavery convention was held in 1839 because "some of the abolitionists made the discovery that men and women could do more efficient work together than alone. . . ."

49. Michael J. McTighe, " 'True Philanthropy and the Limits of the Female Sphere': Poor Relief and Labor Organizations in Antebellum Cleveland," *Labor History* 2 (Spring 1986): 227–56.

50. It is recorded, however, that the women who organized the New York Widows Society met with "the ridicule of many, and . . . the opposition of not a few. The men could not allow our sex the steadiness and perseverance necessary to establish such an undertaking. . . . " See Bethune, *The Power of Faith.* Nancy Hewitt found evidence that the Guilford, Connecticut, church women failed to establish a charitable society in 1806 because of the opposition of a Presbyterian minister, the Reverend Mr. Elliott. Letter from Mary Stone to Mabel Hand Ward, 20 Aug. 1806, ms in the Presbyterian Historical Society, Philadelphia, Pa.

51. See Lori Ginsberg, *Women and the Work of Benevolence: Morality and Politics in the Northeastern United States, 1820–1885* (New Haven, 1990), for some thoughtful speculations along the line that men only objected to women as being "out of their sphere" when their activities threatened the established order, which benevolence, for the most part, did not seem to do. This point will come up again in Chapter 2.

52. See Benjamin Rush, "Thoughts Upon Female Education," in his *Essays: Literary, Moral and Philosophical* (1787), in which he argues that in a new country women needed to be educated for a broad range of responsibilities. He prescribed a curriculum that included reading, writing, grammar, arithmetic, bookkeeping, geography, history, astronomy, chemistry, and natural philosophy. He predicted great results from a higher level of education for women.

53. Lebsock, *Free Women,* 201.

54. Anne Boylan has examined this issue in detail in "Women and Politics."

55. Nancy F. Cott, *The Bonds of Womanhood: Woman's Sphere in New England, 1780–1835* (New Haven, 1975); Nancy Hewitt, *Women's Activism and Social Change: Rochester, New York, 1856–1872* (Ithaca, 1984), chapter 2.

56. Papers of the Fragment Society are in the Schlesinger Library, Radcliffe College, Cambridge, Mass.

57. Oscar Handlin, *Boston's Immigrants: A Study in Acculturation* (rev. ed., Cambridge,

Mass., 1979), throws a great deal of light on the Fragment Society minutes. See especially chapter 1, "Social Boston."

58. Robert Dalzell, Williams College, historian of the Boston Associates, surveyed the list of 1812 subscribers to the Fragment Society for me and wrote: " . . . while [the list] clearly included many women from Associate families, it seems to have been much broader in composition." Letter to Anne F. Scott, 10 June 1988.

59. It may be noted that four hundred subscribers represented roughly one out of every sixteen adult women living in Boston at the time. Recipients were in about the same proportion to population as the subscribers.

60. The distinctive color of layettes may have been designed to discourage pawning the clothes. Bonnie G. Smith, *Ladies of the Leisure Class: The Bourgeoisies of Northern France in the Nineteenth Century* (Princeton, 1981), found making layettes to be the principal activity of women's charitable associations in northeastern France in the late nineteenth century. The attitudes and behavior of the women in Smith's study were very similar to those of Fragment Society members despite the large differences in environment.

61. In her study of the records of Petersburg, Virginia, Suzanne Lebsock was very much struck with the uncertainty of economic condition of most of Petersburg's most prominent men; see Lebsock, *Free Women,* chapter 3.

62. In the course of his research on modernization Richard D. Brown identified at least eighty female charitable and benevolent societies in Massachusetts before 1830, and a hundred more in which men or men and women took part. Many of these were in Boston or its suburbs. Professor Brown was kind enough to share his data with me.

63. Anne M. Boylan, after a close examination of the published records of benevolent societies in Boston and New York, argues, among other things, that there was no linear development, that women did not learn from each others' successes or failures, and that some of the earlier groups were more sophisticated than those that came later. See her "Women in Groups: An Analysis of the Women's Benevolent Organizations in New York and Boston, 1797–1840," *Journal of American History* 71, no. 3 (Dec. 1984): 497–523, and "Timid Girls, Venerable Widows, and Dignified Matrons: Life Cycle Patterns among Organized Women in New York and Boston, 1797–1840," *American Quarterly* 38, no. 5 (Winter 1986): 779–97.

64. In the first twenty-seven years of its existence the society spent $20,505.85 in addition to giving away many contributed goods. Members visited 9,000 families, dispensed 28,707 articles of clothing and 6,624 pairs of shoes.

65. Like so much else in benevolent-society history, this idea was destined for a long life. The *New York Times* for 7 April 1988 carried a long story about a San Francisco organization called the Bay Area Women's Resource Center; it included the following quotation from one of the members: "It really makes a difference if they [homeless children who tend to skip school] can wear something brand new."

66. This in spite of the fact that as early as 1834 the society had recorded thanks to certain "benevolent gentlemen" who had organized a kind of charitable clearing-house that permitted the various benevolent societies to compare notes, avoid duplication of effort—and share in the ever-present vigilance against professional beggars. The Association of Benevolent Societies, as it was called, was made up of

delegates from both male and female societies. Its records are in the Boston Public Library.

67. Perhaps when all is said, gratitude is one of the chief rewards of benevolence. In December 1987 a member of the Chapel Hill, North Carolina, Junior Service League was reported to have said [about the Christmas House which the league had established so that poor parents could choose gifts for their children], "one of the nicest things is when you go around with people, they really appreciate it."

68. Could the society have sat for William Dean Howells's scathing portrait of the Social Union of Hatboro in *Annie Kilburn* (New York, 1888)? Certainly Howells would have found grist for his mill had he been able to read the minutes of the Fragment Society. On the other hand it is well to remember that male novelists, Henry James and Charles Dickens to name two, have tended to caricature women's societies.

69. One remembers the legendary, possibly mythical, New England gentleman to whom his neighbors never spoke after it was revealed that he had "gone into his capital."

70. Of course it is quite possible that some members joined other, more reform-minded groups while keeping the Fragment Society as a social base. I have learned not to be surprised to find seemingly radical social activists who are also members of the DAR or the United Daughters of the Confederacy. Some of the names on Fragment Society rolls appear also in the records of the Boston Female Anti-Slavery Society.

Chapter 2

1. An old book by Alice Felt Tyler, while only descriptive and outdated in many particulars, nevertheless conveys the spirit of the times; see *Freedom's Ferment* (New York, 1944). See also David B. Davis, ed., *Ante-bellum Reform* (New York, 1967), for a useful bibliography of the literature of reform movements. Davis's "interpretive anthology," *Antebellum American Culture* (New York, 1979), provides a wide and provocative sampling of ideas stimulated by the rapidly changing American experience.

2. Hewitt, *Women's Activism*, 97–98. The woman, Mrs. Thomas Kempshall, described in colorful terms her discouraging efforts to help families deserted by fathers and mothers who spent all they got for whiskey, destroyed the goods supplied by the Charitable Society, and mistreated their children.

3. The most useful and detailed discussion of the history of moral reform is Larry Howard Whiteaker, "Moral Reform and Prostitution in New York City, 1830–1860" (Ph.D. diss., Princeton University, 1977); for the first Magdalene Society see 45–46.

4. Barbara Meil Hobson, *Uneasy Virtue: The Politics of Prostitution and the American Reform Tradition* (New York, 1987), 21–22.

5. Carroll Smith-Rosenberg and Barbara Berg have written in detail about the New York FMRS; each found there a vigorous protofeminism. See Smith-Rosenberg, *Religion and the Rise of the American City: The New York City Mission Movement 1812–1870* (Ithaca, 1970), and Berg, *The Remembered Gate: Origins of American Feminism: The Woman and the City* (New York, 1978).

6. *The New York Commercial Appeal* on 8 August 1836 wrote about "females . . . so blinded by their fanaticism as to forget the delicacy and reserve of their sex—to

overleap the modesty of nature—and to enter upon a course . . . from which we are free to proclaim, every pure-minded woman . . . would have recoiled"; quoted in Berg, *Remembered Gate,* 185–86. It is important to note, however, that male supporters of moral reform were also attacked.

7. Flora L. Northrup, *The Record of a Century* (New York, 1934), is an in-house history of the American Female Guardian Society, successor to the New York Female Moral Reform Society.

8. Interest in moral reform ideas had begun to show up outside the city before the New York FMRS was established. See Mary F. Ryan, "The Power of Women's Networks: A Case Study of Female Moral Reform in Antebellum America," *Feminist Studies* 5 (Spring 1979): 70.

9. Berg, *Remembered Gate,* 216.

10. Carroll Smith-Rosenberg, "Beauty, the Beast, and the Militant Woman: A Case Study in Sex Roles and Social Stress in Jacksonian America," *American Quarterly* 23 (1971): 562–84.

11. Northrup, *Record,* details the later history of the Guardian Society.

12. Smith-Rosenberg, *Religion and the Rise of the American City,* 202–4.

13. See below, Chapter 5.

14. Constitution of the Female Moral Reform Society of Erie, 1839 (no state given), Schlesinger Library, Radcliffe College, Cambridge, Mass.

15. Minutes and Annual Reports of the Grafton, Mass., Female Moral Reform Society, in the Library of the American Antiquarian Society, Worcester, Mass.

16. Reports to the *Advocate of Moral Reform* and *Friend of Virtue* suggest that in small towns large numbers of women signed on at the beginning, but that in comparatively short order attendance at meetings (and eventually payment of dues) began to drop off. The reports are remarkable for their frank admission that the societies were criticized for promoting rather than preventing sexual irregularity (by talking about seduction, prostitution, and the like) and that they had difficulty in holding members.

17. Ryan, *Cradle of the Middle Class,* 119–23.

18. See Hewitt, *Women's Activism;* Ryan and Hewitt both found a wider range of social classes represented in the moral reform societies than had been the case in the benevolent societies. Artisan wives and wage-earning women joined the wives of merchants and professional men. I am puzzled by the fact that although Andrea Hinding, ed., *Women's History Sources: A Guide to Archives and Manuscript Collections in the United States* (New York, 1979), contains thousands of references to collections of voluntary association documents, not one moral reform society appears in the index. Was the subject considered so sensitive that minutes were not preserved? Were depositories not interested? At any rate an ingenious historian might find it interesting to try to solve this puzzle.

19. Early-nineteenth-century activists shared an extraordinary faith in the written word as a tool of reform. Our contemporary complaints about junk mail must have had their precursor among the hapless recipients of so many didactic tracts.

20. For the antebellum temperance movement I have drawn on Ian Tyrrell, *Sobering Up: From Temperance to Prohibition, 1820–1860* (Westport, Conn., 1979), and W. J. Rorabaugh, *The Alcoholic Republic* (New York, 1979). For specific information about women's temperance activities I have used Jed Dannenbaum, "The Origins of

Temperance Activism and Militancy Among American Women," *Journal of Social History* 15, no. 2: 235–47, and his *Drink and Disorder: Temperance Reform in Cincinnati from the Washingtonian Revival to the WCTU* (Urbana, 1984); also Susan Dye Lee, "Evangelical Domesticity: The Origins of the Woman's National Christian Temperance Union under Frances E. Willard" (Ph.D. diss., Northwestern University, 1981), and the personal documents of some temperance women.

21. Lyman Beecher's powerful *Six Sermons on the Nature, Occasions, Signs, Evils and Remedy of Intemperance* (Boston, 1829) was surely not directed at the poor and uneducated. New York City records show that by 1835 there was one saloon for every fifty people; Whiteaker, "Moral Reform," 55.

22. Mary Blewett, *Men, Women, and Work: Class, Gender, and Protest in the New England Shoe Industry, 1780–1910* (Urbana, 1988), 78–80. Blewett found women in the families of journeyman shoemakers who were active in the Washingtonian movement.

23. Rorabaugh, *Alcoholic Republic,* appendix, table A1.2. Rorabaugh delineates the hazards in making such estimates. He is also careful not to attribute the decline directly to the reform movement.

24. Hewitt, *Women's Activism,* 101, quoting Elizabeth Selden Eaton.

25. We know about Cincinnati because Jed Dannenbaum has studied the Daughters of Temperance there. We also know that in Cleveland the Martha Washington and Dorcas Society combined temperance with traditional benevolence in one organization. Doubtless the link appeared in many places not yet examined.

26. In her first public speech delivered to the Daughters of Temperance in Canajoharie, New York, when she was twenty-nine, Anthony said: "In my humble opinion, all that is needed to produce a complete Temperance and Social reform in this age of Moral Suasion is for our Sex to cast their United influence into the balance." See I. H. Harper, *Life and Work of Susan B. Anthony,* (Indianapolis, 1898), 1:64–65.

27. Rorabaugh's figures show a modest rise in 1855 but nothing like the amount (7.1 gallons per capita) he calculated for 1830.

28. Dannenbaum, *Drink and Disorder,* 196–200; idem., "Origins of Temperance Activism," 247.

29. Blanche Glassman Hersh, *The Slavery of Sex: Feminist Abolitionists in America* (Champaign, 1978), is an excellent summary of the female antislavery movement. See also Gerda Lerner, "The Political Activities of Anti-Slavery Women," in *The Majority Finds Its Past* (New York, 1979), 112–28, and Aileen Kraditor, *Means and Ends in American Abolitionism* (New York, 1969). The latter book deals with the split in the antislavery movement partly over "the woman question." See also Judith Wellman, "Women and Radical Reform in Antebellum Upstate New York: A Profile of Grassroots Female Abolitionists," in Mabel E. Deutrich and Virginia C. Purdy, eds., *Clio Was a Woman: Studies in the History of American Women* (Washington, 1980). Frederick Sanborn, friend of John Brown and dedicated abolitionist, asserted in his late-life memoirs that antislavery activism was confined to a few families and "in them chiefly to the women of the household." *Recollections of Seventy Years* (Boston, 1909), 1:446.

30. Dorothy Sterling, *We Are Your Sisters* (New York, 1984), 113–19. It is worth noting that in 1830, three years before the organization of the American Anti-Slavery Society, forty African Americans had assembled in convention to denounce slavery and call for "the speedy elevation of ourselves and brethren to the scale and standing of men." *Minutes and Proceedings of the First Annual Convention of People of Color* (Philadelphia, 1831).

31. Minutes of the Philadelphia Yearly Meeting of Women Friends, 1830–1840, Friends Historical Library, Swarthmore College, quoted in Otelia Cromwell, *Lucretia Mott* (New York, 1971), 52. Friends were in the habit of making decisions by consensus—the "sense of the meeting"—hence Mott's unfamiliarity with resolution and voting.

32. Figures drawn from the third and fourth annual reports of the American Anti-Slavery Society (New York, 1836 and 1837).

33. *Right and Wrong in Boston: Report of the Boston Female Anti-Slavery Society* (Boston, 1836), 4. The Boston Society had at least two hundred members when this was written; by 1840 six hundred women had joined. See Debra Gold Hansen, "Bluestockings and Bluenoses: Gender, Class, and Conflict in the Boston Female Anti-Slavery Society, 1833–1840" (Ph.D. diss., University of California, Irvine, 1988).

34. Jane H. Pease and William H. Pease, "The Role of Women in the Antislavery Movement," *Historical Papers Presented at the Annual Meeting of the Canadian Historical Association,* 7–10 July 1967, 174.

35. The following references, sustaining this view, were drawn from the Weston papers in the Boston Public Library and graciously provided by Lee Chambers-Schiller, who is writing about the Westons: Louisa Phillips to Maria W. Chapman, 31 July 1837; Rachel A. Hunt to Maria W. Chapman, 9 Mar. 1840; A. A. Cox to Maria W. Chapman, 19 Nov. 1836; and a number of others that underscore the independence of the women. Professor Chambers-Schiller, on the basis of her wide knowledge of the sources, agrees that the women felt themselves to be quite autonomous. However, as Debra Gold Hansen shows, one wing of the Boston Female Anti-Slavery Society worked closely with men. See again, Hansen, "Bluestockings and Bluenoses."

36. A. A. Cox to Maria W. Chapman, Nov. 19 1836, Weston Papers, Boston Public Library. I am indebted to Lee Chambers-Schiller for this quotation.

37. Hansen, "Bluestockings and Bluenoses." Although Hansen's data is important, the divisions she ascribes to class seem to me to have much more to do with religion.

38. Lee Chambers-Schiller, "A Good Work Among the People: The Role of the Boston Antislavery Fair in Politicizing Abolitionist Women," in John Van Horne and Jean Yellin, eds., *An Untrodden Path: Antislavery and Women's Political Culture* (Ithaca, forthcoming).

39. The minutes of the Philadelphia Female Anti-Slavery Society are included in the microfilm collection of papers labeled Pennsylvania Abolition Society Papers, Historical Society of Pennsylvania, Philadelphia. My interpretation is more positive than that of Jean M. Sonderlund, "The Philadelphia Female Anti-Slavery Society: Priorities and Power," in Van Horne and Yellin, eds., *An Untrodden Path.*

40. G. W. Smith and Charles Judah, *Life in the North during the Civil War: A Source History* (Albuquerque, 1966), 157.

41. Amy Sverdlow, "Abolition's Conservative Sisters: The Ladies' New York Anti-Slavery Societies, 1834–1840" (Paper Delivered at the Berkshire Conference of Women's Historians, 1976).

42. Minutes of the Female Anti-Slavery Society, Lynn Historical Society, Lynn, Mass. All direct quotations are from these minutes.

43. Blewett, *Men, Women, and Work*, 368.

44. See membership lists for all three groups in the Lynn Historical Society.

45. This was the first Anti-Slavery Convention of American Women. It met for three days with black as well as white women among the delegates, and adopted a number of highly controversial resolutions, which the women debated carefully. See Dorothy Sterling, ed., *Turning the World Upside Down: The Anti-Slavery Convention of American Women Held in New York City, May 9–12, 1837* (New York, 1987).

46. Deborah Bingham Van Broekhoven, " 'Let Your Name Be Enrolled': Process and Ideology in Female Anti-Slavery Petitioning," in Van Horne and Yellin, eds., *An Untrodden Path,* says that in Ohio signatures to antislavery petitions tripled when women took over from paid male agents. She cites *Pennsylvania Freeman,* 22 Nov. 1838, and Gilbert Barnes, *Antislavery Impulse* (New York, 1933), chapter 13.

47. The minutes show that both Grimké sisters, Abby Kelley, and Anna Weston spoke in favor of this resolution. It is intriguing that so many leading women abolitionists who lived elsewhere (Weston, Buffum, the Grimkés, Kelley, for example) were so often at Lynn meetings and took such a leading role in them.

48. Minutes of the Greater Lynn Anti-Slavery Society, Lynn Historical Society, Lynn, Mass. This was an all-male society.

49. Blanche Hersh, in *The Slavery of Sex,* notes that women abolitionists exhibited "missionary zeal" for temperance, education, improved health, freedom for the Greeks, and almost any other cause that showed up. They tended to be all-purpose reformers.

50. Mrs. Clara Moore, "The Ladies Educational Society of Jacksonville, Illinois," *Illinois State Historical Society Journal* 18 (1925): 196–200.

51. Susan Porter Benson, "Business Heads and Sympathizing Hearts: The Women of the Providence Employment Society, 1837–1858," *Journal of Social History* 12, no. 2 (Winter 1978): 302–12. This article is as tantalizing as it is interesting; Benson was not able to turn up any evidence of what brought this particular group of women to concern themselves so directly with the central problem of all working-class women: wages. Benson and I would like to know a great deal more about this group and how it actually functioned.

52. As Chapter 6 will show, this concern became almost commonplace among women's organizations in the years after 1890, but the Providence society, like the Boston Seaman's Aid Society, as far as my evidence goes, was unusual in the antebellum period.

53. Philip Foner, *Women and the American Labor Movement: From the First Trade Unions to the Present* (New York, 1982), 41–46.

54. Blewett, *Men, Women, and Work,* 34–39; Foner, *Women and the American Labor Movement,* 5–8.

55. McTighe, " 'True Philanthropy.' "

56. See *Signs* 1, no. 1 (Spring 1976): 777–808, for a series of documents drawn up by various working women's associations.

57. Dorothy B. Porter, "The Organized Educational Activities of Negro Literary Societies, 1828–1846," *Journal of Negro Education* 5 (Oct. 1936): 555–76.

58. Ellen C. DuBois, *Feminism and Suffrage: The Emergence of an Independent Women's Movement in America, 1848–1869* (Ithaca, 1978), chapter 1.

59. *Letters on the Equality of the Sexes and the Condition of Women Addressed to Mary S. Parker* (Boston, 1838).

60. Susan B. Anthony et al., *History of Woman Suffrage* (Rochester, 1887), 1:79–81. Cited hereafter as *HWS*.

61. The words of a man described as a liberal southerner were not atypical: "This most impudent clique of unsexed females." John Hartwell Cocke to William H. McGuffey, 23 Sept. 1854. Cocke Papers, Alderman Library, University of Virginia.

62. *HWS* 1:93–94. Collins's later history is instructive. She turned up in Rochester, where she tried to introduce the subject of suffrage into the deliberations of a moral reform society. This effort produced, she said, "profound agitation." Twenty years later she was in Louisiana, where she joined Elizabeth Lyle Saxon in asking the constitutional convention to enfranchise women. No one knows how many such itinerant suffragists there were, stirring things up in various parts of the country.

63. These two women would be found eleven years later lecturing for the Woman's Loyal National League.

64. Nelson A. Aull, "The Earnest Ladies: The Walla Walla Woman's Club and the Equal Suffrage League of 1886–89," *Pacific Northwest Quarterly* 42, no. 2 (Apr. 1951): 27.

65. See Andrew M. Scott and Anne Firor Scott, *One Half the People: The Fight for Woman Suffrage* (Urbana, 1982), 164–65, for a collective biography of eighty-nine suffragists, some of whom were members of the second and third generation. Biographies of the first generation are found in James, James, and Boyer, eds., *Notable American Women,* and in *HWS,* especially the first three volumes.

66. The phrase is Estelle Freedman's, in a much-cited article, "Separatism as Strategy: Female Institution Building and American Feminism 1870–1930," *Feminist Studies* 5 (Fall 1979):251–53.

Chapter 3

1. This account is based on *Our Acre and Its Harvest: Historical Sketches of the Soldiers' Aid Society of Northern Ohio* (Cleveland, 1869); the Papers of the United States Sanitary Commission, Cleveland Branch, which include account books; and the Papers of Adella Prentiss Hughes, all in the Western Reserve Historical Society, Cleveland.

2. Rebecca Rouse is virtually the heroine of Ingham, *Women of Cleveland.* She also comes through very immediately in the Rouse papers, which are part of the Adella Prentiss Hughes Collection at the Western Reserve Historical Society. Her "unconquerable desire to do good" is amply documented in her account books. Though never well-to-do, and indeed often hard up for money, her benefactions usually exceeded her outlay for personal expenses. Benjamin Rouse's letters and diary, as well as his manuscript autobiography, are revealing. He had little opportu-

nity for formal education, but after his conversion he educated himself with enormous diligence in order to carry out what he perceived to be his Christian duties. He admired his wife partly because she had more formal education than he did, though oddly enough his penmanship is markedly better than hers.

3. *Our Acre and Its Harvest*, 27.

4. Ingham, *Women of Cleveland*, 133.

5. It is important to note that many of these devices were in use in Cleveland before the Sanitary Commission got underway, since it would be possible to believe, if one read only the commission papers, that it had initiated most of these ideas. See Rejean Attie, "'A Swindling Concern': The United States Sanitary Commission and the Northern Female Public, 1861–1865" (Ph.D. diss., Columbia University, 1987). The commission's papers are in the New York Public Library.

6. Rebecca Rouse was clearly delighted, as she put it, to have the chance to see something of "this glorious country." The "wider sphere of usefulness" to which so many women referred was obviously exciting, despite—in this case—danger and hard work.

7. *Our Acre and Its Harvest*, 135.

8. Ingham, *Women of Cleveland*, 130.

9. Ibid., 133.

10. *Our Acre and Its Harvest*, 91.

11. *Troy Daily Whig*, May 13, 1861.

12. Katherine Prescott Wormeley, *The Other Side of the War* (Boston 1889), 5–6.

13. William Quentin Maxwell, *Lincoln's Fifth Wheel* (New York, 1956), 1–2.

14. Schuyler's admirers were fond of pointing out that she was a great-granddaughter of Alexander Hamilton; it was certainly true that, like him, she displayed a tendency to take charge of any enterprise in which she was involved. For a brief biography see Robert D. Cross, "Louisa Lee Schuyler," in James, James, and Boyer, eds., *Notable American Women*, 3:244–46.

15. Though the Crimean campaign was a particularly shocking case, until World War I most armies experienced more death from disease than from battle, and even in the case of World War I, the flu pandemic may have tipped the balance. In 1861, however, the Crimean War was fresh in mind.

16. Maxwell, *Lincoln's Fifth Wheel*.

17. Charles J. Stillé, *History of the United States Sanitary Commission* (Philadelphia, 1866), is the official report, written by a member of the commission. It contains detailed descriptions of every aspect of the commission's work except the work of the local soldiers' aid societies, which Stillé mistakenly believed had all been created by the commission. Maxwell's *Lincoln's Fifth Wheel* is based on a dissertation written under the direction of Allan Nevins, who wrote in the foreword that Maxwell, "using sources never before scrutinized by a historian, has brought together all the important facts...." Maxwell, like Stillé (and Nevins), did not understand how local women's societies functioned or how they had come into being in the first place. He does note, however, that the women thought Bellows a "monument of self-praise" who was "avid for power." These two authoritative books are a dramatic example of the tendency to trivialize women's work and therefore ignore its historical significance. They provide excellent evidence for the point

made in Anne F. Scott, "On Seeing and Not Seeing: A Case of Historical Invisibility," *Journal of American History* 71, no. 1 (June 1984): 7–21.

18. George Fredrickson, *The Inner Civil War: Northern Intellectuals and the Crisis of Union* (New York, 1965).

19. No one knows how many there were at one time or another on either side. Estimates range from seven thousand to twenty thousand; some societies died, others were reconstituted more than once. It is impossible to estimate how many on both sides continued steadily through the war, except to suggest that since the impressive flow of supplies and money continued, many must have done so.

20. It is something of a historical irony that even now Florence Nightingale is far better known for her service in the Crimea ("the lady with the lamp") than for her work in reorganizing the medical department of the British army. Anyone interested in administrative history, or the history of women, should read Cecil Woodham-Smith's magnificent biography. For the work of American Civil War nurses see Wormeley, *The Other Side of the War;* Mary E. Massey, *Bonnet Brigades* (New York, 1966); L. P. Brockett and Mary C. Vaughn, *Women's Work in the Civil War* (Boston, 1867); Hannah Anderson Ropes, *Civil War Nurse: The Diary and Letters of Hannah Ropes* (Knoxville, 1980). For southern nurses see Phoebe Yates Pember, *A Southern Woman's Story* (New York, 1879); Richard B. Harwell, ed., *Kate: The Journal of a Confederate Nurse* (Baton Rouge, 1959); "Sally Louisa Tompkins," in *Dictionary of American Biography* (New York, 1936), 18:584.

21. Wormeley, *The Other Side of the War,* a book by a woman who became a leader in the women's work in hospitals, is interesting for more than her autobiographical account. She was intent on recording the important part women played in the whole enterprise; she noted, "Little circles and associations of women were multiplying, like rings in the water . . . " (5). At the same time she greatly admired Olmsted.

22. Lori Ginsberg, *Women and the Work of Benevolence,* and Attie, " 'A Swindling Concern,' " have begun to dispel the ignorance on this subject.

23. See introduction to Jane Turner Censer, ed., *Defending the Union: The Civil War and the U.S. Sanitary Commission, 1861–1863,* vol. 4 of *The Papers of Frederick Law Olmsted* (Baltimore, 1986), for a detailed and illuminating discussion of the administrative methods Olmsted applied to the task at hand. He was in the forefront of the search for ways to make large-scale organizations effective.

24. For perspective it is well to remember that in the entire United States in 1850 there had been only 101 places of over 10,000 inhabitants. The vast majority of the societies, then, were in small towns and villages. Even if we assume that half the associations were ineffective, this still bespeaks an extraordinary amount of local leadership in small places.

25. The best study of the WCRA and its work is Attie, " 'A Swindling Concern.' "

26. Stillé, *History,* 180–84.

27. Mary E. Livermore, *My Story of the War* (New York, 1887), 158, notes that the gentlemen of the commission laughed when the women said they would raise twenty-five thousand dollars. Some commission members thought the whole thing a mistake. Their reasoning was that news of so much money being raised would discourage further contributions. The record suggests that the commissioners

wanted the women to work hard and do as they were told, but that they had considerable ambivalence when women, as in the case of Livermore and Hoge, proved highly successful without even pretending to take masculine direction. I gather from Maxwell's and Stillé's slighting comments that Livermore and Hoge, particularly, irritated the commissioners. There is little doubt from all the testimony of the women in the Middle West, however, that they *were* the Northwestern Sanitary Commission. It is instructive to compare Stillé's and Maxwell's perceptions of what went on in the Northwestern Branch with that of its official historian, Mrs. Sarah Edwards Henshaw, who wrote *Our Branch and Its Tributaries: Being a History of the Northwestern Sanitary Commission* (Chicago, 1868). Henshaw had been a member of the LaSalle County Aid Society, and she asserted without qualification that the work accomplished by the Northwestern Branch was almost entirely due to the efforts of the aid societies. It was she who wrote that the men who had been appointed to the Chicago Sanitary Commission had discovered—to their surprise—that the task would require a good deal of their valuable time and therefore turned it over to the women. She emphasized the intelligence and energy of the women who formed the aid societies, adding, "The northwest is full of wonderful women" (24–25, 34–35).

28. Censer, *Defending the Union,* 626.

29. *Ebony,* June 1963, and Marilyn Dell Brady, "The Kansas Federation of Colored Women's Clubs, 1900–1930," *Kansas History* 9 (Spring 1986): 1, 21.

30. Information for this paragraph came from Leslie Rowland, editor of the Freedmen and Southern Society Project at the University of Maryland. Dr. Rowland has collected an impressive mass of data about African American voluntary associations.

31. Kathleen C. Berkeley, " 'Colored Ladies Also Contributed': Black Women's Activities from Benevolence to Social Welfare, 1866–1896," in Walter J. Fraser, Jr., et al., eds., *The Web of Southern Social Relations,* describes the rapid rise of black women's benevolent societies in Memphis before the war ended.

32. Sherry Brown and Debra Goldman, undergraduate paper for History 464 at SUNY Buffalo, based on scrapbooks of the society in the Buffalo Historical Society, deposited in the University Archives of SUNY Buffalo. Brown and Goldman found that the Buffalo group included the most prominent women in town, wives of the mayor, a senator, a bank president, for example. Mrs. Horatio Seymour, one of the leaders, warned that when "artificial excitement" wore off, hard work would remain. This was a problem in many places. Ellen DuBois gave me access to this useful and interesting paper, written in one of her classes.

33. Attie, " 'A Swindling Concern,' " has impressive data that reinforces this point.

34. Bellows, introduction to Brockett and Vaughn, *Women's Work in the Civil War,* 42, is interesting in spirit as well as in substance.

35. Sumner's answer is surprising in view of his long involvement with antislavery women: "Boston, 17th Nov., '66: My dear Sir, I have read with much interest your instructive letter, in which you make a revelation with regard to the cooperative support of the Sanitary Comm'n by women, which takes me by surprise. Accept my thanks, and believe me, dear sir, Very truly yours, Charles Sumner." This letter is

reproduced in a printed pamphlet called "Women's Work in the War: A Letter to Senator Sumner," in Bloor Papers, New-York Historical Society. I am indebted to Rejean Attie for a copy of this pamphlet.

36. Francis Butler Simkins and James Welch Patton, *The Women of the Confederacy* (New York, 1936), 18–19. I am grateful to Kim Fayssoux who has allowed me to use a term paper on soldiers' aid societies in the South, which she based on seventeen manuscript collections in the Duke University Library. See also *North Carolina Women of the Confederacy,* written and published by Mrs. John Huske (Lucy London) Anderson, Fayetteville, N.C., 1926.

37. John F. Marszalek, ed., *The Diary of Miss Emma Holmes, 1861–1866* (Baton Rouge, 1979), 68.

38. James Patton and Beth Crabtree, eds., *Journal of a Secesh Lady* (Raleigh, 1979), entry for 6 July 1861.

39. Virginia Ingraham Burr, ed., *The Secret Eye: The Journal of Ella Gertrude Clanton Thomas, 1848–1889* (Chapel Hill, 1990), 185.

40. C. Vann Woodward, ed., *Mary Chesnut's Civil War* (New York, 1981), 194. Later she was kinder, describing the leader as "active and efficient," and the work of the aid society as effective. She recorded that she herself sat with "a poor soldier's wife so this society does good in more ways than one" (203).

41. Kenneth Coleman, ed., "Ladies Volunteer Aid Association of Sandersville, Washington County, Ga., 1861–62," *Georgia Historical Quarterly* 52, no. 1 (Mar. 1968): 78–95.

42. Rev. J. L. Underwood, *The Women of the Confederacy* (New York, 1906), 62–108.

43. Campbell Family Papers, Manuscript Department, Perkins Library, Duke University.

44. H. E. Sterkx, *Partners in Rebellion: Alabama Women in the Civil War* (Rutherford, N.J., 1970), 94–96.

45. Because of this connection a record was made, which Sterkx found and upon which he bases his extremely useful chapter on this subject.

46. Edwin B. Coddington, "Soldiers' Relief in the Seaboard States of the Southern Confederacy," *Mississippi Valley Historical Review* 37 (June 1950): 17–38. Coddington analyzes in detail the wastefulness and other consequences of decentralization and local control.

47. See *When the World Ended: Emma LeConte's Wartime Diary* (New York, 1957), 12–13, for a typical situation.

48. Rebecca Dennis to Governor John Gill Shorter, 25 May 1862. Cited in Sterkx, *Partners,* 108.

49. Letter from Lavia to her uncle, 16 Jan. 1862, Lenoir Family Papers, Southern Historical Collection, University of North Carolina. Heather Streets found this letter.

50. *South Carolina Women in the Confederacy: Records Collected by Mrs. A. T. Smythe, Miss M. B. Poppenheim and Mrs. Thomas Taylor* (Columbia, S.C., 1902), 31.

51. *South Carolina Women,* 58.

52. Mary Elizabeth Massey, *Ersatz in the Confederacy* (Columbia, S.C., 1952).

53. Kenneth Coleman, *Confederate Athens* (Athens, Ga., 1967), 55–63.

54. Drew Gilpin Faust, "Altars of Sacrifice: Confederate Women and the Narratives of War," *Journal of American History* 76, no. 4 (Mar. 1990): 1200-1228.

55. Underwood, *Women of the Confederacy*, gathered in one volume hundreds of saccharine tributes to this glorious creature who resembled no real woman. There is something here that requires analysis, however, for the tone is much like that of Bellows, Brockett, et al. in the North. What did the men intend to accomplish by burying these hard-working women in such lofty and unrealistic praise?

56. Elizabeth Cady Stanton, Susan B. Anthony, and Matilda Joslyn Gage, *HWS*, 2: 3-50.

57. Mari Jo Buhle and Paul Buhle, eds., *Concise History of Woman Suffrage* (Urbana, 1976), 198.

58. The range of opinions on this subject is represented in letters to Stanton and Anthony, inspired by their May 1863 call and printed in the appendix to *HWS*, vol. 2.

59. Wormeley, *The Other Side of the War*, 66.

60. Benjamin Rouse to Ellen Rouse, 30 July 1865, Hughes Papers, Western Reserve Historical Society.

61. Heather Streets, "As Thy Days So Shall Thy Strength Be: Kinship and Faith in the Civil War Experience of North Carolina Women" (Senior Honors Thesis, Department of History, Duke University, 1990), offers a powerful picture of southern women moving from enthusiasm to stoicism to despair as it became increasingly difficult to believe that their cause was just, or that it would triumph.

62. Max Lerner, ed., *The Mind and Faith of Justice Holmes: His Speeches, Essays, Letters and Judicial Opinions* (Boston, 1946), 16.

63. "Memorial Day Address," 30 May 1888, Clara Barton Papers, Sophia Smith Collection, Smith College, Northampton, Mass.

64. Biographical data is drawn from James, James, and Boyer, eds., *Notable American Women*. It might prove illuminating to make an effort to examine systematically all 1,359 biographies in these volumes to identify women who were active both during and after the war.

65. In the mid-nineteenth century there were a striking number of parallel independent efforts to accomplish certain things. Thus at the beginning of the war Clara Barton was doing precisely what the Sanitary Commission meant to do, but she resisted any affiliation. So here we see Abby Gibbons setting up a separate group to do work also being undertaken by various soldiers' aid societies. This kind of duplication would continue through the century in benevolent societies, missionary societies, clubs, temperance groups, and woman's rights organizations. Our modern sense that such duplication of effort should be avoided apparently had yet to be born.

66. This is in part an artifact of the way evidence has been collected. For all their splendid contribution it is clear that the initial three volumes of *Notable American Women* are inadequate for the South.

67. A. D. Mayo, "Southern Women in the Recent Educational Movement in the South," *Bureau of Education Circular of Information*, no. 1 (Washington, 1892), 38-39.

68. Grace Elmore Diary, Southern Historical Collection, University of North Carolina at Chapel Hill. See especially entries for 1864-65.

Part 2

1. Even on farms that were tied to the national or international market, women produced eggs, butter, garden stuff, poultry, and fruit for home use or for sale or barter in nearby towns. They also preserved food for winter use, and they made much family clothing. See Joan M. Jensen, *Loosening the Bonds: Mid-Atlantic Farm Women, 1750–1850* (New Haven, 1986), for excellent documentation of this point.

2. Many freedmen wanted their wives to stay out of the fields, but the exigencies of making a living often frustrated them. See Charles S. Johnson, *Shadow of the Plantation* (Chicago, 1934), 115–18.

3. Commissioner of Labor, Sixth Annual Report of the Commissioner of Labor, 1890, "Cost of Living," pt. 3, House Executive Document no. 265, 51st Cong., 2d sess., 1890–91, contains intriguing data drawn from a household survey of families of iron, steel, or coal workers. The statistics show wives contributing a significant part of the family income in these working-class families. See also Allen C. Kelley, "Savings, Demographic Change, and Economic Development," *Economic Development and Cultural Change* 24, no. 4 (July 1976): 683–93.

4. Max Lerner, ed., *The Portable Veblen* (New York, 1948), 124–27. Veblen's wonderful analysis of the wife as status symbol is not time-bound. One can imagine how he would have skewered the jet set had he lived to observe it.

5. A number of women made a living instructing women's organizations in the principles of parliamentary procedure. The papers of Emma Fox in the Bentley Library, University of Michigan, are a graphic example. Fox's correspondence with many women's societies is extremely illuminating.

6. For women like Florence Kelley and Martha Carey Thomas, studying in Europe was a formative experience. But how many Isabel Archers (the heroine of Henry James's *Portrait of a Lady*) there were—women for whom European travel was a way of increasing their own sophistication—there is no way to know.

7. See Elizabeth Payson Prentiss, *Stepping Heavenward* (New York, 1869), and her *Life and Letters* (New York, 1882), for an excellent example of a woman committed to the most evangelical concept of woman's sphere who was at the same time a radical critic of the way married women's lives were structured for them rather than by them.

8. Hope Summerall Chamberlain, "What's Done and Past," manuscript autobiography, Manuscript Department, William R. Perkins Library, Duke University.

9. "The unremitting ethic of self-improvement has been the sepulchre of all mid-Victorian fiction except *Wuthering Heights* . . . " (V. S. Pritchett, "George Eliot," in *A Man of Letters: Selected Essays* [New York, 1985], 74). No wonder so many late-nineteenth-century American women were drawn to George Eliot's novels, for self-improvement was their most driving motivation.

10. Stuart Blumin, *Emergence of the Middle Class,* 191. John Gilkeson, *Middle-Class Providence,* makes a conscientious effort to write about men and women as he describes the part he thinks voluntary associations play in the shaping of his middle class, but his interest clearly lies with the men. After noting that the Providence Temperance Society had twice as many women as men, he defines the membership solely in terms of male occupations. He does the same with antislavery societies. In

neither case does he pay enough attention to the separate all-female societies. Gilkeson equates the middle class with respectability, thus detaching it from any necessary economic status. One can be respectable on a tiny income, as many women demonstrated. He also sees public education as "remaking middle-class culture" (76).

11. Having said this, one should also recognize how different "middle-class" life might be depending on region, ethnic group, cultural background, or race.

Chapter 4

1. Catholic and Jewish women were part of this general outburst of organizing, and a complete history of the subject will have to include analysis of their work as well as that of the Protestant groups. The basic research for such study has just begun.

2. See for example Caroline Merrick, *Old Times in Dixie Land: A Southern Matron's Memories* (New York, 1901): "Everywhere we found the W.C.T.U. the underpinning (not one would have dared to think of herself as a 'pillar') of the church. Very many of them had in tow the whole church structure—Missionary societies, pastor's salary, the choir, the parsonage and the debt on the church . . . " (181–82).

3. The phrase is that of R. Pierce Beaver, *All Loves Excelling* (Grand Rapids, 1968). The revised edition is called *American Protestant Women in World Mission: A History of the First Feminist Movement in North America* (Grand Rapids, 1980). Denominational histories, such as Noreen Dunn Tatum, *A Crown of Service: A Story of Woman's Work in the Methodist Episcopal Church South from 1878 to 1940* (Nashville, 1960), document Beaver's assertion. Patricia R. Hill, *The World Their Household: The American Woman's Foreign Mission Movement and Cultural Transformation, 1870–1920* (Ann Arbor, 1985), is a recent effort to understand the significance of the foreign missionary societies. There are mountains of primary documents on the subject awaiting the attention of a patient social historian. See, for example, Hinding, ed., *Women's History Sources,* for hundreds of entries listing manuscript records and personal documents of women's missionary societies. The libraries of the various Protestant denominations and of the divinity schools are also filled with unexamined data.

4. For Doremus, see Hill, *The World Their Household,* 45–47.

5. *Heathen Woman's Friend* 1 (May 1869): 2, cited in Hill, *The World Their Household,* 37.

6. 1888 General Conference Journal, 51–52, 63, 97–98, 103–6, 112, 483, cited in Theodore L. Agnew, "Reflections on the Woman's Foreign Missionary Movement in Late 19th Century American Methodism," *Methodist History* (Lake Junaluska, N.C.) 6 (January 1968): 1–14. Agnew has fascinating data though he does not develop its implications.

7. Evelyn Brooks, "The Women's Movement in the Black Baptist Church, 1880–1920" (Ph.D. diss., University of Rochester, 1984), is a splendid study on several counts. Brooks shows that as early as the 1870s black women had begun to show interest in separate organizational work, and attributes this move for independence in part to the educational philosophy of the black colleges committed to creating leaders among freed women. Since missionary women helped to create the colleges in the first place, this was an interactive influence.

8. This story is the central theme of Beaver, *All Loves Excelling,* and of Hill, *The World Their Household.* Jane Hunter, *Gospel of Gentility* (New Haven, 1984), focuses on the women missionaries themselves. Joan Jacobs Brumberg, *Mission for Life: The Story of the Family of Adoniram Judson* (New York, 1980), uses one family of missionaries "as demonstration and symbol of the workings of evangelical religious culture."

9. Beaver, *All Loves Excelling,* 129.

10. Recollections in my family suggest that my grandmother prepared for her missionary meetings as a good student would prepare for a class. When her daughters went to Boston (from Georgia) to go to college, she went with them and enrolled in what appears to have been a kind of graduate program in church work.

11. Joan Jacobs Brumberg, "Zenanas and Girlless Villages: The Ethnology of American Evangelical Women, 1870–1910," *Journal of American History* 69, no. 2 (September 1982): 347–71. Brumberg's thesis is provocative, and her data fascinating. Evidence that might sustain part of her thesis abounds in the diary of Martha Foster Crawford, a missionary to China, whose comments on the depravity of Chinese men reflect the missionary society view of the status of women there. The diary is in the Manuscript Department of Perkins Library, Duke University. Brumberg's overall interpretation differs somewhat from the one offered here.

12. Peggy Pascoe, *Relations of Rescue: The Search for Female Moral Authority in the American West, 1874–1939* (New York, 1990), presents an intriguing view of the work of associations that she variously designates as missionary and benevolent societies in the west.

13. For Haygood, see Oswald E. and Anna M. Brown, *Life and Letters of Laura Askew Haygood* (Nashville, 1904). Ruth Esther Meeker, *Six Decades of Service: A History of the Woman's Home Missionary Society of the Methodist Episcopal Church* (Cincinnati, 1969), is a labor of love by a member of the northern Methodist church. Though not a scholarly monograph, it contains many important bits of information. See also Helen Emery Falls, "Baptist Women in Mission Support in the Nineteenth Century," *Baptist History and Heritage* 12 (Jan. 1977): 26–36, and Lois A. Boyd and R. Douglas Breckenridge, *Presbyterian Women in America: Two Centuries of a Quest for Status* (Westport, Conn., 1983), chapters 2, 3, and 13.

14. See especially Virginia Lieson Brereton, "Preparing Women for the Lord's Work: The Story of Three Methodist Training Schools, 1880–1941" in Hilah F. Thomas and Rosemary Skinner Keller, *Women in New Worlds* (Nashville, 1981), 178–99.

15. Lella A. Clark, "History of the Home Missionary Society of Vineville Mulberry Church" (in Macon, Georgia), manuscript in the James Osgood Andrew Clark Papers, Emory University, Department of Special Collections, Atlanta, Georgia. The strange use of the passive voice suggests that she wanted to communicate proper female modesty.

16. The Methodist church had split over the issue of slavery in 1844 and was not to be reunited until 1939.

17. Arabel W. Alexander, *The Life and Work of Lucinda Helm* (Nashville, 1904), 13.

18. Hill, *The World Their Household,* describes the reaction of women dedicated to the foreign missionary movement who argued that theirs was the form of

missionary work which provided the greatest opportunity for women to contribute to the Christianization of the world. See 56–57. Lella Clark, "History of the Home Mission Society," discusses the way this issue was perceived in her local society.

19. *Our Homes* 3 (May 1894): 8, quoted in John Patrick McDowell, *The Social Gospel in the South: The Woman's Home Mission Movement in the Methodist Episcopal Church, South, 1886–1939* (Baton Rouge, 1982), 20.

20. Clark, "History of the Home Mission Society," 8–12.

21. *Our Homes* 11 (Feb. 1902): 3, quoted in McDowell, *Social Gospel*, 41.

22. Bertha Payne Newell, "Social Work of Women in the Churches: I. Methodist Episcopal Church, South," *Journal of Social Forces* 1 (Mar. 1923): 310.

23. See Anne F. Scott, "Most Invisible of All: Black Women's Voluntary Associations," *Journal of Southern History* 56, no. 1 (Feb. 1990): 9–13.

24. Philip A. Bruce, *The Plantation Negro as a Freeman: Observations on His Character, Condition and Prospects in Virginia* (New York and London, 1889), 5. See also Beverly Guy-Sheftall, "Daughters of Sorrow: Attitudes Toward Black Women, 1880–1920" (Ph.D. diss., Emory University, 1984), which is the best available study of the attitudes of white people (and black men) toward black women during the years 1880 to 1920.

25. Earl Porter, *Trinity and Duke* (Durham, N.C., 1964), chapter 4, "The Bassett Affair."

26. A simple listing of the women's missionary societies in the African Methodist Episcopal Church fills twenty pages in *The Encyclopaedia of the African Methodist Episcopal Church*, 2d ed. (Philadelphia, 1947), 424–43. A splendid research project awaits the historian who investigates this largely unexamined body of data.

27. Barbara Sicherman and Carol Hurd Green, eds., *Notable American Women: The Modern Period* (Cambridge, Mass., 1980), 125–27.

28. *Our Homes* 6 (Jan. 1897): 5, cited in McDowell, *Social Gospel*, 84. It took remarkable courage for women to assert their religious convictions on a subject so deeply and emotionally imbedded in the mores of their own communities. See Lily H. Hammond, *Southern Women and Racial Adjustment* (Lynchburg, Va., 1917).

29. See Lily H. Hammond, *In Black and White* (New York, 1914), 65. "The women of the Southern Methodist church are the only ones in the South as yet carrying on organized work for Negroes," Mrs. Hammond wrote. She went on to draw the connection between this and the social gospel. (Typically, given the year, Hammond completely failed to see the work of black women's own associations.) She wrote frequently for southern Methodist publications, and, with Belle Bennett, Mary and Lucinda Helm, Bertha Payne Newell, and Carrie Parks Johnson, would make a splendid focus for a collective biography of southern Methodist women.

30. See Mary Frederickson, "Shaping a New Society," in Thomas and Keller, *Women in New Worlds*, 345–61; Jacquelyn Hall, *Revolt Against Chivalry* (New York, 1979); also McDowell, *Social Gospel*, chapter 4. Lester Salamon, "The Time Dimension in Policy Evaluation: The Case of the New Deal and Reform Experiments," *Public Policy* (Spring 1979), suggests an important consideration: how long do you have to wait before deciding that some policy initiative had a significant effect? Salamon discusses the New Deal experiments in promoting home ownership, and relates them to strong male participants in the civil rights movement in Holmes

County, Mississippi—all of whom owned their own land. Similarly, one might study these early efforts and what the white women called "interracial work" and relate them to the later participation in civil rights and school integration.

31. Robert T. Handy, *We Witness Together: A History of the Cooperative Home Missions* (New York, 1956), 33.

32. Beaver, *All Loves Excelling*, 143–45.

33. Tatum, *A Crown of Service*, 37–40 and ff.

34. See section 4, "The Status of Women in Institutional Church Life," in Thomas and Keller, *Women in New Worlds*. Many members of the congress opposed woman suffrage on the grounds that "the women of my state do not want to vote."

35. Both the Crusade and the WCTU have been the subject of important recent scholarship. Among the best works are: Ruth Bordin, *Woman and Temperance: The Quest for Power and Liberty, 1873–1900* (Philadelphia, 1980); idem., *Frances Willard* (Chapel Hill, 1986); Barbara Epstein, *The Politics of Domesticity: Women, Evangelism, and Temperance in Nineteenth-Century America* (Middletown, 1980); Jack S. Blocker, *"Give to the Winds Thy Fears": The Woman's Temperance Crusade, 1873–1874* (Westport, Conn., 1985); Norman Clark, *Deliver Us from Evil: An Interpretation of American Prohibition* (New York, 1976); and Susan Dye Lee, "Evangelical Domesticity: The Origin of the Woman's National Temperance Union Under Frances E. Willard," (Ph.D. diss., Northwestern University, 1980).

36. Readers will recall that exactly these tactics had been used in the early days of the antebellum Moral Reform crusade.

37. Helen Macbeth, writing to her Glessner relatives in Chicago, Glessner Papers, 1874, Chicago Historical Society, copies in the possession of Percy Maxim Lee of Mystic, Connecticut. Macbeth went on, speaking of her sister-in-law: "Rache is so absorbed with Temperance (but I do believe saturated would be a better word) I think if you asked her for a receipt for cake or how to clean house . . . and her mouth would be open to reply, Temperance would force itself out. . . . Good is being done and I ought not to say a word against any of it." She added that her brother, Rache's husband, was trying to stop drinking. Helen herself said she did not have the courage to march, but finally she took part in entertaining men who came to the temperance coffeehouse, and was surprised to find among them one who "looked like an idiot" but who was a "fine Shakespeare scholar."

38. Mary Austin, *Earth Horizon* (New York, 1932). The whole of chapter 6 bears on the temperance movement. Austin understood the multiple meanings of the WCTU to its members and writes eloquently on the subject.

39. Blocker, *"Give to the Winds,"* 97–98, gives these figures. Bordin, *Woman and Temperance,* 28, is the source for the proportion of saloons in Ohio. Bordin thinks Blocker's figures are uncertain. See *Woman and Temperance,* 185 n. 52; see also 25–26 for her thoughts about why women marched. W. J. Rorabaugh, reviewing Blocker's book, also found the statistics problematical. He says that the number of licensed liquor dealers is not related to consumption. Overall, however, he called Blocker's book "rich in data and insights." *American Historical Review* 91, no. 2 (Apr. 1986): 473.

40. Blocker, *"Give to the Winds,"* 24.

41. Patricia Hill takes issue with this description, saying that the missionary societies, taken together, encompassed more women. However, they were divided by

denomination, race, and region, while the WCTU was a single organization. See *The World Their Household,* 8.

42. Bordin, *Woman and Temperance,* xiii–xiv. It was discovering this fact, Bordin says, which led to her interest in writing about the temperance movement. In a parallel case, Rebecca Latimer Felton in Georgia joined the WCTU because she thought it the only way to secure a juvenile correction facility.

43. Judith MacArthur, "Children and Women First: the Texas Women's Christian Temperance Union and Social Welfare Reform," an unpublished paper in the possession of the author, which argues that the Texas WCTU was the leader in social reform in that state well into the twentieth century. Also Carolyn DeSwarte Gifford and June O. Underwood, "Intertwined Ribbons: The Equal Suffrage Association and the WCTU: Kansas 1886–1896" (Paper delivered at a conference on "The Female Sphere: Dynamics of Women Together in Nineteenth-Century America," New Harmony, Indiana, 8–10 Oct. 1981), for further evidence on this point.

44. *Zion's Herald,* 21 Apr. 1937, quoting from an address given forty years before. Clipping in the Susan B. Anthony file of the National American Woman Suffrage Association Papers, Library of Congress, Box 76.

45. Bordin, *Frances Willard,* 11.

46. Minutes of the Wellfleet, Mass., WCTU, Schlesinger Library, Radcliffe College, Cambridge, Mass.

47. What follows is drawn from the manuscript minutes of the Ladies Temperance League of Oberlin, Ohio, in the archives of Oberlin College. The minutes run from March 1874 to April 1882, with a gap of two years between late 1875 and 1877, and are written by several hands. One secretary was careful to report in detail what the women said. Later secretaries were less conscientious, and so conveyed less of the full spirit of the meetings. Even so the style and values of the women are reflected in their record. It is worth noting that the president of the LTL had been first principal of the Ladies Department of Oberlin College, and was a graduate of Zilpah Grant's school in Ipswich, Mass.

48. Both records are in the Schlesinger Library, Radcliffe College, Cambridge, Mass. Most of the history of women's associations so far compiled has been based on state and national records, or on printed annual reports, which are more accessible than local records. Yet local records do exist, as is evident in Hinding, ed., *Women's History Sources;* until we know more of what was going on in communities, our understanding of these associations will be incomplete.

49. WCTU Record Book in the Special Collections of Berea College Library.

50. Austin, *Earth Horizon,* 142–43. See also Mrs. J. J. Ansley, *History of the Georgia Woman's Christian Temperance Union* (Columbus, Ga., 1914), chapter 3.

51. Belle Kearney, *A Slaveholder's Daughter* (New York, 1900), 149.

52. Ansley, *History,* 144. The quotation in the next paragraph is from Ansley, 145.

53. Anastasia Sims, "'The Sword of the Spirit': The WCTU and Moral Reform in North Carolina, 1883–1933," *North Carolina Historical Review* 64, no. 4 (Oct. 1987): 394–415.

54. Convention of 1889, 23, quoted in Sims, "'The Sword.'"

55. Merrick, *Old Times,* 15–16.

56. Quotations are from Lee, "Evangelical Domesticity," 159–60. See also Carolyn

DeSwarte Gifford, "For God and Home and Native Land: The W.C.T.U.'s Image of Woman in the Late Nineteenth Century," in Thomas and Keller, *Women in New Worlds,* 310–27.

57. See Mari Jo Buhle, "Politics and Culture in Women's History," in *Feminist Studies* 6, no. 1 (Spring 1980): 37–42, for evidence of the WCTU functioning as a training ground for socialist women.

58. Though the YWCA has been a major institution in American life since the last quarter of the nineteenth century, there is as yet no comprehensive scholarly history of the organization. In 1975 the New York City YWCA had an NEH grant to produce its own history, and managed to organize its archives, but the historian chosen to write the monograph apparently gave up in despair. The sources are voluminous, which may be part of the problem. Mary S. Sims, *The Natural History of a Social Institution: The YWCA* (New York, 1936), is filled with information. Though she used principally printed sources, Sims was a sensitive observer, and recognized many of the problems inherent in the life of an association that aspired to work across class lines. What follows is based largely on Sims's work. I hope that a scholarly history—or histories—will soon emerge from the work of several young scholars who are studying various aspects of the YWCA.

59. Carroll Wright, *Working Girls of Boston* (Washington, 1889), provides a good overview of the needs of such women. Their situation aroused great interest among middle-class women in many associations—it will indeed emerge as a theme of much that follows here.

60. Sims, *Natural History,* 12.

61. Ibid., 16.

62. Ibid., 18–19. This self-image has lived on: in the winter of 1987 the YWCA in California advertised its purpose as "equality for women and racial justice."

63. Sims, *Natural History,* 71.

64. This idea is fully developed in Chapter 7.

65. Records are in the Schlesinger Library, Radcliffe College, Cambridge, Mass., beginning in the minutes book of the Cambridgeport WCTU for 1889–92.

66. The distinction between "ladies" and "girls" carries overtones of class, but it may have begun because most wage-earning women were very young, while most organizers of the WCTU or the YWCA were at least in their thirties.

67. Joanne Meyerowitz, *Women Adrift: Independent Wage Earners in Chicago, 1880–1930* (Chicago, 1988), offers a very important analysis of the interaction between middle-class women and young working women who were the major beneficiaries of the low-cost boarding houses.

68. Frances Saunders Taylor, " 'On the Edge of Tomorrow': Southern Women, the Student YWCA, and Race, 1920–1944" (Ph.D. diss., Stanford University, 1984), suggests just how rich this topic can be. Taylor found that on southern campuses in the twenties and thirties a handful of young white women, working with the black women hired to be staff members for the campus-based Y, pioneered in ways their elders did not risk in the areas of race relations and social equality. It was not easy, and the effort was characterized by much backsliding and community opposition. Yet the young women persisted and in so doing prepared the way for white student participation in the civil rights movement in the 1960s.

69. Ken Fones-Wolf, "Gender, Class, and the Industrial Work of the Philadelphia YM and YWCA, 1900–1920" (Paper delivered at the American Studies Association Convention, Philadelphia, Pa., November 1983).

70. See also Ken Fones-Wolf, *Trade Union Gospel: Christianity and Labor in Industrial Philadelphia, 1865–1915* (Philadelphia, 1989).

71. One recent study is Nancy Boyd, *Emissaries: The Overseas Work of the American YWCA 1895–1970* (New York, 1987).

Chapter 5

1. Mrs. Jane Cunningham Croly, *History of the Woman's Club Movement in America* (New York, 1898), 218.

2. A typical example, also from Little Rock: "In thinking of woman, her club days and ways, and rejoicing in both there comes an echo from the past—that clubless past of our grandmothers. Have you ever considered their voiceless condition and been thankful in your day and generation?" Croly, *History*, 227.

3. In "The 'New Woman' in the New South," *South Atlantic Quarterly* 61 (Autumn 1962): 417–83, I pointed to the importance of women's clubs in the development of southern progressivism. Darlene Roth, "Matronage: Patterns in Women's Organizations, Atlanta, Georgia, 1890–1940" (Ph.D. diss., George Washington University, 1978), was a pioneering work of considerable originality. Roth is still the only scholar who has undertaken cross-racial comparison of women's organizations. Unfortunately her study has never been published, but it is available from University Microfilms. Karen Blair, *The Clubwoman as Feminist* (New York, 1980), was the first extended published treatment of the club phenomenon. Recently there has been an upsurge of interest in the subject as the footnotes in this and the following chapter will suggest.

4. Dorothy Porter, "The Organized Activities of Negro Literary Societies," *Journal of Negro Education* 5 (Oct. 1936): 555–76.

5. It is easy to forget how many of the men who shaped both local and national politics in the nineteenth century were self-educated. Even leading intellectuals sometimes had very little formal education. Possibly the most extreme example was Lester Ward, one of the founders of American sociology, but there were many others.

6. AB to LS, dated "Wednesday." From internal evidence 1847. Blackwell Papers, Schlesinger Library, Radcliffe College, Cambridge, Mass.

7. Manuscript diary, Manuscript Department, Perkins Library, Duke University.

8. The deeply felt desire for and the value placed on formal education emerge clearly from the thousands of biographical sketches collected by the Emma Willard Association in the 1890s. Many diaries and letters also bear witness to the sense of deprivation many women felt and to their envy of their brothers' opportunities.

9. It is not easy to say exactly what constituted a "college" in the nineteenth century. Certain ambitious female seminaries had called themselves colleges in the antebellum years, but none of them came as close to matching the curriculum of the male colleges as did the best seminaries. Vassar at least aspired to the standards of a male college.

10. Years later Caroline Severance, one of the founders of the NEWC, reflected

upon the choice of name: "The title of 'club' had been chosen after considerable discussion as being broad, significant and novel, and with the hope ... that it would be redeemed from the objectional features of so many of the clubs of men. ... It was a 'woman's club'—an unknown quantity heretofore. ... " See Ella Giles Ruddy, ed., *The Mother of Clubs: Caroline M. Seymour Severance* (Los Angeles, 1906), 22. It is difficult for a twentieth-century person to grasp the excitement which these early clubs engendered in their members. Records of the New England Woman's Club in the Schlesinger Library, Radcliffe College, and Jane Croly's introduction to her *History of the Woman's Club Movement* as well as many of the reports contained therein give some sense of the widespread excitement of the first generation of clubwomen as they embarked on this new adventure.

11. Minutes of the New England Woman's Club, 6 Nov. 1868, vol. 2, box 3, Schlesinger Library, Radcliffe College, Cambridge, Mass.

12. Louisa May Alcott, who moved in the same circle, dramatized these burdens in her novel *Work* (New York, 1977). Jane Addams must have listened to many of these self-righteous conversations; at the turn of the century she published an impassioned discussion of the situation from the domestic servant's point of view in *Democracy and Social Ethics* (New York, 1902).

13. Claudia L. Bushman, *"A Good Poor Man's Wife," Being a Chronicle of Harriet Hanson Robinson and Her Family in Nineteenth-Century New England* (Hanover, 1981), chapter 11. See also the manuscript diary of Harriet Hanson Robinson, Schlesinger Library, Radcliffe College, Cambridge, Mass., for much more detail with respect to Robinson and women's clubs.

14. Papers of this extraordinary association are in the Schlesinger Library, Radcliffe College. In all the publicity about the Woods Hole Oceanographic Institution, I have yet to see any reference to its origin as an experiment in adult education for women.

15. Croly, *History*, 15–16.

16. "Memories of Jennie June Croly," manuscript in Caroline Severance Papers, Huntington Library, San Marino, California, and her essay on Sorosis, in Croly, *History*.

17. Kate Gannett Wells, writing in *The Arena* 6, no. 33 (Aug. 1892): 270, as part of a "Symposium on Women's Clubs," remembered that "mild sarcasm, staid rebukes and uplifted eyebrows of conservatism" had greeted the founding of the NEWC; she added, "Society stood aloof but the well-known intelligence and public spirit of the founders compelled recognition." The quotation from the *Boston Transcript* is preserved in the NEWC Papers, Box 11, Schlesinger Library, Radcliffe College.

18. Croly, *History*, 21.

19. There is an excellent, detailed discussion of the Association for the Advancement of Women in Blair, *Clubwoman*, 39–56. Carolyn J. Stefanco, "Pathways to Power: Women and Voluntary Associations in Denver, Colorado, 1876–1893" (Ph.D. diss., Duke University, 1987), describes the energizing effect of an AAW meeting in Denver in 1889.

20. Sallie Southall Cotten to Kate Connor, 12 Aug. 1884. Cotten Papers, Southern Historical Collection, University of North Carolina, Chapel Hill, N.C. A year earlier her letters to her dear friend Connor had dwelt upon entering her pickles in

the county fair, and on hog killing. Cotten fits the description of a woman who all her life yearned for ever more education. As a busy farm wife with nine children she somehow found time to read, and to discuss her reading with Connor, a single woman teacher.

21. Croly, *History,* 379.

22. Theodora Penny Martin, *The Sound of Our Own Voices: Women's Study Clubs, 1860–1910* (Boston, 1987). Martin has made good use of the material in Croly's book. She sees principally the very best side of the study clubs.

23. Marilyn Dell Brady, "Kansas Federation of Colored Women's Clubs, 1900–1930," *Kansas History* 9, no. 1 (Spring 1986): 19–30.

24. Chamberlain, "What's Done and Past."

25. Croly, *History,* 54–60.

26. Stella L. Christian, ed., *History of the Texas Federation of Women's Clubs* (Houston, 1919), 37.

27. Croly, *History,* 51 and 314.

28. *History of the Chicago Woman's Club.* Printed by order of the Board, 26 Sept. 1888.

29. Croly, *History,* 1080.

30. *The Arena* 32 (Aug. 1892): 365–66.

31. Marion Talbot and Lois Kimball Mathews Rosenberry, *The History of the American Association of University Women, 1881–1931* (Boston, 1931). A modern study of this very interesting organization is badly needed.

32. The manuscript records of the Mothers' Club are in the Schlesinger Library and run from 1881 to 1941. I was led to read these records by an excellent seminar paper written by Martha Hodes for my course, The Social History of Women's Voluntary Associations, at Harvard in the spring of 1984. Some of Hodes's formulations appear in what follows. Forty years earlier, mothers' associations had met to consider the best way to achieve salvation for their children; forty years later, activities of this sort would engage many clubs under the label "child study."

33. Health reformers since the 1840s had been insisting upon the virtues of whole wheat flour and the evils of sugar.

34. This summary narrative can hardly convey the amount of detailed work the women undertook in order to bring about the results here described. Material in the papers of the Mothers' Club and the Almy Family Papers provides a graphic picture of the steady effort required to bring such a project to life and then to sustain it.

35. In this club of academic and professional wives, located in the town where the Harvard Annex was beginning to function, one would expect to find a disproportionate number of daughters, born in the 1880s and 1890s, going to college. The minutes reveal the mothers' intense admiration (tinged with envy) of their daughters' accomplishments.

36. Years later the Chicago Woman's Club would claim credit for having initiated the idea of federation. The idea was an obvious one; it is curious that various groups cared so much about priority. See Henriette Greenebaum Frank and Amalie Hofer Jerome, *Annals of the Chicago Woman's Club for the First Forty Years of Its Organization: 1876–1916* (Chicago, 1916).

37. Papers of Agnes Morris, Archives of Louisiana State University Library. Morris herself had initiated the formation of a Louisiana federation of women's clubs.

38. Brady, "Kansas Federation," 21.

39. It is hard not to look back in dismay at the road not taken. If the white clubwomen had seen this opportunity to cross the racial divide and set up integrated federations, the history of the nation for the next century might have been very different. As one traces the conflicts over racial issues that surfaced in the WCTU, the YWCA, among church women, clubwomen, and suffrage women, it is clear that there was no white woman leader, however "progressive" she considered herself on this issue, who was completely emancipated from the pervasive racism of the time beyond the level of *noblesse oblige.* Many had not come even that far. As an organization the YWCA probably came closest to a serious effort to incorporate black women, but even there it was 1946 before real integration was achieved. See Paula Giddings, *When and Where I Enter: The Impact of Black Women on Race and Sex* (New York, 1984), chapters 5–7, and "The Colored Work of the YWCA," typescript in the National YWCA Archives, a copy of which is in the Schlesinger Library, Radcliffe College, Cambridge, Mass.

40. Anna Garlin Spencer, *The Council Idea: A Chronicle of Its Prophets and a Tribute to May Wright Sewall* (The National Council of Women, 1930).

41. May Wright Sewall, ed., *The World's Congress of Representative Women* (Chicago, 1894), 2 vols., contains the papers under the headings of education, literature, science and religion, charity, philanthropy and religion, moral and social reform, civil and political status of women, civil law and government, industry and occupations.

42. Mary Kavanaugh Oldham Eagle, *The Congress of Women Held in the Women's Building, World's Columbian Exposition* (Chicago, 1894), 2 vols. There is a marked similarity between the subjects discussed at the Congress of Representative Women and those presented in the Woman's Building during the following summer.

43. Ann Massa, "Black Women in the 'White City,'" *American Studies* 8, no. 3: 319–37. See also Alfreda M. Duster, ed., *Crusade for Justice: The Autobiography of Ida B. Wells* (Chicago, 1970), 115–19.

44. Sandra Hardin, "The World's Columbian Exposition of 1893: American Women's Door to Opportunity," Honors Paper in History, Duke University, 1980, has a perceptive chapter on the multiple effects of the fair on the women who took part.

45. James, James, and Boyer, eds., *Notable American Women,* 2: 181–82. Henrotin's papers in the Schlesinger Library are disappointingly thin; if records could be found she would offer an important subject for a biography.

46. Kate Brannon Knight, *History of the Work of Connecticut Women at the World's Columbian Exposition* (Hartford, 1898). The experience of gathering all this data and putting it together for the rest of the world to see must have had a considerable influence on the women who did it.

47. Faith Rogow, "'Gone to Another Meeting': The National Council of Jewish Women" (Ph.D. diss., State University of New York, Binghamton, 1988).

48. Eagle, ed., *Congress of Women,* 1:175.

49. Ibid.

50. Ibid., 2:710.

51. See James, James, and Boyer, eds., *Notable American Women*, 3: 374–76.

52. Eagle, *Congress of Women*, 2: 708–12.

53. Gayle Gullett, " 'The Great Opportunity': Women Advancing Women's Work at the Chicago Columbian Exposition, 1893" (Paper delivered at the Berkshire Conference of Women Historians in 1987), documents the effect on California women, who went home to organize a local exposition very much along the lines of the Chicago one, and who then created an ongoing Congress of Women which in time became a suffrage organization. All this emphasis on the power of organization, of course, reflected one of the dominant emerging strands of American culture in the nineties. Hardin, "World's Columbian Exposition," also offers a good bit of evidence on this point.

54. Sallie Southall Cotten Papers, Southern Historical Collection, University of North Carolina, Chapel Hill, N.C. See also Chamberlain, "What's Done and Past": [Mrs. Cotten] was a woman of "remarkable insight, well known and highly regarded. She had wrought nobly, accomplishing a great change in the ideas of the women of our State."

55. Gullet, "Great Opportunity," argues that the women who set the tone at the fair "linked women's advancement with maintaining the social order" and therefore failed. The question must be, Failed to do what? A thousand local communities were improved by the municipal housekeeping encouraged by the fair experience, and some of the leaders who would shape the Progressive movement were brought into national visibility by its agency. This is a complex issue, however, which requires detailed analysis.

56. Sewall, *World's Congress*, 463.

57. Louise Noun, *Strong-Minded Women* (Ames, Iowa, 1969), 42–52.

58. A. Elizabeth Taylor, "The Texas Woman Suffrage Movement," *Journal of Southern History* 27, no. 2 (May 1951): 194–95.

59. It is hard to know how much of the seeming progress was illusory and how much was a function of postwar euphoria. In Texas the constitutional convention rejected the majority report in favor of a thoroughly confused minority report. It may also be important that organized antisuffragism had not yet appeared though it soon would.

60. Ellen DuBois, the expert on this phase of the suffrage movement, says she is beginning to believe that "national" as Stanton and Anthony used it meant that the society was focused on national suffrage rather than assuming that their organization was truly national.

61. Because it is so seldom recognized I want to point out that the *Woman's Exponent*, published by the Woman's Relief Society of the Mormon church, was a staunch woman's rights journal that reported every aspect of the woman's movement, and supported suffrage. However, this journal did not reach much beyond the Mormon community. Utah had granted suffrage to women in its territorial days, and came into the union as a suffrage state. See Scott, "Mormon Women, Other Women," 2–49.

62. In practice local, state, and any other suffrage associations were quite autonomous except insofar as ties of friendship led women to take advice from the leaders

of one or the other of the so-called national associations. The structure that would permit real coordination was far in the future.

63. Lois Merk, "Massachusetts and the Woman Suffrage Movement," (Ph.D. diss., Northeastern University, 1961), 9–39.

64. It is intriguing to observe that the rivalry between New York and Boston, exemplified in the Sorosis-New England Woman's Club exchanges, was replicated in the suffrage movement. Members of the NEWC were active in the organization of the AWSA; Charlotte Wilbour and Celia Burleigh of Sorosis were involved in the NWSA.

65. Perhaps this activity owed something to the courageous prewar visits of women to brothels and saloons.

66. *The History of Woman Suffrage* is a major resource for modern historians, especially since it reprinted letters and speeches that might otherwise have been lost. However, it is well to be aware of the editing that Stanton and Anthony imposed upon reports they solicited from the various states. Amelia Bloomer, who wrote the Iowa section for volume 2, said bitterly that her work had been distorted. The American Woman Suffrage Association had no such historians and has suffered accordingly. Its history would have to be reconstructed from *The Woman's Journal*, the Blackwell Family papers, and the papers of other leading AWSA women, such as Mary E. Livermore. Merk, "Massachusetts and the Woman Suffrage Movement," is excellent on the AWSA, but a book is waiting to be written on it; when it is, a good deal of the conventional wisdom may have to be modified.

67. See Clifton J. Phillips, "Helen M. Gougar," in James, James, and Boyer, eds., *Notable American Women*, 2: 69–70.

68. Lois Scharf, "The Woman Movement in Cleveland from 1850," in David D. Van Tassell and John J. Grabowski, *Cleveland: A Tradition of Reform* (Kent, Ohio, 1986), 71–72.

Chapter 6

1. *The Ladies Home Journal*, January 1910.

2. Quoted from *The Crisis* in Eileen Boris, "The Power of Motherhood: Black and White Activist Women Redefine the 'Political,' " *Yale Journal of Law and Feminism* 2, no. 1 (Fall 1989): 25.

3. The term "Progressive movement" came into wide use by 1910 but it has been applied retroactively by historians who perceive it as beginning sometime in the 1880s or 1890s—depending on the historian. See John D. Buenker, John C. Burham, Robert M. Cruden, *Progressivism* (New York, 1977), for a succinct discussion of the ongoing debate as to just what progressivism was and was not.

4. The corruption of the city council is described in Lloyd Wendt and Herman Kogan, *Lords of the Levee* (Indianapolis, 1943). See also Anne Firor Scott, "Saint Jane and the Ward Boss," *American Heritage* 12, no. 1 (Dec. 1960): 12–17.

5. The first president, who had insisted on the long preparation, wrote that "no one acquainted with the difficulty of managing large interests by means of a body of untrained women, without business habits or parliamentary experience, can feel that these years of preparation and education were wasted. It is my firm conviction that without this preliminary training we should never have attained that steadiness

of purpose and that broad habit of looking at all sides of a question which has made us a power in the community." Caroline Brown, quoted in *History of the Chicago Woman's Club,* printed by the board, 26 Sept. 1888, 5.

6. Frank and Jerome, *Annals of the Chicago Woman's Club;* and Belle Short Lambert, "The Woman's Club Movement in Illinois," *Transactions of the Illinois State Historical Society for the Year 1904.* Fifth Annual Meeting of the Society, Bloomington, 27–29 Jan. 1904. Published by the Authority of the Board of Trustees of the Illinois State Historical Library. Also Bertha Damaris Knobe, "What the Chicago Woman's Club Has Done for Chicago," *Woman's Home Companion* (Mar. 1907).

7. The in-house history of the Chicago Woman's Club is unusually revealing for such a document. See Frank and Jerome, *Annals of the Chicago Woman's Club.* Allen Davis, *Spearheads of Reform* (New York, 1967), and idem., *American Heroine* (New York, 1973), provide a thorough analysis of Hull House, the intellectual center of the Chicago woman's movement.

8. See the essay on Stevenson in *Notable American Women,* 3: 375–76.

9. "An imperative rule of the New Century Club has been from the first that no public reports should ever be made of its work or its meetings. This rule has been relaxed of late years. But in the beginning, in so conservative a city as Philadelphia, it was necessary to woman's club life and growth." Croly, *History,* 1023. By 1893 the club was ready to go public, but thought a new organization necessary to that end.

10. Croly, *History,* 1044–46.

11. Mary S. Cunningham, *The Woman's Club of El Paso* (El Paso, 1978).

12. Elizabeth Hays Turner, "Benevolent Ladies, Club Women, and Suffragists: Galveston Women's Organizations, 1880–1920" (Ph.D. diss., Rice University, 1990).

13. See June O. Underwood, "Civilizing Kansas: Women's Organizations, 1880–1920," *Kansas History* 7, no. 4 (Winter 1984–85): 291–306; Eagle, *The Congress of Women,* 280. Underwood finds all kinds of organizations, including the WCTU and the missionary societies, engaged in what I am here calling—following the women's own nomenclature—municipal housekeeping. There is a vast amount of evidence for this activity. As one striking example: Megan Seaholm, "Earnest Women: The White Woman's Club Movement in Progressive Era Texas, 1880–1920" (Ph.D. diss., Rice University, 1988), exceeds five hundred pages. Many state federations have published their own histories while the General Federation of Women's Clubs has a large archive in Washington, D.C.. One of the most perceptive studies so far is Janice Stanschneider, " 'Not a New Woman, but an Improved Woman': The Wisconsin Federation of Women's Clubs, 1895–1920" (M.A. thesis, University of Wisconsin–Madison, 1983).

14. Janet G. Humphrey, ed., *A Texas Suffragist: Diaries and Writings of Jane Y. McCallum* (Austin, 1988), 21.

15. Mary I. Wood, "Civic Activities of Women's Clubs," *Annals of the American Academy of Political and Social Science* 28 (Sept. 1906): 79.

16. A recent article that provides a particularly graphic description of the prevailing racial attitudes is Wayne Mixon, "The Ultimate Irrelevance of Race: Joel Chandler Harris and Uncle Remus in Their Time," *Journal of Southern History* 56, no. 3 (Aug. 1990): 457–80.

17. Charles H. Wesley, *The History of the National Association of Colored Women's Clubs: A Legacy of Service* (Washington, 1984).

18. Quoted in Beverly Jones, "Mary Church Terrell and the National Association of Colored Women, 1896 to 1901," *Journal of Negro History* 67, no. 1 (Spring 1982): 28.

19. Jacqueline Anne Rouse, *Lugenia Burns Hope: Black Southern Reformer* (Athens, Ga., 1989), is a careful study of Hope and the Neighborhood Union.

20. Jane Edna Hunter, *A Nickel and a Prayer* (Nashville, 1940).

21. Gerda Lerner, "The Community Work of Black Women's Clubs," in *The Majority Finds Its Past* (New York, 1982), 83–93; Lynda Faye Dickson, "The Early Club Movement Among Black Women in Denver, 1890–1925" (Ph.D. diss., University of Colorado, 1982); Darlene Clark Hine, *When the Truth Is Told: A History of Black Women's Culture and Community in Indiana, 1875–1950* (National Council of Negro Women, 1981); Tullia Kay Brown Hamilton, "The National Association of Colored Women" (Ph.D. diss., Emory University, 1978); Susan Lynn Smith, "The Black Women's Club Movement: Self-Improvement and Sisterhood, 1890–1915" (M.A. thesis, University of Wisconsin—Madison, 1986).

22. Dorothy Salem, "To Better Our World: Black Women in Organized Reform, 1890–1920" (Ph.D. diss., Kent State University, 1985); Cynthia Neverdon-Morton, "Self-Help Programs as Educative Activities of Black Women in the South, 1895–1925: Focus on Four Key Areas," *Journal of Negro Education* 51, no. 3 (Summer 1982): 207–21.

23. Historians of white voluntary associations will find much to ponder in Wesley, *History of the National Association of Colored Women's Clubs*, as well as the growing number of dissertations on black women's organizations.

24. Forty years ago C. Vann Woodward made the point that progressives were blind to justice in matters of race, but he failed to note the existence of black progressives, much less black women who were trying to do what the white people would not. C. Vann Woodward, *The Origins of the New South, 1877–1913* (Baton Rouge, 1951), chapter 14, "Progressivism for Whites Only." Woodward did not notice the work of white women in creating southern progressivism either.

25. Adair's story and those that follow are found in the Black Women's Oral History Project, Schlesinger Library, Radcliffe College, Cambridge, Mass. This project collected an extraordinary series of life histories.

26. Anne F. Scott, "Women and Libraries," in Donald G. Davis, Jr., ed., *Libraries, Books and Culture: Proceedings of Library History Seminar 7* (Austin, 1986), 400–405.

27. Barbara M. Solomon, *The Company of Educated Women* (New Haven, 1986).

28. Moore, "Educational Work of Women's Clubs," 29.

29. As early as 1890 the treasurer of the General Federation of Women's Clubs, who was also president of the St. Louis branch of the Association of Collegiate Alumnae, wrote a long report on educational work. After numerous detailed examples drawn from all over the country, she added: "Suddenly they [women's clubs] realized that they possessed influences; that as organizations they could ask and gain, where as women they received no attention. . . . " Moore, "Educational Work of Women's Clubs," 33–34.

30. James H. Leloudis II "School Reform in the New South: The Woman's Association for the Betterment of Public School Houses in North Carolina, 1902–1919," *Journal of American History* 69 (March 1983): 886–909.

31. This is one small part of a large, complex, and fascinating story. See Robert L. Reid, ed., *Battleground: The Autobiography of Margaret A. Haley* (Urbana, 1982).

32. Mary Ritter Beard, *Woman's Work in the Municipalities* (New York and London, 1915).

33. Perhaps Beard thought that she was writing for a popular or lay audience, and for clubwomen themselves, and hence did not need to provide detailed documentation, but a citation simply to *The American City* or *The Survey* is enough to make a historian tear her hair. The material itself is compelling, but how far can we trust it? She relied heavily on *The American Club Woman*, published by the General Federation of Women's Clubs, which was unlikely to speak of failures. My intuition is that most of the projects Beard describes were indeed undertaken, but that the success was not as unalloyed as her narrative would suggest, and that the process involved much more conflict than she records.

34. Beard, *Woman's Work*, 49.

35. Ibid., 64.

36. Ibid., 60–61.

37. Martha E. D. White, "The Work of the Woman's Club" *Atlantic Monthly* 93, no. 559 (May 1904): 614–23. Part of the article is a thoughtful analysis of the ever-present problem of the gap between what the General Federation thought local clubs were doing and what they were really doing, and the conclusion is an attempt to diagnose a problem without offering any concrete solution. It perhaps should not have surprised White that women's organizations, like all human institutions, exhibited a wide range of human types.

38. See especially Steinschneider, " 'Not a New Woman, but an Improved Woman.' " This superb study contains a great deal of concrete data about the women leaders in Wisconsin.

39. What follows is a highly impressionistic summary based on thirty-eight biographies in James, James, and Boyer, eds., *Notable American Women*, and on Sicherman and Green, eds., *Notable American Women: The Modern Period*, as well as on published and unpublished biographical material. A collective biography of some of these women, especially one based on manuscript sources, might reveal a good deal more than we now know on this elusive topic. Robert M. Cruden, *Ministers of Reform: The Progressives' Achievement in American Civilization, 1889–1920* (New York 1982), offers an intriguing collective psychobiography of a hundred progressives. Some of his sample were active in women's clubs. Cruden recognizes that women were an important part of the movement but he is not aware of the central importance of voluntary associations. It would be useful to test his thesis using a sample of a hundred leaders of a wide variety of clubs.

40. Robins is one of the few who has been the subject of a thorough biography. Elizabeth Payne, *Reform, Labor and Feminism: Margaret Dreier Robins and the Women's Trade Union League* (Urbana, 1988).

41. The pictures in Croly's volume, as well as in many histories of state federations, and in Wesley, *The History of the National Association of Colored Women's Clubs*, are worth careful study. Few of these early clubwomen could have sat for a portrait by Helen Hokinson, creator of the hilariously funny New Yorker cartoons who made naïve, overweight clubwomen a national stereotype in the 1940s.

42. Memorial service for Grace Abbott, the second head of the Children's Bureau, 18 Oct. 1939. Josephine Roche Papers, University of Colorado Library, Department of Special Collections, Boulder, Colorado. See also Molly Ladd-Taylor, *Raising a Baby the Government Way: Mothers' Letters to the Children's Bureau* (New Brunswick, N.J., 1986).

43. Nancy P. Weiss, "The Children's Bureau: A Case Study in Women's Voluntary Networks" (Paper delivered at the Berkshire Conference of Women's Historians, Bryn Mawr, Pa., 10 June 1976).

44. Jeanette E. Tuve, *First Lady of the Law: Florence Ellinwood Allen* (Lanham, N.H., 1989), 50. Somerville-Howorth Papers, Schlesinger Library, Radcliffe College, Cambridge, Mass.

45. Lori Bernstein, "Moving Beyond Charity: Women and the Creation of North Carolina's Public Welfare System" (Honors Paper, Duke University, 1984).

46. Albion Fellows Bacon, *Beauty for Ashes* (New York, 1914), and Roy Lubove, "Albion Fellows Bacon and the Awakening of a State," *Midwest Review* 4, no. 1 (1962): 63–72.

47. Sophonisba P. Breckinridge wrote a careful, scholarly and admiring biography, discreetly ignoring certain family scandals. *Madeline McDowell Breckinridge: A Leader in the New South* (Chicago, 1921). The Breckinridge Papers in the Library of Congress are a treasure house of information about the way a voluntary-association leader functioned and the long reach of her influence. See also Melba Porter Hay, "Madeline McDowell Breckinridge: Kentucky Suffragist and Progressive Reformer" (Ph.D. diss., University of Kentucky, 1980).

48. *Palo Alto Times*, 29 Jan. 1904.

49. *The Southerner* 28 (January 1912), clipping in Sallie Southall Cotten Scrapbook, Southern Historical Collection, University of North Carolina, Chapel Hill, N.C.

Chapter 7

1. Wood, "Civic Activities of Women's Clubs," 85.

2. See Papers of the Women's Educational and Industrial Union of Boston, Schlesinger Library, Radcliffe College, Cambridge, Mass. Brenda K. Shelton, "Organized Mother Love: The Buffalo Women's Educational and Industrial Union, 1885–1915," *New York History* 67, no. 2: 155–76. Like every other effort to attain cross-class cooperation, the Buffalo Union did not always have smooth sailing, but a thousand women joined and the membership held at that level for thirty years.

3. The name, Women's Educational and Industrial Union, did not carry the same connotation everywhere. A WEIU in Knoxville, Tennessee, founded in 1890 engaged chiefly in municipal housekeeping and some traditional benevolence such as providing work for sewing women and building a day-care center. Croly, *History*, 1080.

4. Blewett, *Men, Women, and Work*, 170.

5. Dorothy Ross, "Socialism and American Liberalism: Academic Social Thought in the 1880s," *Perspectives in American History* 11 (1977–78): 7–79. Richard Ely, John Dewey, John R. Commons, and E. A. Ross in particular were close to Florence Kelley, Jane Addams, Julia Lathrop, and Helen Sumner among others. See Ellen Fitzpatrick, *Endless Crusade: Women Social Scientists and Progressive Reform* (New York, 1990).

6. One could certainly argue that the critics of the eighties called for changes more radical than any that were generally accepted in the broad progressive movement of the late nineties and the early twentieth century. It is in the nature of social movements, I think, that as their adherents become more numerous, assumptions tend to become more middle-of-the-road.

7. Papers of the Los Angeles Woman's Club, Henry Huntington Library, San Marino, California, include some of Severance's long and passionate attacks on industrial capitalism.

8. Frank and Jerome, *Annals of the Chicago Woman's Club*, 120.

9. Kathryn K. Sklar, ed., *The Autobiography of Florence Kelley* (Chicago, 1986), 77–89, tells the story from Kelley's perspective. Mari Jo Buhle, *Women and American Socialism* (Urbana, 1981), 72, examines the same situation from the perspective of the Illinois Woman's Alliance.

10. "Address Delivered by Mrs. Potter Palmer ... on the Occasion of the Opening of the Woman's Building, May 1st, 1893," printed in Eagle, *Congress of Women*, 25.

11. *Bulletin of the Department of Labor*, no. 25 (July 1899).

12. Steinschneider, "Not a New Woman, But an Improved Woman."

13. Abbie Graham, *Grace H. Dodge, Merchant of Dreams* (New York, 1926).

14. Croly, *History*, 83.

15. *The Union Signal*, 23 Feb. 1893.

16. Jane Addams, *Democracy and Social Ethics* (New York, 1902), introduction.

17. Jean Bethke Elshtain, "A Return to Hull House: Reflections on Jane Addams," *Cross Currents* 38, no. 3: 257–67, is an indication that at long last Addams is beginning to be recognized as a significant social theorist. See also Anne F. Scott, *Making the Invisible Woman Visible* (Urbana, 1984), 107–48.

18. Maud Nathan, one of the leaders of the Consumers' League, writing its history in the 1920s noted: "I cannot dwell too strongly upon the fact that the work of the Consumers' League lay along the lines of true economics. Although our sympathies may have been aroused, we were not guided by a false sentiment...." *Story of an Epoch-Making Movement* (New York, 1926).

19. Allen Davis, *Spearheads of Reform: The Social Settlements and the Progressive Movement, 1890–1914* (New York, 1976).

20. The generational links in women's activism are always intriguing. Olivia Sage was a graduate of Troy Female Seminary and so great an admirer of Emma Willard that she paid for the massive survey of Troy alumnae, published as *Mrs. Emma Willard and Her Pupils*, one of the first compilations of data on educated middle-class American women.

21. See papers of Louise Marion Bosworth, Schlesinger Library, Radcliffe College, Cambridge, Mass. Bosworth was a Wellesley graduate who worked for a number of settlement houses; she participated in surveys of workers' living conditions for the WEIU, published in 1911 as *The Living Wage of Women Workers: A Study of Incomes and Expenditures of 450 Women in the City of Boston*, and a survey of housing conditions in Philadelphia. Other studies made under the WEIU auspices included Elizabeth K. Adams, *Women Professional Workers* (New York, 1921); Susan M. Kingsbury, ed., *Labor Laws and Their Enforcement: Studies in the Economic Relations of Women* (New York, 1911); and Lucille Eaves, *A Legacy to Wage-Earning Women* (Boston, 1925).

22. Sharon Hartman Strom, "Leadership and Tactics in the American Woman Suffrage Movement: A New Perspective from Massachusetts," *Journal of American History* 62, no. 2 (Sept. 1975): 296–315, is a very important article which changed the conventional wisdom about the so-called "doldrums" of the first decade of the twentieth century.

23. Eleanor Flexner, *Century of Struggle: The Woman's Rights Movement in the United States*, rev. ed. (Cambridge, 1975), 260–61.

24. Payne, *Reform, Labor, and Feminism;* Nancy Schrom Dye, *As Equals and As Sisters: Feminism, Unionism and the Women's Trade Union League of New York* (Columbia, Mo., 1980).

25. Florence Kelley, "Twenty-five Years of the Consumers' League Movement," *The Survey* (27 Nov. 1915).

26. Buhle, *Women and American Socialism,* 106–11.

27. For an interesting comparative study, see Alisa Klaus, "Women's Organizations and the Infant Health Movement in France and the United States," in Kathleen D. McCarthy, ed., *Lady Bountiful Revisited: Women, Philanthropy, and Power* (New Brunswick, N.J., 1990), 157–73.

28. Lillian Wald, *The House on Henry Street* (New York, 1915), 163–65.

29. Nancy P. Weiss, "The Children's Bureau: A Case Study in Women's Voluntary Networks" (Paper delivered at the Berkshire Conference of Women's Historians, Bryn Mawr, Pa., 10 June 1976). The women who supported the Children's Bureau were "determined that human welfare, human conservation, be made the first concern of, the first charge on government," said Josephine Roche at a memorial service for Grace Abbott, the second head of the bureau, 18 October 1939. Josephine Roche Papers, University of Colorado Library, Department of Special Collections, Boulder, Colorado. The bureau remains unique in the history of the federal government in the degree of personal attention it gave to the concerns of mothers all over the country who wrote to it almost as if it were a personal friend. See Ladd-Taylor, *Raising a Baby the Government Way.*

30. See Clarke A. Chambers, *Paul U. Kellog and The Survey: Voices for Social Welfare and Social Justice* (Minneapolis, 1971).

31. Darlene Clark Hine, " 'We Specialize in the Wholly Impossible': The Philanthropic Work of Black Women," in McCarthy, *Lady Bountiful,* 70–89.

32. Gloria T. Hull, ed., *Give Us Each Day: The Diary of Alice Dunbar-Nelson* (New York, 1984), reveals something of these relationships. See especially Dunbar-Nelson's records of visits of black delegations to President Warren G. Harding. In 1920 Dunbar-Nelson was the first black woman to serve as a member of the Republican state committee in Delaware. She was also very active in the National Association of Colored Women's Clubs. This diary is a significant document for anyone interested in the gradually developing political influence of black women.

33. Lily H. Hammond, *In Black and White: An Interpretation of Southern Life* (New York, 1914), 217. This is a remarkable book to have been written by a southern white woman, daughter of slaveholders, in the second decade of the twentieth century. Hammond foreshadows women like Dorothy Tilley and other southern women of the later twentieth century who were out front on issues of civil rights. Like most books this one reflects the time in which it was written, for example, in its

view of Reconstruction, but it should stand with a number of the much better known works of women in the social justice movement.

34. *The Independent* 63, no. 3082 (26 Dec. 1907), reprinted in Gerda Lerner, ed., *Black Women in White America: A Documentary History* (New York, 1972), 460–61.

35. *Brooklyn Eagle,* 6 Aug. 1912. Clippings from this and the other newspapers quoted are in the Jane Addams Papers, Swarthmore College Peace Collection.

36. Telegram to Jane Addams, 13 Aug. 1912, Jane Addams Papers, Swarthmore College.

37. In a new book which arrived as this book was in production Ellen Fitzpatrick writes: "American women had yet to win the vote, but . . . the cause they held dear had finally penetrated the dense rhetoric of national politics. The hour of women social reformers, and their male compatriots, seemed finally at hand." *Endless Crusade: Women Social Scientists and Progressive Reform* (New York, 1990), xi.

38. A copy of this letter is in the Jane Addams Papers, Swarthmore College.

39. Henry S. Commager, ed., *Documents of American History* (New York, 1958), 254–55.

40. *New York Evening Mail,* 11 Oct. 1912.

41. 5 Oct. 1912.

42. Mary Cooke Branch Munford Papers, Virginia State Library, Richmond, Virginia. See also Steinschneider, "Not a New Woman."

43. The most recent study of the National Woman's Party is Christine A. Lunardini, *From Equal Suffrage to Equal Rights: Alice Paul and the National Woman's Party* (New York, 1986). Lunardini, like nearly every historian of woman suffrage, is a strong partisan, and is convinced that Alice Paul was principally responsible for the passage of the Nineteenth Amendment. The weakness of her argument is that it is built on Alice Paul's own recollections, recorded late in her life, for which no contemporary evidence seems to exist. The book is useful for the detailed information about what Alice Paul, Lucy Burns, and their colleagues were doing between 1912 and 1920.

44. Named for Morris Sheppard, a Democratic senator from Texas, and Horace Towner, a Republican congressman from Iowa, the bill had originally been introduced by Jeanette Rankin, the first woman member of Congress, but she had been defeated before it was placed on the calendar. Its full title was the Maternity- and Infancy-Protection Act. See Louise M. Young, *In the Public Interest* (New York and Westport, Conn., 1989), 59–61, for a very important discussion of the act and the part women played in its execution. Young's is the indispensable study of the League of Women Voters.

45. League of Women Voters Papers, Georgia file, Manuscript Division of the Library of Congress, letters of Mrs. Elliott Cheatham.

46. Papers of Adele Clark, Virginia State Library, Richmond, Virginia. Interview with Miss Clark, Oct. 1963.

47. J. Stanley Lemons, *The Woman Citizen: Social Feminism in the 1920s* (Urbana, 1973); Anne F. Scott, "After Suffrage: Southern Women in the 1920s," *Journal of Southern History* 30 (August 1964): 298–318; Clarke A. Chambers, *Seedtime of Reform: American Social Service and Social Action* (Minneapolis, 1963); Felice Gordon, *After Winning: The Legacy of the New Jersey Suffragists, 1920–1947* (New Brunswick, 1946);

Carole Nichols, "Votes and More for Women: Suffrage and After in Connecticut," *Women and History* 5 (Spring 1983).

48. Jacquelyn Hall, *Revolt Against Chivalry,* 56, 59, 62, 64–94, and ff. Hall's book is an excellent study, and virtually the only one that focuses in detail on a post–Civil War woman's voluntary association.

49. Young, *In The Public Interest,* chapter 8. State league records in the Library of Congress are filled with data about these citizenship schools.

50. The New Orleans Woman's Club was a dramatic case in point. Founded in the 1880s by and for "working women," broadly defined, and politically effective in the following decades, by the middle teens it had lost its drive and was mostly social and cultural. See scrapbooks for 1884–1934, Tulane University Archives.

51. Susan Ware, *Beyond Suffrage: Women in the New Deal* (Cambridge, 1981), 87. See chapter 5, "Women and Social Welfare Policy," for a detailed discussion of the way women functioned in working for major New Deal policies: the NRA, the 1935 Social Security Act, the 1938 Fair Labor Standards Act, and the relief programs for women in the Works Progress Administration. There is an important study yet to be made of the women who served in relief agencies in the states and cities.

Chapter 8

1. By the 1980s the AAUW had opened its doors to men, but it remained for most purposes a woman's organization.

2. Jane Addams, *Democracy and Social Ethics,* rpt. (Cambridge, Mass., 1964), 11.

3. "Address Delivered by Mrs. Potter Palmer . . . on the Occasion of the Opening of the Woman's Building, May 1st, 1893," in Eagle, *Congress of Women,* 25.

4. Lynn Dumenil, *Freemasonry and American Culture, 1880–1930* (Princeton, 1984); Hall Barron, *Those Who Stayed Behind* (Cambridge, 1984); Don Harrison Doyle, *The Social Order of a Frontier Community: Jacksonville, Illinois, 1825–1870* (Urbana, 1978), are all useful on the functions of male voluntary associations in community life.

5. Daniel Rodgers, "In Search of Progressivism," in Stanley L. Kutler and Stanley N. Katz, eds., *The Promise of American History* (Baltimore, 1982), and Richard L. McCormick, "The Discovery that 'Business Corrupts Politics': A Reappraisal," *American Historical Review* 86, no. 2 (April 1981): 247–74, are among the best recent discussions of the much-disputed question: What was progressivism? It was, of course, as Rodgers makes clear, many things. He is not much aware of what women were doing.

6. Of course many women were vehemently, one might say rabidly, opposed to school integration, but none of the major organizations discussed here opposed and some worked vigorously to promote enforcement of *Brown.*

7. Ryan, *Cradle of the Middle Class,* 119–23.

8. *Bonds of Womanhood* (New Haven, 1975), 138.

9. *Fin de Siècle Vienna* (New York, 1980), 187.

10. *Bonds of Womanhood,* 138.

11. *Cradle of the Middle Class* (New York, 1982), chapter 3, "The Era of Association."

12. *Women's Activism and Social Change* (Ithaca, 1984), chapter 2, "A Profusion of Pathways."

Index

A Note on the Author

ANNE FIROR SCOTT is W. K. Boyd Professor of History Emerita in Duke University. She is the author of *The Southern Lady: From Pedestal to Politics, 1830–1930* and *Making the Invisible Woman Visible*. She is the coauthor (with Andrew MacKay Scott) of *One Half the People: The Fight for Woman Suffrage* and is the editor of *Women in American Life* and *The American Woman: Who Was She?* Prof. Scott has contributed numerous articles to scholarly journals and anthologies.

Books in the Series
Women in American History

Women Doctors in Gilded-Age Washington:
Race, Gender, and Professionalization
Gloria Moldow

Friends and Sisters: Letters between Lucy Stone
and Antoinette Brown Blackwell, 1846–93
Edited by Carol Lasser and Marlene Deahl Merrill

Reform, Labor, and Feminism: Margaret Dreier Robins
and the Women's Trade Union League
Elizabeth Anne Payne

Private Matters: American Attitudes toward Childbearing
and Infant Nurture in the Urban North, 1800–1860
Sylvia D. Hoffert

Civil Wars: Women and
the Crisis of Southern Nationalism
George C. Rable

I Came a Stranger: The Story of a Hull-House Girl
Hilda Satt Polacheck
Edited by Dena J. Polacheck Epstein

Labor's Flaming Youth: Telephone Operators and
Worker Militancy, 1878–1923
Stephen H. Norwood

Winter Friends: Women Growing Old
in the New Republic, 1785–1835
Terri L. Premo

Better Than Second Best:
Love and Work in the Life of Helen Magill
Glenn C. Altschuler

Dishing It Out: Waitresses and Their Unions
in the Twentieth Century
Dorothy Sue Cobble

Working Women of Collar City: Gender, Class,
and Community in Troy, 1864–86
Carole Turbin

Natural Allies: Women's Associations in American History
Anne Firor Scott

Beyond the Typewriter: Gender, Class,
and the Origins of Modern American Office Work, 1900–1930
Sharon Hartman Strom